DIGITAL COPYRIGHT

The first edition of this book in 2002 was the first UK text to examine digital copyright together with related areas such as performers' rights, moral rights, database rights and competition law as a subject in its own right. Updated editions have included the UK implementation of the 2001 Information Society Directive and commentary on user-generated content and the development of Web 2.0 and beyond. Now in its fourth edition, the book has been updated and revised to take account of legal and policy developments in copyright law and related areas, in particular the increasing role of the Court of Justice of the European Union in shaping EU copyright law.

The book helps put digital copyright law and policy into perspective and provides practical guidance for those creating or exploiting digital content or technology, whether in academia, the software, information, publishing and creative industries, and other areas of the economy. The focus is on the specifics of the law in this area together with practical aspects, including precedents and precedent checklists dealing with common digital copyright transactions. The latest edition has been expanded to include a discussion of Open Access, eBooks and App development and licensing. Both academics and practitioners will find the book an invaluable guide to this rapidly developing field of law.

Digital Copyright

Law and Practice

Fourth Edition

Simon Stokes

Solicitor
Partner, Blake Lapthorn; Visiting Research
Fellow, Bournemouth Law School

·HART·
PUBLISHING
OXFORD AND PORTLAND, OREGON
2014

Published in the United Kingdom by Hart Publishing Ltd
16C Worcester Place, Oxford, OX1 2JW
Telephone: +44 (0)1865 517530
Fax: +44 (0)1865 510710
E-mail: mail@hartpub.co.uk
Website: http://www.hartpub.co.uk

Published in North America (US and Canada)
by Hart Publishing
c/o International Specialized Book Services
920 NE 58th Avenue, Suite 300
Portland, OR 97213-3786
USA
Tel: +1 503 287 3093 or toll-free: (1) 800 944 6190
Fax: +1 503 280 8832
E-mail: orders@isbs.com
Website: http://www.isbs.com

First edition published 2002 by Butterworths Tolley. Second edition published by Hart
Publishing 2005. Third edition published by Hart Publishing 2009. Fourth edition published
by Hart Publishing 2014.

Simon Stokes has asserted his right under the Copyright, Designs and Patents Act 1988, to be
identified as the authors of this work.

Hart Publishing is an imprint of Bloomsbury Publishing plc

British Library Cataloguing in Publication Data
Data Available

ISBN: 978-1-84946-402-4

Typeset by Compuscript Ltd, Shannon
Printed and bound in Great Britain by
TJ International Ltd, Padstow, Cornwall

PREFACE TO THE FOURTH EDITION

This book was first published in the Spring of 2002 by Butterworths Tolley and a second edition (published by Hart Publishing) came out in 2005. The intention was to provide a readable introduction to digital copyright and related areas (moral rights, database rights, and competition law) and provide practical guidance. As far as the author is aware it was the first book in the UK to treat digital copyright as a subject in its own right.[1] The book seeks to be a practical guide to the area—whilst the ongoing and often heated debate about the scope and purpose of copyright law is noted (in particular in chapter one), the author's intention has been to provide a guide to the law for students, researchers, creators and users of copyright and practitioners.

Since the previous, third edition of 2009 there have been a number of significant legal developments, not least proposals for copyright law reform in the UK and the increasing number of cases referred by the UK courts to the Court of Justice of the European Union (CJEU/ECJ). There is now a developing European copyright jurisprudence driven by digital developments—whether in databases, software, copyright, online infringement and intermediary liability. At the same time digital technology moves apace with the use of mobile devices, tablets, and eReaders becoming widespread. This is changing how copyright-protected content is delivered and consumed, and also created. The law and commercial practice struggle to catch up. This has encouraged the UK Government to seek to legislate in this area.[2]

This latest edition is a snapshot of the position as at the end of 2012, with important later developments up to June 2013 noted where possible.

Simon Stokes
Clerkenwell
24 June 2013

---

[1] Jessica Litman's *Digital Copyright* (Amherst, New York, Prometheus Books, 2001) is written from a US perspective and is still worth reading to understand the debate in the US and why stronger copyright laws are not necessarily the answer to the challenges of digitisation.

[2] In particular, the Hargreaves Review and its follow-up (in particular the December 2012 HM Government response to consultation on copyright exceptions and clarifying copyright law entitled 'Modernising Copyright: A Modern, Robust and Flexible Framework', IPO, December 2012, and also the provisions in the Enterprise and Regulatory Reform Act 2013 dealing with orphan works and extended collective licensing). Draft legislation dealing with a number of copyright exceptions was made available for comment by the IPO in June 2013 (see www.ipo.gov.uk/types/hargreaves.htm (accessed 21 June 2013). These are discussed in section 2.4.1 of this book).

ACKNOWLEDGEMENTS (FOURTH EDITION)

The continued support of my colleagues at Blake Lapthorn is appreciated. In particular I would like to thank the Information Enquiries team, Andrea Hayes and Stephen Reeves.

ACKNOWLEDGEMENTS (THIRD EDITION)

I am grateful for the assistance of my colleagues at Blake Lapthorn (formerly Blake Lapthorn Tarlo Lyons) and in particular Adeline Cantais, Suzanne Hughes, David Jones, the Information Enquiries team, and Sara Shreeves in helping me to update this edition. I am also grateful for the assistance of the personnel at the various collecting societies noted in chapter nine for helping to further update the section on collecting societies.

The book remains dedicated to my family, current and future users and creators of user-generated content.

ACKNOWLEDGEMENTS (SECOND EDITION)

I am grateful to Butterworths Tolley for permitting the publication of a second edition, and to Hart Publishing for agreeing to publish the new edition and for their encouragement throughout.

Tarlo Lyons have continued to provide support: Antonia Tarnoy helped with the updating of the text and generally, Maeve Mullally got the text into shape and Helen Dewar tracked down a number of the cases cited. I am also grateful for the assistance of personnel at the various collecting societies noted in chapter eight (see footnote 6 of chapter eight) for helping to update the section on collecting societies.

The book is dedicated to my family.

ACKNOWLEDGEMENTS (FIRST EDITION)

This book is the outcome of ten years spent practising digital copyright law. I am grateful to my clients and colleagues over the years for their help in deepening my understanding of this area. Needless to say I am responsible for any errors or omissions. I am also very grateful to Anand Shukla of Butterworths Tolley for being receptive to the idea of a book on the subject and for his support throughout.

I would like to thank various past and present members of Tarlo Lyons for their help with the book. Cheryl Wright helped to get the manuscript into shape. Lisa Carter and Charlotte Hennessey helped to proof read the text and provide references, as did Nynke Wisman (of Kennedy van der Laan, Amsterdam and a secondee at Tarlo Lyons), who also helped with some Dutch cases. Jeffrey Eneberi helped with the sections on Open Source and mobile phone ring tones, Jamie Lyford researched into Internet standards, David Varney provided general research assistance and looked in particular at licensing issues, and Luvisa Rains helped with the precedents. Helen Dewar also helped throughout in providing cases and materials. The Library of the Law Society provided comfortable and efficient surroundings in which to finish the manuscript.

Preparation of the book largely coincided with the expected arrival of our second child Dominic. This book is dedicated to Dominic and also to my wife and daughter for their patience and support in yet another publishing project.

TABLE OF CONTENTS

GLOSSARY

This glossary lists some of the more common terms used in digital copyright law and in the book.

ADSL: a telecommunications line that enables the fast downloading of data. Stands for asymmetric digital subscriber line.

Analogue: information/data that is represented in a non-**Digital** form that is continuous (as opposed to being comprised of discrete **Bits**).

API: application programming interface—in non-technical terms this can be considered to be a specification that allows computer programs to communicate with each other.[3]

App: short for application software ie software that performs specific tasks or functions. Also commonly used to refer to smartphone or tablet computer applications (being application software developed to perform specific functions or tasks or play games and usually highly branded) that are downloaded to the phone from the relevant online store or market, for example Google Play (from Google—for **Smartphones**, **Tablets** or other devices running the Android operating system) or the App Store (from Apple—for devices running the iOS operating system).

Atom: a format used for **Web Feeds** and an alternative to **RSS**.

Bandwidth: in effect the speed of data transmission; the higher the bandwidth the faster the transmission measured in **Bits** per second.

Berne Convention: The Berne Convention for the Protection of Literary and Artistic Works (Paris Act, 24 July 1971).

Berne Three Step Test: the approach the Berne Convention takes to exceptions to copyright (see section 2.4 of chapter two).

Bits: See **Digital**.

Blog: this is a website, usually maintained by an individual, often as an online diary, with individual comments, opinion and other content (eg video), and it may also allow readers to post their own comments. It is short for web log. The blogosphere is the collective community of all blogs.

Broadband: a transmission channel with a high **Bandwidth**.

Browse Wrap: an online contract, licence agreement or terms of use visible on a website (eg via a **Hyperlink**) but which the user does not have to accept

---

[3] See www.eff.org/cases/oracle-v-google (accessed 24 June 2013).

affirmatively or assent to (eg by clicking 'I agree' etc). It is debatable how enforceable such terms are (see chapter seven).

Browser: software which enables the display of web pages and **HTML** text generally. For example, Firefox or Microsoft's Internet Explorer program.

Burning: recording data or other source material (video, audio) onto an optical disk (eg CD or DVD).

Bytes: eight **Bits**.

Cache; Caching: an information store available for easy and swift access, usually temporary.

CC: see **Creative Commons**.

CDPA: Copyright, Designs and Patents Act 1988. The current UK copyright statute.

CD ROM: a read only memory (**ROM**) embedded in a compact disk (CD).

CJEU: the Court of Justice of the European Union (also previously referred to as the 'European Court of Justice' (**ECJ**)).

Click Wrap: a form of online contract or licence entered into by the user ticking or otherwise 'clicking' on an 'I agree' or similar box (which will refer to the actual licence terms agreed to either by displaying them (eg to be scrolled through) or via a **Hyperlink**). Agreement to the terms is required before the user is able to download the product in question.

Cloud [the]: 'the cloud' is a metaphor for the **Internet**. So **Cloud Computing** is a nebulous term for computer services delivered over the cloud eg through **Servers** which **Host** applications accessed remotely (rather than use of software within the user's own physical location)—it includes the concept of 'software as a service' (**SaaS**).

Collecting Society: an organisation which collectively administers and/or licences copyright (See section 9.3 of chapter nine for more information). A proposed EU law definition is 'any organisation which is authorised by law or by way of assignment, licence or any other contractual arrangement, by more than one right-holder, to manage copyright or rights related to copyright as its sole or main purpose and which is owned or controlled by its members.'[4]

Communication to the Public Right: see **Right of Communication to the Public**.

Compress/Compression: the process of reducing the size of a digital file/ program whether text, media or both. Compression is typically effected by removing unnecessary information from the file. Some compression techniques lose some data eg **MP3**.

Conditional Access Directive: Directive 98/84/EC on the legal protection of services based on, or consisting of, conditional access.

---

[4] See definition in proposed Directive on collective management of copyright and related rights and multi-territorial licensing of rights in musical works for online uses in the internal market (11 July 2012).

Copyleft: this is a requirement contained in a number of **FLOSS/FOSS** licences that seeks to ensure that derivatives of the software continue to be available as **Open Source** under the **Free Software** principles: 'Copyleft is a general method for making a program (or other work) free, and requiring all modified and extended versions of the program to be free as well.'[5]

Copyright Hub: a proposed not for profit industry-led initiative in the UK to facilitate rights clearance, provide information on rights owners (including as regards searches for **Orphan Works**), information on copyright generally, and link to or facilitate **Digital Copyright Exchanges**. See section 9.4 of this book.

Co-regulation: a development of self-regulation that involves both industry and the government (or a regulator) administering and enforcing a regulatory solution in a variety of ways—in other words self-regulation but with active oversight by a regulator or government.

Creative Commons (CC): is a nonprofit corporation founded in 2001 in the USA. It provides free standard form 'Creative Commons' licences discussed in section 9.5.5 of this book that a creator can use so that others can share, remix, use commercially, and so on, their works, as set out in the licence terms chosen by the creator.

CSS: encryption code used to protect **DVDs**—stands for 'Content Scramble System'.

Database Directive: Directive 96/9/EC on the legal protection of databases.

Decrypt/Descramble: the opposite of **Encrypt/Scramble**.

De CSS: program devised by hackers (allegedly by reverse engineering **DVD** player (Xing DVD) software in breach of the manufacturer's licence) to overcome **CSS** and copy **DVDs**.

Deep Linking: Linking that points to a specific page on another web site and not to the home page of that site.

Digital: information/data that is represented as binary digits (1010 etc) (or **Bits**). These in turn make up **Bytes**.

Digital Copyright Exchange (DCE): as envisaged by the **Hargreaves Review** a DCE is an automated e-commerce website or network of websites which allows licensors to set out the rights they wish to license and allows licensees to acquire those rights from the licensors.[6] The intention is to aid those seeking to clear rights and reduce licensing costs and provide online payment and other features. See also **Copyright Hub**. See section 9.4 of this book.

Digital Rights Management (DRM): technology designed to track and/ or copy protect digital copyright content. It includes **Secure Distribution**

---

[5] www.gnu.org/copyleft/ (accessed 15 June 2013).

[6] Definition taken from *Rights and Wrongs: Is Copyright Licensing Fit for Purpose for the Digital Age?, The First Report of the Digital Copyright Exchange Feasibility Study* (Intellectual Property Office, London 27 March 2012) 4 (www.ipo.gov.uk/dce-report-phase1.pdf (accessed 4 April 2013)).

mechanisms which generally use **Encryption** and **Digital Watermarks**. DRM typically controls the exploitation of content by 'meta tagging' content with the relevant usage rules (licence rights) prior to the content being encrypted. It can only be unlocked by a user who has access to the necessary **Decryption** technology and used within the permitted usage rules.

Digital Watermark: data embedded in digital content—this will identify the copyright proprietor and usage rules. It also refers to code placed into a content file (text, audio, visual etc) which makes the content difficult to copy or destroys it if an attempt is made to copy or use the content without permission.

DMCA: US law of 1998 amending the US Copyright Act 1976 and entitled the 'Digital Millennium Copyright Act' which deals with the liability of **Service Providers** and the protection of copyright protection systems and cryptography, among other things, and implements the **WIPO Treaties**.

Download: copying a file from one computer (typically a **Server**) to another (typically a PC) via transmission.

DVD: digital versatile disk. An optical storage disk with much greater capacity than a **CD-ROM**.

E-books: electronic books readable on PCs, PDAs, e-readers, or proprietary hardware; reader software eg Microsoft Reader software or proprietary hardware is required for this.

ECJ: see **CJEU**.

EEA: the European Economic Area. This comprises the 27 EU member states plus certain other states (Norway, Liechtenstein and Iceland).

Electronic Commerce (or **E-Commerce**) **Directive:** European Directive 2001/31EC 'on certain legal aspects of information society services, in particular electronic commerce, in the Internal Market'. This deals among other things with **Service Provider** liability.

Electronic Commerce Regulations: the Electronic Commerce (EC Directive) Regulations 2002, SI 2002/2013.

Encrypt/Scramble: to convert into unreadable form (without the right **Decryption** key).

ERMI: electronic rights management information.

EU: European Union. In general, for competition law and IP policy matters the EU equates to the **EEA** in practice.

EULA: short for End User Licence Agreement (ie the licence terms applying to the end user (eg a consumer or employee of a business) who actually uses the licensed digital product).

Extended Collective Licensing (ECL): schemes which allow collecting societies and other rights management entities to manage rights without the consent of rights owners (who would typically be members of the society but under ECL non members' rights are also dealt with by the society) (rights owners being able to opt out of such schemes but in effect are automatically 'opted in'). ECL is often proposed in the context of **Orphan Works** but can potentially be broader than this.

File Sharing: the use of **P2P** technology to share audio, video or data files.

Filter: to control access to **Internet** content through the use of Internet filtering software that is designed to restrict access to certain websites or files considered dangerous, unlawful or inappropriate for a user or a group of users.

Finch Report: Report of the Working Group on Expanding Access to Published Research Findings (entitled 'Accessibility, Sustainability, Excellence: How to Expand Access to Research Publications'), June 2012, chaired by Dame Janet Finch CBE. This recommended among other things that a clear policy direction should be set towards support for publication in **Open Access** or hybrid journals, funded by article processing charges (APCs), as the main vehicle for the publication of research, especially when it is publicly funded.

FLOSS: acronym for **Free, Libre** and **Open Source Software**.

FOSS: acronym for both **Free** and **Open Source Software**. Such software is not necessarily made available free of charge—'free' refers to certain freedoms users have (see **Free Software**).

Free Software: software made available as **Open Source** with licence terms that seek to preserve four freedoms to run the program, study how it works and adapt it, to redistribute copies of the program, and to improve the program and release improvements to the public.[7]

GIF: a **Compression** method for graphic images. Such files are called .gif files. Stands for graphic interchange format.

GPL: 'general public licence'—a major **Open Source** licence (see chapter nine).

Hargreaves Review: Hargreaves Review of Intellectual Property and Growth (Intellectual Property Office, London, May 2011).[8]

Host: to 'host' information or software eg a **Server** may host a website.

Hyperlink/Link: text with embedded **HTML** code which allows links between web pages.

Hypertext/HTML: language used to create web pages. Stands for hypertext markup language. By clicking on 'Source' on a typical web browser the HTML code will be displayed.

Information Society Directive: European Directive 2001/29/EC 'on the harmonisation of certain aspects of copyright and related rights in the information society'. This implements in part the **WIPO Treaties** and deals generally with digital copyright matters, although it also refers to analogue issues as well.

---

[7] www.gnu.org/philosophy/free-sw.html (accessed 15 June 2013).
[8] www.ipo.gov.uk/ipreview-finalreport.pdf (accessed 4 April 2013).

In-line Linking: the importation of graphics or other material from one website ('source website') to another ('second web page') via the use of a **Hyperlink** so that the material appears as a seamless part of the second web page (but is nevertheless linked content. It is *not* copied onto the server hosting the second web page—the person browsing the second web page downloads the material from the source website onto *their* computer in order to view it by clicking on the **Hyperlink**).

Internet: a global network of networks communicating using **TCP/IP**.

Internet of Things: the wireless interaction between machines, vehicles, appliances, sensors and many other devices taking place using the Internet. An example would be electronic travel cards. It is predicted that such technology will be in more than one billion phones by 2015.[9]

Internet Service Providers (ISPs): entities which provide **Internet** access and usually email accounts to their customers.

IP/IPR: short for 'intellectual property rights' ie patents, design rights and trade marks (whether registered or unregistered), copyrights, database rights, moral rights, trade secrets and other rights in confidence together with related rights.

IPO: The UK's Intellectual Property Office (www.ipo.gov.uk).

ISP: Internet Service Provider.

JPEG: a **Compression** method for graphic images. Such files are called .jpg files. Stands for Joint Photographic Experts Group.

Libre: 'free'—another word used for **Free Software** (ie free as in 'freedom' not free as in having no monetary cost/free of charge).

Linking: see **In-line Linking**.

Media Player: software used to play **Digital** media (audio, video) files; examples include Windows Media Player (from Microsoft), Quicktime Player (from Apple), iPlayer (from the BBC), and RealPlayer (from Real Networks).

Meltwater: an important UK digital copyright case appealed to the Supreme Court[10] and decided in April 2013 and at the time of writing referred to the CJEU. The case among other things explores the scope of the Article 5(1) exception for transient/incidental copies in the Information Society Directive, the Supreme Court finding that website browsing can benefit from this exception (see section 1.5.1).

Mere Conduit: transmitting information without selecting the information transmitted, the receiver of the information or initiating the transmission.

---

[9] European Commission press release IP/08/1422 (Brussels, 29 September 2008): Commission consults on how to put Europe into the lead of the transition to Web 3.0.

[10] *Public Relations Consultants Association Ltd v The Newspaper Licensing Agency Ltd* [2013] UKSC 18.

Meta tag: **HTML** information ('tag') which identifies and categorises a web page.

MPEG: Motion Pictures Experts Group—an industry research group developing standards for **Compression**, etc of audio and moving pictures.

MP3: a very popular standard for audio **Compression**. Stands for **MPEG**-1, audio player 3. Other technologies for audio files include Microsoft Windows Media file format and Real Networks' Real Jukebox Media Player. These potentially offer greater security against copying than **MP3**. See also **MP3i**.

MP3i: technology developed by First International Digital which allows additional content (eg synchronised lyrics) to be used alongside **MP3** audio files.

Notice and Takedown: a procedure for a website operator or other 'service provider' to escape from legal liability by expeditiously removing ('taking down') allegedly infringing or otherwise unlawful content once it has notice of the offending content.

Object Code: machine-readable software code typically compiled from **Source Code**.

On-Demand Transmission: the making available to the public of a work by electronic transmission in such a way that members of the public may access it from a place and at a time individually chosen by them (see **Information Society Directive** Article 3 as implemented in section 20 of the **CDPA** by the **2003 Regulations**).

Open Access: the practice of making scholarly publications (eg peer-reviewed journals) freely available over the Internet, usually without the user having to pay. However, often the author or the author's institution or funding body will pay for the costs of this instead. This area is discussed in section 8.4.3 of this book.

Open Source: in the context of software, software that is made available in **Source Code** as well as **Object Code** form so that users can evaluate and further collaboratively develop and/or correct the code, typically under the terms of an open source or similar licence (see chapter nine).

Orphan Works: copyright works whose rights owners cannot be traced after a diligent search.[11] See section 9.4 of this book.

Packet: content or data sent over the **Internet** is transported in discrete *packets* of data which are routed accordingly. The routing is done by the **TCP/IP** protocol.

Peer-to-Peer/P2P: systems which enable direct communications and filesharing/swapping between PCs ('peers') without the need for a central **Server** storing the files.

Platform: a combination of hardware and software that allows **Apps** to be run.

---

[11] See eg definition in Article 2(1) of Directive 2012/28/EU on certain permitted uses of orphan works.

Podcast: digital media files (audio, video) available for downloading and playback on portable devices (such as the Apple iPod device) and PCs through **Web Feeds**.

RAM: computer memory which can be both read and written into. Stands for random access memory. Memory which is only read only is called **ROM**—read only memory.

Repertoire Imbalance: content (film, music) only being available in physical form (eg on DVD/video/vinyl) and not online and so available for **Downloading** or **Streaming**.

Right of Communication to the Public: Article 3 of the **Information Society Directive** refers to a general right of communication to the public (which the UK has interpreted to include broadcasting and cable programmes) and in addition a more specific right to authorise or prohibit **On-Demand Transmissions**.

RightsWatch: An EU-funded project to develop codes of conduct and procedures to remove copyright infringing material from the **Internet**.

Ripping: extracting a file from a CD and copying it into an audio file (eg in MP3 format) which can then be easily shared through **File Sharing** and played using a **Media Player**.

ROM: see **RAM**.

Rome Convention: International Convention for the Protection of Performers, Producers of Phonograms and Broadcasting Organisations (Rome, 26 October 1961).

Router: see **TCP/IP**.

RSS: a format used for **Web Feeds**—on web browsers RSS feeds are indicated by an icon consisting of an orange square with white radio waves. 'RSS' stands for really simple syndication—which describes the ease with which the format can be used to access syndicated and other information and data.

Scan/Scanning: to convert an image (text/graphic work) into electronic form eg a **GIF** or **JPEG** file by using a piece of hardware and related software called a scanner.

SDMI: 'Secure Digital Music Initiative'—a forum to develop specifications for protected/secure digital music distribution technologies.

Secure Distribution: a means of distributing digital content. Typically the content file is encrypted and contains embedded usage rules. A 'trusted device' is then required to access the content. The device may only be activated, for example, once payment for the content has been made.

Semantic Web: this describes a development of the **World Wide Web** that allows data to be shared and reused across application, enterprise, and community boundaries (see www.w3.org/2001/sw/).

Server: a computer system (hardware and software) providing services to other systems.

Service Provider: at its most general, any person providing information services. It is a term of art in the **DMCA** and **Electronic Commerce Directive**.

Shrink Wrap: a printed contract, licence agreement or terms of use included with a tangible copy of software or other digital media often with a notice along the lines that opening the product (eg the shrink wrap containing it on eg a **CD-ROM**—hence its name) the user will be deemed to accept the contract terms. It is debatable how enforceable such terms are (see chapter seven).

Smartphone: a mobile phone with advanced computing capability, typically running **Apps** and with **Wi-Fi** capability.

SNS: Social Networking sites.

Social Bookmarking: an offshoot of **Social Networking** where users post news links and other items to a site such as Digg or reddit which then take into account the views of other users to rate them.

Social Media: see **Social Networking**.

Social Networking: the use of the **Internet** to create networks of social inter-action between users, typically through the use of social media/networking sites (SNS) (such as Facebook, LinkedIn) where users register in order to be able to post and share content and communicate with each other.

Software as a Service (SaaS): see **Cloud**.

Software Directive: Directive 91/250/EEC on the legal protection of com-puter programs (this Directive is now repealed and codified as Directive 2009/24/EC).

Source Code: human-readable software code (eg written in a human read-able computer program language). This is compiled into code executable by a computer (ie machine-readable code—**Object Code**) in order for the soft-ware to be run. Access to the source code is required in order to develop and modify the software in question.

Streaming/Stream: the real time delivery of sound or video to be played in real time.

Tablet: a mobile computer with a flat touch screen, typically running **Apps** and with **Wi-Fi** capability (and possibly mobile connectivity as well).

TCP/IP: the protocol used to transmit data over the **Internet**. Data is sent in **Packets** and directed (routed) by a **Router**. Stands for transmission control protocol/**Internet** protocol.

Thumbnail: a reduced size version of an image.

TRIPS: Agreement on the Trade Related Aspects of Intellectual Property Rights.

2003 Regulations: The Copyright and Related Rights Regulations 2003, SI 2003/2498.

UCC: Universal Copyright Convention (as revised at Paris, 24 July 1971). Also refers to **User-Created Content**.

UGC: user-generated content (see chapter eight).

Upload: the opposite of **Download**.

URI/URL: uniform resource identifier/uniform resource locator—a description of where an object (eg a web page) can be found on the Internet. An example of a URL would be http://www.bllaw.co.uk.

User-Created Content (UCC): the same as **User-Generated Content**.

User-Generated Content (UGC): this primarily refers to content created by the end-users of websites (who are not usually media professionals) but can also include content that end-users copy from others (such as music or video files) and **Upload**. The Internet encyclopedia *Wikipedia* is a good example of UGC; other such sites include **Social Networking** sites and **Virtual World Content** sites.

Virtual World Content: content created (often but not necessarily by users) in the context of an online game-like 3D environment, typically a website; such sites include Second Life.

Webcasting: the online distribution of content (audio, visual, etc)—akin to broadcasting by satellite or terrestrial means; typically used to refer to the operation of Internet (music) radio stations.

Web Crawler/Trawler/Spider: software technologies used to search the web for information or content. For example, Digimarc developed a web trawler that looks for Digimarc **Digital Watermarked** files.

Web Feeds: these are data formats which allow the automated delivery of news and other frequently updated content (music, video etc) from a web link (the feed link, which is subscribed to by the user); a feed reader, aggregator or **RSS** reader is used by the user to subscribe to web feeds from the feed links and the reader checks the various feeds subscribed to for new content and allows ease of user access to this content, typically through a web browser.

Web Scraping: the use of a **Web Crawler** to extract information from various web sites—this information can then be used to create a scraper site built from this information.

Web 1.0: the **World Wide Web** as it was between 1994 and 2004, categorised by limited **Bandwidth** and the lack of interactivity, and before the advent of **Web 2.0**.

Web 2.0: a term dating from 2004 which describes the currently evolving **World Wide Web** with the rapid growth of **Blogs**, **Web Feeds**, **Social Networking**, and **UGC** and other interactive sites.

Web 3.0: how the **World Wide Web** will evolve after **Web 2.0**—this will be driven by increasing **Bandwidth**. How the web will evolve is open to debate but it is likely to include increased use of networks, distributed databases, the increased use of artificial intelligence and intelligent systems, and it may also include the development of the **Semantic Web**. Another definition has been given by the European Commission: 'Web 3.0 means seamless "anytime, anywhere" business, entertainment and social networking over fast reliable and secure networks. It means the end of the divide between mobile and fixed lines. It signals a tenfold quantum leap in the scale of the digital universe by 2015' (Commissioner Viviane Reding).[12]

Wi-Fi: a wireless local area network ie a local network (in a shop, at home) which can be accessed wirelessly using radio frequencies and gives access to the **Internet** eg through a wireless hotspot (Wi-Fi and its familiar logo are trade marks/certification marks of the Wi-Fi Alliance).

Wiki: a website that allows others to add, change, remove and/or edit content (most often text) in a collective and/or collaborative manner, for example the online encyclopedia *Wikipedia*.

WIPO Treaties: two international copyright treaties adopted by a diplomatic conference in December 1996: WIPO Copyright Treaty and WIPO Performances and Phonograms Treaty. These set out the 'digital agenda' for copyright and related rights.

World Wide Web (the web): the linked **Hypertext** documents that can be accessed via the **Internet** using a **Browser**.

XML: a language similar to **HTML** but different in that it describes both the presentation of the information and what the actual information is ('metadata'). Stands for eXtensible mark-up language.

---

[12] IP/08/1422 (Brussels, 29 September 2008): Commission consults on how to put Europe into the lead of the transition to Web 3.0.

TABLE OF CASES

TABLE OF LEGISLATION

National Legislation

France

Germany

United Kingdom

Primary Legislation

1

Why Digital Copyright Matters

1.1 OVERVIEW OF THIS BOOK

Copyright is the property right the law gives authors/creators and those taking ownership from them to control the copying and other forms of exploitation of their creations or 'works'. The traditional view is that copyright arose out of lobbying by printers to prevent the piracy of their books. So in one sense it was a response by vested economic interests to the growth of a new technology. The first UK copyright statute dates back to 1709. The current statute, the Copyright, Designs and Patents Act (CDPA), dates from 1988. A lot may have changed in 300 years but it remains the case that those who exploit their creativity (or that of others) continue to use copyright to fight a battle against piracy and the pirates become ever more sophisticated in their approach. Digitisation is yet another new technology copyright is coming to terms with. The most significant recent legislative development was the adoption in Europe of the so-called Information Society Directive[1] in May 2001 and its implementation into UK law by the Copyright and Related Rights Regulations 2003.[2]

This book argues that digitisation continues to pose fundamental challenges to copyright which have only been partially addressed by the 2003 Regulations, important though these are, although as noted case law continues to develop and the possibility of further legislation in this area arises from current UK and EU consultations and initiatives. The book's aim is to help educate rights owners, users, and their lawyers of these challenges so that they can better protect and exploit their copyrights. Other texts tend to

---

[1] Directive 2001/29/EC of the European Parliament and of the Council of 22 May 2001 on the harmonisation of certain aspects of copyright and related rights in the information society, OJ L 167/10 22 June 2001. This Directive is referred to throughout this book as the 'Information Society Directive' albeit that it applies to non-digital issues as well.

[2] SI 2003/2498 ('2003 Regulations').

focus on all aspects of copyright, or deal only with specific digital rights or works such as software, databases and so on. This book treats digital copyright law as a subject in its own right. The basic rules of the game may be derived from the real, analogue world. Yet how those rules are applied and what businesses and their lawyers do with the proliferation of additional rules to address digitisation will determine in part the success of the digital economy. It focuses on the private rather than the public sector although in most cases the rules will be the same.[3] If this book helps creators, businesses and their lawyers through the maze of digital copyright it will have served its purpose.

The focus is on copyright and related rights such as database rights which protect digital content. The book does not deal with non-digital copyright matters such as design rights and the protection of semiconductor chip designs by topography rights.

1.1.1 This Chapter and the Book

This chapter looks at why copyright remains important, the challenges posed by digitisation and the history of legislation relevant to digital copyright. Later chapters look in more detail at the legal rules underpinning digital copyright, the constraints on how these rights can be exercised and four very important digital copyright-based industries: databases, software, e-commerce and e-publishing. The book concludes with practical advice on how to protect, manage and exploit digital copyright assets across a range of industries.

1.2 COPYRIGHT: ITS SCOPE AND RATIONALE

1.2.1 Why Have Copyright?

Most of us take copyright for granted. We may choose to ignore it when we photocopy materials, duplicate software or perform works protected by copyright. But when pressed, most lawyers and business people would at least acknowledge that the law ought to grant authors property rights in their works. Surely authors should have the right to prevent the 'theft' of their works and their creativity ought to be rewarded?

---

[3] But see eg Directive 2003/98/EC of the European Parliament and of the Council of 17 November 2003 on the reuse of public sector information for specific rules dealing with the exploitation of public sector information.

1.2.2 The Case Against Copyright and Copyright Reform

Some argue that copyright ought not to exist or at least it should be severely limited in its application. The 'open source' or 'copyleft' movement discussed later in this book is one example of this. We all stand on the shoulders of giants—if all copying were outlawed how would society advance? A novel or a painting is self-evidently not the same as a piece of real property, to be subject to access and possession to the exclusion of all others. Once made available to the public surely all products of the human intellect should be available to everyone for their use, edification and enjoyment? The great US jurist and Supreme Court Justice Louis Brandeis memorably argued against the privatisation of knowledge and for an 'intellectual commons' in the landmark US case *International News Service v Associated Press*[4]: '[t]he general rule of law is, that the noblest of human productions—knowledge, truths ascertained, conceptions, and ideas—become, after voluntary communication to others, free as the air to common use'.

Concerns have been raised in certain quarters that the effect of strengthening copyright law in recent years to address the digital agenda will be to seriously and unjustifiably restrict the dissemination of speech, information, learning, and culture while not providing any decisive incentives to the creator.[5] On this analysis copyright law needs to be reassessed in light of its premises and pared back to a right of much more limited scope and duration.

Such a wholesale reassessment of copyright law is in the author's view unlikely, at least in the short to medium term. For example, the European Commission launched a consultation in 2004 on its Staff Working Paper 'On the Review of the Legal Framework in the Field of Copyright and Related Rights'.[6] The Working Paper indicated that the Commission's view was that current EU copyright legislation was generally effective and consistent, but would benefit from fine-tuning in certain areas. In 2008 the European Commission published a Green Paper on copyright,[7] but the scope of areas under consideration for review was relatively limited. In the words of the Commission:

> In its review of the Single Market[8] the Commission highlighted the need to promote free movement of knowledge and innovation as the 'Fifth freedom' in the single

---

[4] 248 US 215, 250 (1918).

[5] Kretschmer, 'Digital Copyright: The End of an Era' [2003] *EIPR* 333. Professor Kretschmer cites the US Supreme Court in *Eldred v Ashcroft* 537 US (2003) S Ct 01-618 and in particular the comments of Justice Breyer.

[6] SEC (2004) 995; Brussels, 19 July 2004.

[7] Commission of the European Communities, Green Paper: 'Copyright in the Knowledge Economy', Brussels, 2008 (COM (2008) 466/3).

[8] COM 2007 724 final of 20.11.2007: 'A Single Market for 21st Century Europe'.

market. The Green Paper will now focus on how research, science and educational materials are disseminated to the public and whether knowledge is circulating freely in the internal market. The consultation document will also look at the issue of whether the current copyright framework is sufficiently robust to protect knowledge products and whether authors and publishers are sufficiently encouraged to create and disseminate electronic versions of these products.

This consultation is targeted at everyone who wants to advance their knowledge and educational levels by using the Internet. Wide dissemination of knowledge contributes to more inclusive and cohesive societies, fosters equal opportunities in line with the priorities of the renewed Social Agenda.

With this Green Paper, the Commission plans to have a structured debate on the long-term future of copyright policy in the knowledge intensive areas. In particular, the Green Paper is an attempt to structure the copyright debate as it relates to scientific publishing, the digital preservation of Europe's cultural heritage, orphan works [i.e. works where the copyright owner cannot be traced], consumer access to protected works [i.e. works protected by DRM] and the special needs for the disabled to participate in the information society. The Green Paper points to future challenges in the fields of scientific and scholarly publishing, search engines and special derogations for libraries, researchers and disabled people. The Green paper focuses not only on the dissemination of knowledge for research, science and education but also on the current legal framework in the area of copyright and the possibilities it can currently offer to a variety of users (social institutions, museums, search engines, disabled people, teaching establishments).[9]

On 6 December 2006 the UK Treasury under the Labour Government published the findings of the Gowers Review, a review of the UK IP system, and certain recommendations were made which, if followed up, would have made limited changes to UK copyright law.[10] Then under the current Coalition Government the Hargreaves Review of Intellectual Property and Growth reported in May 2011.[11] The government has been acting on the Hargreaves Review—the Enterprise and Regulatory Reform Act 2013[12] among other things enables the Secretary of State by regulations to introduce schemes to allow lawful use of orphan works and extended collective licensing by collecting societies under appropriate conditions, and to regulate collecting societies through codes of practice. Other actions following the Hargreaves Review include steps to establish a Digital Copyright Exchange (now called

---

[9] Commission Press Release, IP/08/1156 Brussels, 16 July 2008. Other recent EU consultations and relevant policy documents have included a Consultation Paper 'Creative Content in a European Digital Single Market: Challenges for the Future A Reflection Document of DG INFSO and DG MARKT' (22 October 2009) and the Commission Communication 'Copyright in the Knowledge Economy' Brussels, 19.10.2009 COM(2009) 532 final.

[10] *Gowers Review of Intellectual Property*, HM Treasury, December 2006 (www.hm-treasury.gov.uk).

[11] www.ipo.gov.uk/ipreview.

[12] 2013 c. 24.

a 'Copyright Hub') under Richard Hooper and proposals for legislative change in October 2013 to amend and expand the exceptions under UK copyright law and to introduce a new non-statutory system to help clarify copyright law by Copyright Notices issued by the Intellectual Property Office (IPO).[13]

1.2.3 Limits on Copyright

In any event, whatever the criticisms of the copyright system, copyright does not protect ideas as such. The courts have developed the so-called 'idea/expression' dichotomy to help set the boundary between what is in the 'public domain' and so common to others to freely copy and exploit, and what can be proprietary and 'privatised'.

So copyright is said to only protect the expression of ideas, not ideas themselves. Take a famous painting such as *The Bathers* by the Neo-Impressionist painter Seurat. Anyone is free to copy the idea or style behind the picture (a river scene depicted using small coloured spots of paint: pointillism). But if it were in copyright the painting itself would be protected from being copied whether by photography or some other means.

Of course this all sounds simple enough but what if someone copies a piece of software not by literally copying the code but by writing a new program which nevertheless replicates the features and functions of the existing software? As we shall see later, such examples challenge the idea/expression dichotomy. In such a case it is difficult not to argue that what has been copied are 'ideas' but nevertheless that in certain cases the law ought to protect them.

Both the common law and latterly the legislature have also recognised that not all copying and exploitation of copyright works ought to be treated as infringements of copyright. In the UK there are currently certain 'fair dealing' exceptions to copyright, such as the right to copy materials for private study and research, for criticism and review, and for news reporting, although the Gowers Review (and Hargreaves Review) have made suggestions for additional exceptions.[14] In the USA the courts have developed a broader 'fair use' defence to copyright infringement and this was enshrined in statute in the 1976 Copyright Act. As we shall see in this book these defences are being tested to the limit in the digital environment: is it fair use, for example, to copy millions of Internet images in order to operate an Internet 'visual search engine'? Or to operate an Internet music service such as MP3.com so

---

[13] See 'Modernising Copyright: A Modern, Robust and Flexible Framework', IPO, December 2012. These are discussed in ch 2.

[14] www.ipo.gov.uk/policy/policy-issues/policy-issues-gowers/policy-issues-gowers-flexibility. htm.

that users can listen to their CDs whenever they want to without necessarily having direct access to them? Indeed, will the very concepts of fair use and fair dealing survive in the digital economy?

1.2.4   Justifying Copyright

Copyright can be justified on several grounds. These are no mere philosophical speculations. The two major world copyright systems, the Anglo-American 'copyright' system and the continental 'authors' rights' system stand on different philosophical bases. To make sense of copyright law it is necessary to understand what these bases are and their implications for protecting digital products.

In the UK and the USA copyright is frequently justified on the basis of some or all of the following:

(a)   there would be no incentive for authors to create or innovate unless in return they are granted the exclusive rights to exploit their works: innovation is good both for economic and public policy reasons and therefore we ought to have copyright;

(b)   the efforts (labour) of the creative artist deserve to be rewarded in their own right, regardless of any economic benefits;

(c)   the fruits of intellectual labour should be classed as property just in the same way that the products of industry or agriculture are property;

(d)   it is unjust to reap where others have sown ('unjust enrichment');

(e)   by reference to the Bible and the Ten Commandments ('Thou shalt not steal').

For example, in the UK database rights case, *British Horseracing Board v William Hill*,[15] the judge looked back to the express purpose behind database rights in order to determine whether there was infringement. The judge made clear that following recitals 39 and 40 of the Database Directive[16] the object behind database rights is to protect against the misappropriation of the investment made by the creator of a database in obtaining, verifying or presenting the contents of a database. The investment protected could be financial or simply the time, effort and energy spent in obtaining and collecting the database contents. This analysis was fundamental to how the judge applied database law to the facts in this case.

---

[15] High Court, Chancery Division 9 February 2001; J Laddie; [2001] RPC 31.

[16] Directive of the European Parliament and of the Council on the legal protection of databases 96/9/EC, OJ L 77, 27.3.96, 20.

1.2.5   Originality and Copyright

In the UK a frequent justification for copyright protection cited by the courts is the unjust enrichment argument. For example, this was referred to by the House of Lords in a leading copyright case, *Designers Guild Limited v Russell Williams (Textiles) Limited*:[17]

> [t]he law of copyright rests on a very clear principle: that anyone who by his or her own skill and labour creates an original work of whatever character shall, for a limited period, enjoy an exclusive right to copy that work. No one else may for a season reap what the copyright owner has sown ...[18]

So the law ought to protect any independent skill and effort ('originality') by an author in creating their works. This is also a variant of the so-called 'sweat of the brow' justification for copyright. The work need not be 'original' or creative in any novel sense—it simply has to have involved some, even a very modest, amount of effort to create and not be slavishly copied from something else.

In contrast, countries such as France and Germany have traditionally protected the works of authors on the basis they embody or bear the stamp of the author's personality. As a number of European Directives discussed later in this book put it, works which 'constitute the author's own intellectual creation' are entitled to copyright protection. So for certain classes of work, software, databases, photographs and so on, the standard of originality appears higher in the continental system as opposed to the UK system, although moves made by the European Commission to harmonise copyright across the EU are diminishing such differences. Indeed, since the last edition of this book it is clear that the Court of Justice of the European Union (CJEU) is in effect developing a copyright jurisprudence that will inevitably bring UK law closer to continental law here.[19]

1.2.6   Moral Rights

One lasting influence of the continental approach to treating works as sacrosanct and embodying the 'spirit' of the author/creator, has been the development of moral rights. In addition to the 'economic rights' underlying copyright which may be freely transferred ('assigned') or licensed, such as the right to copy and distribute copyright protected works, authors also have the moral right to be identified when their works are exploited and to object to derogatory treatment of their works. So the author of a photograph,

---

[17] [2000] 1 WLR 2416.
[18] *Per* Lord Bingham of Cornhill at 2418A.
[19] See in particular *Infopaq International A/S v Danske Dagblades Forening* (C-5/08) as applied in eg *Newspaper Licensing Agency Ltd v Meltwater Holding BV* [2010] EWHC 3099 (Ch).

regardless of whether he owns the copyright in it (ie the economic rights) may have the right to be identified when the photograph is exhibited or reproduced; he may also have the right to object should the photograph be poorly reproduced. Moral rights have also recently been extended to performers.

Unlike the economic rights, moral rights cannot be assigned and not all countries will permit them to be waived either, which is what the UK permits. Moral rights are often ignored in the digital world but as we shall see later in this book, there is no reason why they do not apply to digital works.

1.2.7　Copyright and Other Intellectual Property (IP) Rights

Copyright simply protects against copying and dealing in illegal copies. If the allegedly infringing work was created without reference to the earlier work then there can be no copyright infringement: if two people write substantially similar software programs independently from each other there can be no copyright infringement. In contrast, if one of the pieces of software was patented then the other could still infringe the patent. Patents create absolute monopoly rights: copyright does not.

Copyright must also be distinguished from laws which protect against unfair competition, such as the English law tort of passing off, or laws which protect brands, such as trade mark law. For example, copying a copyright-protected logo by placing it on a website can amount to copyright infringement even if the logo is not being used as a trade mark and so there is no trade mark infringement or passing off.

These other intellectual property rights are not the subject of this book. Nevertheless rights owners need to bear them in mind where the copyright claim may be weak and where the other IP rights offer additional protection.

1.3　THE INTERNATIONAL ASPECT OF COPYRIGHT

1.3.1　Background

There is no such thing as an 'international copyright'. Copyright is a national property right. It was only in the late nineteenth century when the international piracy of books and other printed materials became a pressing problem that the major industrialised nations got together to grant authors and publishers from other countries the same rights and remedies their own authors and publishers received. This so called principle of 'national treatment' underpins the international copyright system.

The first major international convention to establish the principle of national treatment was the Berne Convention, which dates back to 1886.

It has been revised on a number of occasions but remains the leading international treaty. The USA only agreed to the Berne Convention in 1989. Before that the USA had pressed for countries to sign up to the Universal Copyright Convention (UCC) either instead of, or most frequently in addition to, Berne. The challenges of digitisation resulted in the two latest international copyright treaties: the WIPO Copyright Treaty and the WIPO Performances and Phonograms Treaty, both of December 1996.

The international copyright system is notoriously complex. Readers who require a fuller treatment of this area are referred to the specialist texts in this area.[20] Nevertheless when faced with a digital copyright problem with an international dimension it is worth bearing in mind the following very rough 'rules of thumb':

(a) The law where the work is created (ie its country of origin) is likely to be relevant when determining who owns the copyright in the work or who the author is;

(b) The law where the infringing acts are taking place is likely to be relevant to the questions of the subsistence and infringement of copyright in the work; and

(c) Which courts will hear and resolve any international copyright dispute is likely to be addressed by reference to a number of international conventions dealing with jurisdiction and the enforcement of judgments including the 1968 Brussels and the 1988 Lugano Conventions on Jurisdiction and Enforcement of Judgments in Civil and Commercial Matters.

1.3.2   An Example

By way of an example consider the case of a British software developer who writes code for his employer, a UK company, in the course of his employment. His employer then exploits the code by posting it on their web-server in England as an upgrade to be downloaded by authorised users anywhere in the world. Someone else in England then downloads this code and in breach of his licence copies it and sells it with his own program in the UK.

As discussed in the next chapter, in the UK copyright can be infringed when all or a substantial part of a work protected by copyright is copied without the permission (express or implied) of the copyright owner. As the unlawful copying in this case is taking place within England the matter will

---

[20] For example, Goldstein, *International Copyright: Principles, Law and Practice* (Oxford, Oxford University Press 2001).

be dealt with under UK copyright law. Also it is clear the UK courts would be prepared to hear the case and give judgment, in other words 'seize jurisdiction', if the employer (as copyright owner in the UK) sued the infringer. As previously noted, the court would apply UK copyright law.

But what if the developer were Indian and the code was developed in India in the course of his employment, but still effectively first published in the UK and the English company publishing the code got an assignment of copyright from the Indian employer? Or what if the infringer were located in the USA but was distributing the pirated software in the UK via the Internet? Who would own the copyright, the developer or his employer? Which courts would have jurisdiction, the UK or US courts? Which law would they apply—US or UK?

To answer these questions it is first necessary to note again that copyright is a national right. So the general rule is that infringement will be determined by reference to the law of the country where the infringing act is taking place. Which courts will seize jurisdiction will depend on various factors as elaborated by international convention including whether the plaintiff (claimant) or defendant has a trading presence in the jurisdiction and whether the infringing act takes place within the jurisdiction.

For example, let us assume that the English company sues the US infringer in the English courts and the English courts seize jurisdiction. At the outset of the case the English company will need to show it owns the copyright being infringed: as the work was created in India the general principle is that Indian law will apply to this question. So Indian employment and copyright law will need to be considered. On the basis that the Indian employer was in fact the first owner of copyright then there would appear to be no issue here. The English company will then also need to show that a valid UK copyright subsists. This means that the work must have been first published in the UK or another country with which the UK has a relevant copyright treaty (such as the Berne Convention), or the author was a national of a country with which the UK has a relevant copyright treaty. Having overcome these two hurdles the court will then consider whether there has been infringement.

1.3.3   The Internet and International Copyright

It is often argued that cyberspace has no 'real' location—it can be everywhere and nowhere. In fact as noted below, the location of the relevant equipment underlying the Internet—the routers, servers, PCs and so on immediately gives a physical presence to any infringing activity. But it may be that a person in another jurisdiction is controlling this equipment. Immediately, difficult issues are likely to arise as to which law applies and which courts have jurisdiction. An international copyright code might solve this problem but this is a long way off.[21] At the moment all we can do is endeavour to apply the existing legal rules discussed earlier to cyberspace.

1.4   THE DIGITAL CHALLENGE TO COPYRIGHT

Digital technology poses a number of challenges to copyright. The two most significant aspects are first the digitisation of copyright works (so a photograph, for example, can be scanned into an image file) and the creation of new purely digital products (such as software). Second, the growth of networks such as the Internet which allow the rapid global transmission of digital information.

A useful summary of the challenges is the six characteristics of digital technology identified by a leading US copyright lawyer Professor Pamela Samuelson,[22] to which a seventh can be added—the lack of a human author:

1. *Ease of replication*—the technology used to create and view/use a digital work can be used to make multiple 'perfect' copies of that work.

2. *Ease of transmission and multiple use*—networked computers potentially facilitate the widespread piracy of works. The ongoing development and implementation of broad bandwidth fixed and mobile networks to deliver content-rich 'multimedia' works facilitates this further.

3. *Plasticity of digital media*—users can easily modify, enhance or adapt works in digital form. This has come to the fore with the growth of Web 2.0 discussed in chapter eight.

4. *Equivalence of works in digital form*—all works look alike once in code: this means it is easy to combine digital works into new products such as 'multimedia'. This is also an aspect of *convergence*—the merger of media, technology and networks in areas such as the Internet, digital broadcasting, cable services and so on.

5. *Compactness of works in digital form*—a whole library can be stored on a few CD-ROMS or a storage device; this feature also assists in the creation of new works or assemblages of printed and graphic materials.

6. *New search and link capabilities*—Internet sites can be easily linked, for example.

---

[21] Sterling, *Draft International Copyright Code* (Queen Mary Intellectual Property Research Institute, University of London, 31 May 2001).

[22] Samuelson 'Digital Media and the Changing Face of Intellectual Property Law' (1990) 16 *Rutgers Computer and Technology Law Journal* 323.

7. *No human author (sometimes)*—the digital work may be computer-*generated* as opposed to being created with the *aid* of a computer; copyright law is rooted in the concept of an identifiable, personal author.

This book is about these challenges and how best to exploit the opportunities they present.

1.5 INTERNET TECHNOLOGY AND COPYRIGHT

To understand digital copyright law it is essential to look in general terms at how the Internet works.

1.5.1 How the Internet Works

To illustrate how the Internet works from a digital copyright perspective, consider what steps take place when an image is loaded onto a website—the discussion here centres on the use of a PC by the user but it equally applies to the use of a tablet, smartphone or other mobile device. When the image in question, a photograph ('Work'), is scanned into computer memory using a digital scanner the Work will be copied and if the Work is in copyright, this will amount to an infringement of copyright.[23] Once in electronic form numerous further copies of the Work can be made, for example onto floppy disk, hard disk—they would also infringe copyright under the CDPA. Also, transitory copies of the Work will be made—for example, if the work is viewed on-screen a copy of the Work will be made in computer RAM memory—both this copy but *not necessarily* the on-screen 'copy' will potentially infringe copyright.

Also, let us assume the electronic copy of the Work is loaded onto a computer server (itself an act of copying) made accessible on the worldwide web. A person browsing the relevant website would, through instructions sent by that person's computer, download a copy of the work into RAM in his PC. Again this would be an act of copying.

The Internet is best viewed as a global computer network which allows computers to talk to each other. The viewer's ('browser's') computer transmits a request to the server computer holding the website which is being browsed to forward a copy of some particular material that it is storing. This material is not passed directly to the browser's computer. It is broken into packets, each with an address, and sent across the Internet. It is then passed from one computer on the Internet to another, all of which could be said to make a copy, until all the packets are received at the browser's computer. So the Internet works by copying.

---

[23] s 16 CDPA.

Thus the exploitation of works in digital form is likely to involve the generation of a number of potentially infringing copies. Copying may also take place in several countries; for example, if the server in question is located in Country A and the person browsing in Country B then if the copyright laws of A and B differ this may lead to a different degree of protection between countries.

In practice, however, provided the digital copy of the work is lawfully made available for browsing then those browsing ought to benefit from an implied licence—ie the law will imply a licence from the circumstances. But query the scope of this licence—this is considered further in chapter seven. Having said that, regardless of any implied licence, in light of the recent UK Supreme Court judgment in *Public Relations Consultants Association Limited (Apppellant) v The Newspaper Licensing Agency Limited and others (Respondents)*[24] (and assuming the CJEU takes the same view as the Supreme Court when it gives its ruling on the case) then browsing the Internet will not in any event infringe copyright, as any cached or other copies made in order to do so will be lawful under section 28A CDPA (which gives effect to an exception for temporary copies under Article 5(1) of the Information Society Directive).

Other copyright-related issues which arise in connection with the Internet include:

Caching

A cache is a computer (generally a server) which holds copies of information (eg, the most popular pages on the worldwide web), so that users do not have to return to the original server. In general terms cached material can be stored:

(a)   at a geographically closer site; or
(b)   on a more powerful computer; or
(c)   on a computer with a less congested path to the user.

Typically, Internet service providers (ISPs) store ('cache') frequently-accessed web pages onto their own servers to speed up users' connection times.

A cache is also created by web browsers (such Microsoft's Internet Explorer software), which can create a cache on the hard disk of the user's computer in addition to the transient RAM copies created whilst browsing. This means that users have easier and quicker access to particular websites. Thus caching can occur both on the user's computer and at server level (so-called 'proxy caching').

Caching clearly involves copying a substantial part of a copyright work and (assuming the work is protected by copyright) would appear to require a licence from the copyright owner to avoid a claim of infringement. Although

---

[24] [2013] UK SC 18.

convenient for users, caching is by no means necessary and therefore it can be argued that no licence will be implied from the circumstances.

Regardless of its legal status, caching facilitates the copying of entire websites, throwing up obvious copyright issues. The cache site may not be updated as frequently as the original site. Therefore infringing information may have been removed from the original site but not the cache, rendering the website owner and/or the person operating the cache still potentially liable for any infringement actions.

Linking and Framing

Hypertext links enable a website browser to jump from one website to another, facilitating the accessing of related information. 'Hyper-link' means a connection between two items of hypertext (the HTML language used to build websites and converted into readable English by browser software). The hyper-link often appears on a page of information displayed when browsing a website as an underlined keyword, which if clicked on will take you to another document or website. Whether hyper-linking amounts to copyright infringement is considered in chapter seven. In any event, viewers are often unaware that having clicked onto a particular word or phrase (usually highlighted and underlined) they have accessed another website.

There is still debate about the extent to which the use of hypertext links requires the consent of the person whose site is being linked and/or of the copyright owner. In particular, what if such linking is:

(a)   misleading (eg by 'framing' someone else's content so that it appears on-screen as your own, although in fact it is from a hypertext linked site with no connection to your site);

(b)   defamatory; or

(c)   facilitates copying in circumstances such that a licence permitting such copying cannot be implied from the copyright owner? For example, a search engine automatically provides a link to a site hosting infringing content.

Liability of ISPs and Others

Internet service providers (ISPs) may charge subscribers for the right to access the Internet, for the use of their bulletin boards and other services and/ or for the rental of pages/space on their server on which they host content on behalf of third parties. ISPs can therefore be viewed as intermediaries in the sense they do not themselves determine what appears on the websites they host. A much debated question is whether an ISP can be held liable for copyright infringement occurring on its site and if so what (if any) knowledge of or participation in the infringement must the ISP have to be liable? This area is considered in more detail in chapters two and seven.

Various other intermediaries are involved in facilitating the transmission of content over the Internet: telecommunications operators may provide the backbone/pipe (in this case they may be said to be acting as a 'mere conduit') and may (or others may) provide the intermediate servers and proxy caches. It is clearly debatable to what extent such activities may infringe copyright.

ISPs and other intermediaries concerned that their activities may be held to infringe copyright (including the Internet Service Providers' Association in the UK) have been vociferous in lobbying to seek to ensure that copyright law does not impose liability on them unfairly. To a large extent their concerns are now dealt with by the Electronic Commerce Directive.

Transmission Right

A major issue regarding the Internet is to what extent 'transmissions' via the Internet are protected by copyright. When a person browses a website, then, as discussed above, instructions sent from the browser's computer will arrive at the computer ('server') (the physical location of the website) and will set in motion the transmission of the relevant text or image in digitised packets over the Internet. These packets are received by the browser's computer and are then converted into on-screen images.

Such 'on-demand', interactive access to copyright material is considered by some to represent a challenge to existing copyright laws. In the UK, at least, for the act of transmission itself potentially to infringe copyright the position prior to the 2003 Regulations was that the transmission would have to amount to either a broadcast (which it clearly is not) or a cable programme service. However, under the previous law it could be argued that the interactive nature of the Internet might rule out cable programme protection, although some case law suggested otherwise, as discussed in chapters two and seven.[25]

International concerns about the level of protection for online transmissions were addressed in the 1996 WIPO Copyright Treaty, the US Digital Millennium Copyright Act 1998 and in the Information Society Directive. The WIPO Treaty, for example, provides for a new right of communication to the public for authors of literary and artistic works; such persons shall:

> enjoy the exclusive right of authorising any communication to the public of their works, by wire or wireless means, including the making available to the public of their works in such a way that members of the public may access these works from a place and at a time individually chosen by them.[26]

This 'communication to the public right' (or as it is also called, 'transmission right') was included in the Information Society Directive[27] and implemented

---

[25] *Shetland Times v Wills* [1997] FSR 604; *Sony Music Entertainment (UK) Ltd v Easyinternetcafe Ltd* [2003] FSR 882.
[26] Art 8 (Right of Communication to the Public).
[27] Art 3.

into UK law by the 2003 Regulations:[28] this has given rights holders much
clearer control over the use made of their works over the Internet.

1.6   INTERNATIONAL LEGISLATION

Legislative activity in the digital copyright area has tended to address four
issues:

(a)   the implementation of the World Intellectual Property Organisation
      (WIPO) Treaties of 1996 dealing with the challenges of copyright and digi-
      tisation generally—does existing copyright law adequately protect authors
      and others involved in exploiting copyright works over the Internet?;
(b)   clarifying the liability of ISPs and other intermediaries;
(c)   the legal protection of technical steps to prevent copying ie ensuring
      that there are adequate civil remedies (eg damages and/or an injunction)
      and possibly criminal remedies to deter those who would otherwise
      hack copyright protection systems, or distribute devices which facilitate
      illegal copying and so on; and
(d)   more recently strengthening the remedies against online infringement
      (see section 8.3.3).

In Europe two pieces of legislation are particularly relevant:

(a)   the E-Commerce Directive, dealing among other things with the liability
      of intermediaries; and
(b)   the Information Society Directive, which implements the WIPO Treaties
      and deals with certain other matters including copy—protection tech-
      nologies, in particular following on from the 1995 EU Copyright Green
      Paper.

The USA was ahead of Europe in this area with the enactment in 1998 of
the Digital Millennium Copyright Act (DMCA) which deals with the implementation of the WIPO Treaties and other matters, including the liability of
intermediaries.

1.6.1   Electronic Commerce Directive

Among other things this Directive clarifies that an intermediary such as an
ISP would not be liable for:

(a)   acting as a 'mere conduit'
(b)   'caching', or
(c)   'hosting'

---

[28]   Regs 3 6(1).

Nor is it under a general obligation to monitor information it transmits or stores.

The UK implemented this Directive by the Electronic Commerce (EC Directive) Regulations 2002.[29] This is considered further in chapter two.

1.6.2   **Information Society Directive**

The main copyright issues addressed by the Information Society Directive are:

(a)   Clarification of the extent to which the reproduction and distribution rights apply in the digital environment including the scope of fair use/fair dealing exceptions.[30] The exceptions Member States may make to copyright are now constrained. A particular issue for the UK is the limitation of the fair dealing exception for research and private study to research for a *non-commercial* purpose.[31] This is a change from the previous position where commercial research fell within the exception.

(b)   The reproduction right (subject to limited exceptions) is defined so that authors shall have the exclusive right to authorise or prohibit 'direct or indirect, temporary or permanent reproduction by any means and in any form in whole or in part … of their works'.[32] In particular temporary acts of reproduction integral and essential to a technological process but without economic significance of their own are expressly excepted from copyright protection (thus the activities of Internet intermediaries may not necessarily infringe copyright)[33] and indeed, as noted earlier, the Supreme Court in *Public Relations Consultants Association Limited (Appellant) v The Newspaper Licensing Agency Limited and others (Respondents)*[34] recently came to the conclusion that temporary copies made in browsing the Internet do not infringe copyright on the basis of the exception in Article 5(1) of the Information Society Directive.

(c)   A new right of communication to the public (as part of an on-demand service such as the Internet) to be added to the rights of authors—reflecting the discussion above about the need for a 'transmission right' for the Internet:

> Member states shall provide authors with the exclusive right to authorise or prohibit any communication to the public of their works, by wire or wireless means, including the making available to the public of their works in such a way that members of the public may access them from a place and at a time individually chosen by them.[35]

---

[29] SI 2002/2013.
[30] Art 2, 5 and 6(4).
[31] s 29, CDPA.
[32] Art 2.
[33] Art 5 (1).
[34] [2013] UK SC 18.
[35] Art 3 (1).

(d)   Legal protection of anti-copying and rights management systems.[36]

The UK was obliged to implement this Directive before 22 December 2002. In fact, the UK was late in doing this—the 2003 Regulations implementing the Directive came into effect on 31 October 2003. The amendments made to the CDPA by the Directive are considered in greater detail in chapter two.

1.7   THE FUTURE

Digital technology has put copyright at the cross roads. There are two conflicting ways ahead: the death of copyright or the consolidation and revision of copyright to address the digital future.

1.7.1   The Death of Copyright

Unlike a book or a painting which can be viewed or read without any need for infringing copies of it to be made, digitised works require electronic copies to be generated (whether transitory or not) in order to be accessed or used. This raises several possibilities for digital works including:

(a)   The growth of file swapping/peer-to-peer services such as Napster and Gnutella together with their later incarnations (such as Grokster, StreamCast, KaZaa and Newzbin and the use by pirates of service providers such as eBay and Google/YouTube to distribute/communicate infringing material) and also DVD piracy indicate copyright cannot effectively regulate the digital environment in any event. As a result more and more digital content will be encrypted or copy-protected; breaking or hacking the copy protection or encryption to access and use the work will be made illegal or unlawful whatever the motive—to read for personal use or to distribute commercially. Also strong laws will be in force to prevent access to the Internet to those who infringe copyright along the lines of 'three strikes and you are out'. The solution to prevent serial infringers of copyright is to deny them access to the Internet by way of a warning email and then a graduated response with denial of access the ultimate sanction for non-compliance. So in France, for example, there is now the controversial HADOPI law[37] (from 2009) and in the UK from 2010 the Digital Economy Act (further discussed in chapter eight); and

---

[36] Ch III.
[37] www.hadopi.fr/ (accessed 11 May 2013).

(b) Users will also be required to enter into binding licences with rights owners in order to be permitted to access and use digital content—the use of digital material will be regulated by contract not copyright.

In each case technology, contract or stringent anti-piracy laws will effectively prevent users from benefiting from the fair use/fair dealing exceptions to copyright infringement. Copyright will become redundant. Taken to an extreme, digital content could effectively be locked up and no longer be available for legitimate private study or research, criticism or review, etc. Digital information will become privatised. Chapter seven looks in detail at this area.[38]

1.7.2 A New Future for Copyright

Legislators are becoming increasingly aware of the need to preserve the public domain or, as it is often called these days, an 'intellectual commons'. Also is copyright 'fit for purpose'? The Information Society Directive empowers member states to take action to ensure access to copyright-protected works for limited 'public good'-type purposes regardless of technological or contractual restrictions on their use. However, the language in the Directive enabling this is vague and difficult to construe. Much depends on its implementation in the various EU states.

Initiatives such as the Information Society Directive indicate that copyright's power and flexibility as an intellectual property right is not yet dead.

Some argue for a much more simplified copyright system aimed at the digital environment with one key copyright—the right to control the dissemination or exploitation of copyright works. This would replace the existing 'bundle of rights' approach to copyright (ie today copyright covers many rights such as the right to control copying, adaptation, broadcasting, transmission, etc). Such a single right should be technologically neutral whatever digitisation and other new technologies bring. There would also probably be a breakdown between the current classification of copyright works as films, sound recordings, artistic works, etc to one all-encompassing class of 'multimedia' work.[39]

Others see an International Copyright Code as the solution to the harmonisation and effective enforcement of copyright in the digital world.[40]

---

[38] See eg Lucchi, 'Access to Network Services and Protection of Constitutional Rights: Recognizing the Essential Role of Internet Access for the Freedom of Expression' (2011) 19 3, *Cardozo Journal of International and Comparative Law (JICL)*. Available at SSRN: http://ssrn.com/abstract=175624.

[39] Perlmutter, 'Convergence and the Future of Copyright' (2001) *EIPR* 111.

[40] Sterling, *Draft International Copyright Code.*

Digitisation may also lead the way to new collective ways of administering rights. 'Micro payments' and other Internet technologies could play a part in enabling proper remuneration for rights holders. For example, in the UK a digital copyright hub is being established to assist in rights clearance.

Finally, some people want to keep the copyright system in place but construct licensing models to allow the collaborative and open exploitation of digital works. The best known examples of this are the 'open source' or 'copyleft' movement and 'Creative Commons', discussed in chapter nine.

1.7.3   Concluding Thoughts

It is unclear where copyright will end up: an irrelevance in a world of technological and legal locks and keys, or a simplified and rejuvenated intellectual property right. Much will depend on how the courts and legislators balance fair use and free speech arguments against contractual, legal and technological measures restricting access to content. But for the moment at least, news of copyright's demise remains greatly exaggerated. Certainly since the first edition of this book in 2002 when these comments were first made, copyright far from being an irrelevance has taken centre stage with ongoing legislative reform to seek to make it fit for purpose in light of technological change.

Nevertheless, rights owners should take account of the pressures digital copyright protection is facing. In practice digital copyright law *and* a combination of technical and/or contractual steps will need to be applied or at least considered when protecting digital content.

This book endeavours to state the law current in the UK as at 31 December 2012 but where possible, account has been taken of more recent decisions up until April 2013 (and in certain cases up to June 2013). This book does not purport to advise or provide guidance on US law although where helpful US cases are referred to, but these are not necessarily up to date references.

SUMMARY

(a) Digital copyright law involves the application of existing 'analogue' copyright rules to the digital environment and new digital rules.
(b) The primary purpose of digital copyright law is to protect the investment and/or the skill and effort of the creator of the copyright work.
(c) Gaps in the existing copyright rules are being plugged in a piecemeal fashion to deal with digitisation.

(d) The bulk of European legislation dealing with digital copyright is now in place following the adoption of the Information Society Directive.

(e) The UK implemented the Information Society Directive on 31 October 2003.

(f) Unfinished legislative business includes better ways of dealing with international copyright disputes and the ongoing modernisation of copyright law in the UK (see 1.2.2).

(g) The jury is still out whether digital copyright has a long-term future or whether technical locks and keys and/or contract law will displace copyright from protecting digital content.

(h) Content owners will want to use a mixture of digital copyright, technical measures and/or licences (ie contract law) to protect their content.

2

Digital Copyright: The Basics

2.1 INTRODUCTION

2.1.1 Overview

This chapter sets out the basics of digital copyright law. As digital copyright law is built upon analogue copyright law, this chapter explains the existing structure of UK copyright law focusing on the digital aspects. The last section looks at some specific issues thrown up by the implementation of the Information Society Directive and Electronic Commerce Directive into UK copyright law.

Important rights of particular relevance to the digital environment which are either separate from copyright (moral rights, database rights) or are worthy of separate treatment (software copyright), are dealt with in later chapters. Rights in performances (of particular relevance to the music industry and digital music distribution) are covered in this chapter, however.

This chapter is an overview of the area. The chapters which follow go into specific aspects of digital copyright law and their application, with examples and issues in mind.

2.1.2 Sources of Law

In the UK, the copyright statute is the Copyright, Designs and Patents Act 1988 (CDPA) (primary legislation). This has been supplemented and/or amended by various Statutory Instruments or Regulations (secondary legislation) which have sought to implement various EC Directives. It is this legislation and the Directives (which embody the purpose behind the legislation) to which one should look for a statement of UK copyright law, together with relevant cases interpreting and applying this law.

Difficult issues arise where the legislation implementing a Directive is defective in that it clearly fails to implement the Directive properly. This is beyond the scope of this text and readers are referred to specialist texts eg

Laddie, Prescott and Vitoria, *The Modern Law of Copyright and Designs* (Butterworths, London, 3rd edn, 2000) for a full discussion of this area.

International Conventions, Treaties and Agreements to which the UK is a signatory, such as the Berne Convention, Rome Convention and Universal Copyright Convention (UCC), are not self-implementing in the UK. Instead the UK has enacted primary and secondary legislation to deal with their requirements, primarily embodied in the legislation referred to in the preceding paragraphs. Nevertheless, the text of these documents provides useful guidance and is essential in order to understand international copyright. Hence these documents are referred to at various points in the book. The UK is also obliged to give effect to the World Trade Organisation TRIPS Agreement of 1994[1] and again this is noted where relevant.

The UK has sought to implement the provisions of the 1996 WIPO Copyright and Performances and Phonograms Treaties (WIPO Treaties) not already part of UK law as part of the UK implementation of the Information Society Directive and follow-up legislation (The Performances (Moral Rights, etc) Regulations 2006).[2]

2.2   WHAT DIGITAL COPYRIGHT PROTECTS

2.2.1   UK Law

In considering the scope of digital copyright protection under the CDPA it is necessary to consider:

(a)   the classes of work (digital or analogue) protected by copyright—the 'subject-matter' of copyright;
(b)   criteria for protection ie the work must be 'original';
(c)   who the author is (including for computer-generated works)
(d)   the need for fixation/permanence of the work;
(e)   qualifying factors for protection;
(f)   duration of protection; and
(g)   other rights related to or neighbouring copyright.

2.2.2   Digital Copyright Works

It is fundamental to any understanding of copyright that copyright only protects various categories of *works* against copying.[3] These works can be in analogue or (in certain cases) digital form. Unless a work falls within one of the statutory definitions noted below it will *not* be protected by copyright.

---

[1] *Designers Guild v Russell Williams* [2000] 1 WLR 2416 (HL).
[2] 2006 No 18.
[3] s 1(1) CDPA.

The Copyright, Designs and Patents Act 1988 (CDPA) classifies copyright 'works' as follows:[4]

(a)   *original* **literary works:** (defined as any work, other than a dramatic or musical work, which is written, spoken or sung—these include databases and computer programs, including preparatory design material for a computer program);

(b)   *original* **dramatic works:** (including a work of dance or mime) and **musical works** (ie works consisting of music, exclusive of any words or action intended to be sung, spoken or performed with the music);

(c)   *original* **artistic works:**[5] a graphic work (which includes (i) any painting, drawing, diagram, map, chart or plan, and (ii) any engraving, etching, lithograph, woodcut or similar work)[6], photograph, sculpture or collage, in each case *irrespective of artistic quality* [emphasis added]; a work of artistic craftsmanship; a work of architecture (ie a building or a model for a building);

(d)   **sound recordings, films, or broadcasts**; and

(e)   **the typographical arrangement of published editions:** this limited copyright protects the 'image on the page' and protects the publisher (the owner of this right) from exact copying ('facsimile copying'[7]) by photo-lithography, digital scanning or similar means. It arguably only protects works published by analogue means eg a printed newspaper as opposed to an online paper. Section 175 ((1)(b)) CDPA (which deals with electronic publication) does not apply to typographical arrangements, and the new 'communication to the public' right does not apply to typographical arrangements. Also it can be argued that this copyright is aimed at classic, printed, published editions, as used in the publishing trade.[8]

Certain copyright works can only exist in digital form—they are truly 'digital copyright' works:

(a)   **computer programs**—which are classed as literary works

Other copyright works can exist in both analogue and digital form:

(a)   **databases** (discussed in chapter three)

(b)   **photographs**—the CDPA[9] defines a photograph as 'a recording of light or other radiation on any medium on which an image is

---

[4] s 1 CDPA.
[5] s 4 CDPA.
[6] s 4(2) CDPA.
[7] s 17(5) CDPA.
[8] *Newspaper Licensing Agency v Marks & Spencer plc* [2001] 3 WLR 295 (HL).
[9] s 4(2) CDPA.

produced or from which an image may by any means be produced, and which is not part of a film'. Clearly a digital photograph can fall within this definition.

(c) **computer-generated literary, dramatic, musical or artistic works**[10]

(d) **literary works**—under section 178 of the CDPA 'writing' includes any form of notation or code

(e) **dramatic works** (these can include films which record a dramatic work)[11]

(f) **musical works**

(g) **sound recordings**—these are protected regardless of the medium or the method used to make or play the recording[12]

(h) **films**

(i) **broadcasts**—this definition has recently changed: cable programmes now fall within this definition (they are no longer separately defined in the CDPA[13]) and the position of Internet transmissions is dealt with through the new 'communication to the public' right.[14] A broadcast is now defined as an electronic transmission of visual images, sounds or other information which is (i) transmitted for simultaneous reception by members of the public and is capable of being lawfully received by them, or (ii) transmitted at a time determined solely by the person making the transmission for presentation to members of the public, and which is not (with limited exceptions) an Internet transmission.[15]

(j) **typefaces** (artistic works)—the copyright protection for typefaces is effectively limited to 25 years.[16] Query how software fonts are protected—a typeface stored in a computer program is arguably a literary rather than an artistic work.[17] In any event, registered design protection may also be available as discussed in chapter six, section 6.1.

Some copyright works can only exist in analogue form:

(a) **The majority of artistic works apart from photographs, for example, except where they are computer-generated.** In *Anacon Corporation Limited and Another v Environmental Research Technology Limited and Another*[18] Jacob J. said that the essential nature of a graphic work (a

---

[10] s 178 CDPA; s 9(3) CDPA.
[11] *Norowzian v Arks Ltd* (No 2) [2000] FSR 363.
[12] s 5A CDPA.
[13] See former s 7 CDPA.
[14] s 20 CDPA.
[15] s 6(1) CDPA.
[16] ss 54 and 55 CDPA.
[17] Burloch, 'Typography in Law: From Mechanics to Aesthetics' [2001] *ENTLR* 78; Watts and Blakemore, 'Protection of Software Fonts in UK Law' [1995] *EIPR* 133.
[18] [1994] FSR 659.

class of 'artistic work') was that it was a thing to be looked at in some manner or other: '[i]t is to be looked at in itself'.[19] Also as noted above, it can be argued that typographical copyright does not protect on-line books and newspapers.

Of course even if the work does not exist in digital form, copies of it can. For example, consider a painting by Picasso. This is an artistic work (a painting) in analogue form. A digital photograph of it would nevertheless be a *digital copy* of the painting and also a copyright work (a photograph) in its own right.

The Problem of Categorising Digital Works

Many digital works—digital sound recordings or films, digital broadcasts, digital photographs, electronic books and so on—easily fall within the existing definitions of copyright works. But there are certain problem areas. The CDPA does not define 'multimedia' or 'digital media' as such.

As noted in chapter one, digitisation enables the creation of non-traditional works such as:

(a) **multi-media works on CD or available on the web:** when accessed these may display one or more of text, images, moving images and sound/music and they may also be highly interactive—are they software (literary work), films (moving images recorded in electronic form), photographs (still electronic images), literary works (text stored in electronic form), musical works (music stored in electronic form), or even a database (collection of independent works arranged in a methodical way and individually accessible electronically[20])?

(b) **a website:** similar issues arise to those for multimedia works

(c) **titles of web pages and hypertext links:** on the basis of *Shetland Times Ltd v Wills*[21] these might be classed as literary works and hence be protected from copying, although this goes against a long-standing principle of literary copyright that literary works must afford information and instruction or pleasure in the form of literary enjoyment[22]—titles/links might be too short or unimaginative to satisfy this test although recent cases suggest otherwise.[23] The issue of whether hyperlinking and its variants such as deep linking infringe copyright or database right is considered in chapter seven.

(d) **computer games:** similar issues arise to those for multimedia works

---

[19] Ibid 662.

[20] s 3A CDPA—see ch 3.

[21] [1997] FSR 604.

[22] *Exxon Corporation v Exxon Insurance Consultants International Ltd* [1982] RPC 69 (HL).

[23] *The Newspaper Licensing Agency Ltd v Meltwater Holding BV* [2011] EWCA Civ 890.

(e) **Internet transmissions:** prior to the 2003 Regulations it was debat-
able whether transmissions over the Internet (ie the data sent over the
Internet in the course of downloading a web page—see chapter one)
could amount to a cable programme service under Section 7(1) CDPA.
Shetland Times Ltd v Wills[24] and *Sony Music Entertainment (UK) Ltd v
Easyinternetcafe Ltd*[25] are authority that they were. However, now the
Information Society Directive has been implemented in the UK and a
new transmission/communication to the public right introduced into
UK copyright law,[26] this concern is no longer relevant (see later in this
chapter).

The copyright protection for these and similar digital works will be as
follows:

(a) They will be protected by copyright in so far as their parts are protected
by copyright.
(b) The work as a whole might fall within the UK's generous definition of
a 'film'—'a recording on any medium from which a moving image may
by any means be reproduced' and they include the film soundtrack.[27] In
Galaxy Electronics Ltd v Sega Enterprises Ltd[28], the Federal Court of
Australia held that visual images created by playing a video game fell
within the Australian statutory definition of 'cinematographic film'.
(c) The compilation of various works involved might allow for copyright
and/or database rights protection—see chapter three.

2.2.3   Criteria for Protection ie Work Must Be 'Original'

Certain works (literary, dramatic, musical and artistic works) must be *original*
to be protected. Sound recordings and films must also not be copied from
previous recordings and films if they are to be protected by copyright.[29]
Broadcasts are not protected by copyright to the extent they infringe the
copyright in another broadcast.[30]
   The standard required for a work to qualify as *original* is very low under
English law (with the caveat that European developments noted in section
2.6.2 below may reassess this standard). An often-cited case is *University of
London Press Limited v University Tutorial Press Limited*[31] which considered

[24] [1997] FSR 604.
[25] [2003] FSR 48 (page 882).
[26] s 20 CDPA.
[27] s 5B CDPA.
[28] [1997] 145 ALR 21.
[29] ss 5A(2) and 5B(4) CDPA.
[30] s 6(6) CDPA.
[31] [1916] 2 Ch 601.

what was meant by *original* in the context of a literary work. According to the judge:

> The word 'original' does not in this connection mean that the work must be the expression of original or inventive thought. Copyright [A]cts are not concerned with the originality of ideas but with the expression of thought, and, in the case of a 'literary work,' with the expression of thought in print or writing. The originality which is required relates to the expression of the thought. But the Act [Copyright Act 1911] does not require that the expression must be in an original or novel form, but that the work must not be copied from another work—that it should originate from the author.[32]

However, it remains the case that some degree of skill and labour on the part of the author is required to qualify a work as 'original'[33] but no more than trivial effort and skill are required for these purposes.[34] Nevertheless, when the work is derived from another work mere 'slavish' copying, even if it involves considerable skill, labour or judgment cannot confer originality.[35] In cases of copying from another work there needs to be some element of material alteration or embellishment, which suffices to make the totality of the work an original work.[36] But it is still the case that the threshold is a low one: for example, in *Sawkins v Hyperion Records Ltd*[37] the Court of Appeal held that the editing of musical works long out of copyright and in the public domain into performing editions created new copyright works (in this case musical works) even where the editor's intention had not been to write new music but to faithfully reflect the original scores and correct them into a form that could be played.

Certainly the level of originality in the UK appears lower than that required in the USA where, following the Supreme Court in *Feist Publications v Rural Telephone Service Co*[38] the work must possess at least *some minimal degree of creativity*.[39] In Europe the position is different again. Harmonisation of this area has been attempted to a limited extent by the European Commission. For example, in the Term Directive[40] where the concept of originality is

---

[32] *Per* Peterson J at 608–9.

[33] *Interlego AG v Tyco Industries* [1989] 1 AC 217 at 262H.

[34] *Autospin (Oil Seals) v Beehive Spinning* (a firm) [1995] RPC 683 at 694, cited in *SPE International Ltd v Professional Preparation Contractors (UK) Ltd* [2000] EIPR N-19.

[35] *Interlego AG v Tyco Industries and Others* [1989] 1 AC 217 at 262H as cited eg in *SPE International Ltd v Professional Preparation Contractors (UK) Ltd* [2000] EIPR N-19.

[36] *Interlego v Tyco* at 263C.

[37] [2005] EWCA Civ 565.

[38] 499 US 340 (1991).

[39] Ibid 369.

[40] Directive 93/98/EEC of 29 October 1993, OJ L 290/9 (24 November 1993) (Term Directive) [now repealed and replaced by codified and amended version 2006/116/EC].

applied to computer programs, databases and photographs, *the author's own intellectual creation reflecting his personality* is the criterion for protection.[41]

Given the low standard required for 'originality,' this hurdle to copyright protection in the UK is likely to be satisfied for most digital copyright works, including such relatively 'unoriginal' works as digital photographs of paintings or objects in an art gallery's collection, for example. Nevertheless as discussed above, mere mechanical copying will not be sufficient to confer 'originality'—so a digitally scanned image will not of itself benefit from copyright protection. In *The Reject Shop plc v Manners*[42] the Court of Appeal rejected an argument that a slightly enlarged image produced using a photocopier was itself an original artistic work—there was no skill and labour involved in the copying sufficient to confer *originality of an artistic character*.[43] Chapter seven looks at the protection of images in more detail.

2.2.4   Who is the Author (Including for Computer-generated Works)?

Under the CDPA all copyright works need an author (even if unknown). As we shall see later in this chapter, who the author is will help determine who first owns the copyright in a work, how long copyright in the work subsists and if the work qualifies for copyright in the first place. 'Author' is a term of art used throughout the CDPA.[44]

For artistic, musical, dramatic and literary works the 'author' for copyright purposes is the creator of the work in question.[45] The rule is different for sound recordings, films, broadcasts and published editions (in respect of protection for typographical arrangements).[46]

Where a literary, dramatic, musical or artistic work is *computer-generated*, however, the author is the person by whom the arrangements necessary for the creation of the work are undertaken[47]—this will typically be the programmer but not necessarily so.[48] This is to be distinguished from a *computer-assisted or computer-aided* work where the computer is a mere tool, such as the laptop computer and software used to write this book.

For example, a software program is written and implemented to control a web camera (webcam) which then automatically takes pictures and these pictures are relayed back to a website. There is no doubt these images are

---

[41] Art 6 and Recital 17 of the Term Directive.
[42] [1995] FSR 870.
[43] *Per* Legatt LJ at 876.
[44] s 179 CDPA.
[45] s 9(1) CDPA.
[46] s 9(2) CDPA.
[47] s 9(3).
[48] See *Nova Productions Ltd v Mazooma Games Ltd* [2006] EWHC 24 (Ch).

protected by copyright—to ascertain who the author was one would need to apply the rule concerning computer-generated works noted above. In an Austrian case where a web camera was set up to display Alpine weather conditions at a ski resort just such an issue arose. Although Austrian copyright law did not appear to have the concept of a 'computer-generated work' the court had no problem in considering that the author could not be a machine— it had to be the person who made the necessary arrangements for the production of the work.[49]

There are also specific rules concerning works of joint authorship and works of 'unknown authorship'.[50]

2.2.5   The Need for Fixation/permanence of the Work

In the case of a literary, dramatic or musical work, copyright will only subsist in the work if it is recorded in writing or otherwise.[51] As noted earlier 'writing' includes any form of notation or code, whether by hand or otherwise, and regardless of the method by which, or medium in or on which, it is recorded.[52] For example, the text of this book was recorded on the author's laptop RAM and then hard drive initially—at that point it was recorded in writing.

There are no equivalent provisions for artistic works. However on public policy grounds it can be argued that because copyright confers a sort of monopoly, there must be certainty in what copyright protects in order to avoid injustice.[53] US law, for example, requires fixation of original works of authorship 'in any tangible medium of expression, now known or later developed, from which they can be perceived, reproduced, or otherwise communicated, either directly or with the aid of a machine or device'.[54]

2.2.6   Qualifying Factors for Protection and Digital Copyright Formalities

As noted in chapter one, the basis behind the international copyright system as enshrined in the Berne Convention is the principle of 'national treatment'. This means that in the UK, for example, a work originating in a foreign country will in the vast majority of cases be given the same protection as a work

---

[49] Case 4 Ob 15/00k, Austrian Supreme Court (1 February 2000); [2000] *ENTLR* N-91.
[50] ss 10 and 9(4) CDPA, respectively.
[51] s 3(2) CDPA.
[52] s 178 CDPA.
[53] By Farwell LJ in *Tate v Fullbrook* [1908] 1 KB 821 at 822–33.
[54] s 102, Copyright Act 1976.

created in the UK.[55] So in general, a work will be protected by copyright in the UK provided either:

(a) the author was at the material time[56] a 'qualifying person' ie a British national or is resident or domiciled in one of the countries of the Berne Union (ie states which are parties to the Berne Convention) or a country which is a party to the Universal Copyright Convention; or

(b) the work was first 'published' in one of these countries.[57] Section 175 of the CDPA states that 'publication' means the issue of copies to the public, and includes, in the case of a literary, dramatic, musical or artistic work, making it available to the public by means of an electronic retrieval system. So a work can be first published via the Internet.[58]

There is no requirement in the UK to register the work with any official body such as the Stationers' Company or the UK IPO—no such formalities are necessary to secure copyright in the UK. However it is desirable, for international protection and also to help enforce the owner's rights, to include a copyright notice on copies of a work along the lines of © [name of copyright owner], year of first publication.[59] In states such as the USA where the registration of copyright may confer certain benefits, registration of copyright should also be considered.

Phonogram producers should likewise use the (P) notice and year of first publication together with details of the producer or his licensee and principal performers on the copies or containers for the phonogram to benefit from the Rome Convention (see the rights in performances section below). A phonogram is any exclusively aural fixation of sounds of a performance or other sounds (eg CD, record, cassette) and a producer of phonograms is the person who first fixes the sounds of the performance or other sounds.[60]

2.2.7 Duration of Protection

From 1 January 1996 copyright in new and existing literary, dramatic, musical and artistic works, and films was extended as a result of EU harmonisation. In general copyright now lasts for the life of the author and expires at the end of the period 70 years from the end of the calendar year in which the author dies—this is the so-called 70-year *post mortem auctoris* rule.[61] Until 1 January 1996, the term was 50 years *post mortem auctoris*. The introduction

---

[55] Part I, Ch IX, CDPA.
[56] s 154(4) CDPA.
[57] ss 153–6 CDPA.
[58] See also Gringras, *The Laws of the Internet* (London, Butterworths, 2nd edn, 2003) 225.
[59] Art III (1) of the Universal Copyright Convention (UCC).
[60] Rome Convention Arts 3 and 11.
[61] ss 12 and 13(B) CDPA.

of the new copyright term has also 'revived' copyright in works previously out of copyright in the UK but which were protected under the copyright legislation of any other state in the European Economic Area (EEA) on 1 July 1995.

Not all works benefit from the 70 years *post mortem auctoris* rule. Notable exceptions include:

(a)   sound recordings copyright remains subject to a maximum term of 50 years from date of release (this would include by releasing MP3 files over the Internet), although this will be extended to 70 years once the UK implements Directive 2011/77/EU (which the UK must do by 1 November 2013);[62]

(b)   copyright in broadcasts remains subject to a maximum term of 50 years from when the broadcast was made;[63]

(c)   works of unknown authorship—typically a 70-year term from the date of making them available to the public;[64]

(d)   computer-generated works—these are protected by copyright for 50 years from creation;[65] and

(e)   typographical arrangement of published editions—a 25-year term from first publication.[66]

2.2.8   Other Digital Rights Neighbouring Copyright or Related to it

Copyright, more than any other intellectual property right, has been expanded to cover a wide range of objects and activities, and to protect both economic and moral interests, adding to the complexity of the subject. Copyright in its strict sense excludes a number of related or neighbouring rights to copyright, such as rights in performances, rental and lending rights, moral rights, rights protecting the encryption of broadcasts (including cable programme services) or copy protection systems, and *sui generis rights* such as database rights. Because of their importance, database rights and moral rights are dealt with separately in chapters three and four respectively. Encryption and copy protection issues are discussed in chapter seven.

Other neighbouring rights are briefly outlined in this section to the extent they are relevant to the digital world.

---

[62] s 13(A) CDPA; the Directive also extends the duration of performers' rights in sound recordings to 70 years and deals with certain other matters (see www.ipo.gov.uk/consult-2013-copyterm.pdf (accessed 16 June 2013)).

[63] s 14 CDPA.

[64] ss 12(3) and 12(4) CDPA.

[65] s 12(7).

[66] s 15 CDPA.

Publication Right

From 1 December 1996, a new right, 'publication right', equivalent to copyright (but excluding moral rights protection), protecting unpublished literary, artistic, dramatic, or musical works or films in which copyright has expired, was introduced into the CDPA.[67] The first owner of the publication right is the person who 'publishes' such a work for the first time within the European Economic Area (EEA), being a national of an EEA state. The right lasts for 25 years from the end of the calendar year in which the work is first published.

'Publication' is defined to include any communication to the public and includes making the work available by means of an electronic retrieval system, so publication on the Internet would amount to 'publication' in the context of publication right.[68]

Rights in Performances[69]

Performers' rights stand outside the core of copyright. But they are of great importance in the digital environment, especially as the recording industry fights Internet piracy.

These rights seek to protect:

(a) performers; and
(b) those with recording rights in their performances. They are classed into non-property and property rights (see below) and from 1 February 2006 have together been referred to in the CDPA as 'economic rights'[70] (as opposed to performers' moral rights, which are separate and discussed in chapter 4).[71]

The Rome Convention (1961) lays down minimum international standards of protection for performers as well as phonogram producers and broadcasting organisations.[72] The TRIPS Agreement (1994) and the WIPO Performances and Phonograms Treaty (1996) also deal with performers.

It should be noted that the USA has never acceded to the Rome Convention and has always been opposed to the extension of performers' rights beyond music/phonograms to audio-visual works such as films. WIPO is attempting to take forward a possible new Treaty or Protocol to the WIPO Treaties dealing with the protection of audio-visual performances but the progress to date has been difficult.

---

[67] The Copyright and Related Rights Regulations 1996 (SI 1996/2967).
[68] Reg 16(2).
[69] See Arnold, *Performers' Rights* (London, Sweet & Maxwell, 1997).
[70] Part II Rights in Performances—ch 2: Economic Rights (ss 182–205B CDPA).
[71] Part II Rights in Performances—ch 3: Moral Rights (ss 205C–205N CDPA).
[72] The International Convention for the Protection of Performers, Producers of Phonograms and Broadcasting Organisations.

In the UK, until Part II of the CDPA came into force on 1 August 1989, performers only benefited from statutory criminal sanctions for 'bootlegging' and other unauthorised activities and also they had very limited civil rights (ie to claim damages and secure an injunction).[73] The CDPA gave express civil rights to performers and to persons having exclusive recording contracts with performers. Then in 1996, performers were given property rights in recordings of their performances.[74] Criminal sanctions remain.[75]

So in the UK performers have protection under Part II of the CDPA under two regimes provided:

(a)   the performance falls within the appropriate category (ie it is a *live* dramatic (including dance or mime) or musical performance, a reading or recitation of a literary work, or a performance of a variety act).[76] This clearly excludes sporting events but unfortunately the CDPA does not clarify what 'live performance' means—the general view is that this simply means it is not a pre-recorded performance or one that is computer-generated, say. It does not have to be a performance given in front of an audience. So a studio recording will be given the same protection as a recording made in a concert hall, for example; and

(b)   it is a qualifying performance[77] ie it is given by a qualifying individual (ie a person with a connection to a qualifying country)[78] or takes place in a qualifying country (the UK, another EEA country and certain other countries[79]); and

(c)   the recording is a film or sound recording made directly from the live performance or from a broadcast of the performance or made directly or indirectly from another recording of the performance.[80]

Performers' Non-property Rights and Recording Rights

Performers have the right to consent to the recording or live broadcast of their performances.[81] They also have the right to consent to the exploitation (ie public performance, communication to the public (for example by broadcasting or (a new right under the 2003 Regulations) making the work available for downloading over the Internet/on-demand transmission[82]), and importing, possessing and dealing in recordings) of recordings of their

---

[73] *Rickless v United Artists Corpn* [1988] QB 40.
[74] Copyright and Related Rights Regulations 1996 (SI 1996/2967).
[75] ss 198 and 201 CDPA.
[76] s 180(2) CDPA.
[77] s 181 CDPA.
[78] s 206(1) CDPA.
[79] s 206(1) CDPA.
[80] s 180(2) CDPA.
[81] s 182 CDPA.
[82] s 182(b) CDPA.

performances where the recording was made without their consent.[83] These rights cannot be assigned but they are transmissible on death.[84]

Persons with recording rights in relation to a performance (ie they have an exclusive recording contract with the performer or have been assigned the benefit of it) have rights with respect to recordings made without their consent or that of the performer.[85] It is an infringement of recording rights to show or play in public the performance via such a recording or (a new right under the 2003 Regulations) to communicate the performance to the public (eg by broadcasting or Internet access/on-demand transmission) via such a recording. These rights also cannot be assigned except through the mechanism of assigning the benefit of the exclusive recording contract to someone else.[86]

Performers' Property Rights[87]

These are the rights conferred on performers to control the copying of recordings of their performances ('reproduction right'), the issue to the public of copies of such recordings ('distribution right), rental and lending of these recordings ('rental right and lending right') and (a new right under the 2003 Regulations) the making available to the public of a recording of the performance by electronic transmission in such a way that members of the public may access the recording from a place and at a time individually chosen by them—what is often called 'on-demand transmission' ('making available right' or 'communication to the public right')[88]. These rights can be licensed or assigned in whole or part or otherwise disposed of as personal movable property. Like copyright, any assignment must be in writing signed by or on behalf of the assignor[89] and exclusive licences should be in writing.[90]

Performers' rights expire (a) at the end of 50 years from the end of the calendar year in which the performance takes place, or (b) if during that period a recording is released, 50 years from the end of the calendar year in which it is released.[91] A recording is released when it is first published, played, or shown in public, or communicated to the public.[92] Where the performer

---

[83] ss 183 and 184 CDPA.
[84] s 192A CDPA.
[85] ss 185–8 CDPA.
[86] s 192B CDPA.
[87] s 191A CDPA.
[88] s 182CA CDPA.
[89] s 191B CDPA.
[90] s 191D CDPA.
[91] s 191(2) CDPA. Although as noted above Directive 2011/77/EU extends this period for sound recordings to 70 years.
[92] s 191(3) CDPA.

is not a national of an EEA state the duration of protection may be less.[93] There are specific rules for performances given before 1 January 1996.[94]

Performers are also entitled to equitable remuneration from the owner of the copyright in the sound recording in respect of the playing in public, or where it is communicated to the public (eg by broadcasting but not where it is made available over the Internet ie by 'on-demand transmission'[95]), of commercially published sound recordings of the whole or a substantial part of their performances.[96] This right cannot be waived and can only be assigned to a collecting society. If the parties cannot agree on the amount, the Copyright Tribunal is empowered to determine the matter. There are also similar provisions noted below in respect of equitable remuneration in respect of the performers' rental right for sound recordings and films.[97]

The exceptions to digital copyright noted below also broadly apply to rights in performances.[98]

Performers' Rights and the Digital Environment

It is clear that recordings of performances can be in digital or analogue form. Likewise, the exploitation of performances can include Internet transmissions (by analogy to inclusion in a cable programme service[99]). So the same issues which arise in relation to analogue recordings and exploitation apply to digital exploitation. However, the rights management issues surrounding digital exploitation will require continual development. Also there continue to be further international developments in this area.

The 1996 WIPO Performances and Phonograms Treaty is highly relevant to the digital environment. To the extent there was any doubt about whether performers had rights in cyberspace, the Treaty removes these doubts. In particular Articles 10 and 14 of the Treaty effectively allow performers and producers of phonograms to control the exploitation of their phonograms over the Internet by clarifying the existence and scope of the communication to the public right.

For example, this right will control whether or not phonograms may be placed on a website or bulletin board or made available by a peer-to-peer service such as Napster. Also Article 15 provides that performers and

---

[93] ss 191(4) and 191(5) CDPA.

[94] See: s 191 CDPA and the Duration of Copyright and Rights in Performances Regulations 1995.

[95] The right does not apply where the work is made available to the public under 182CA(1) CDPA—see s 182D(1)(b) CDPA.

[96] s 182D CDPA. NB Publication of a sound recording now includes making it available to the public online—see s 182D(1A), which was inserted into the CDPA by the Performances (Moral Rights etc) Regulations 2006, SI 2006/18.

[97] s 191G CDPA.

[98] s 189 CDPA.

[99] *Shetland Times v Wills* [1997] FSR 604.

phonogram producers will also enjoy the right to a single equitable remuneration for any communication to the public of phonograms.

The Treaty also contains obligations dealing with technical protection measures and rights management information.[100] These are discussed generally in chapter seven.

The Treaty requires certain moral rights to be given to performers in respect of the sound element of a performance. In order for the UK to ratify the Treaty, from 1 February 2006, the CDPA was amended to implement performers' moral rights, going beyond what was required by the Treaty.[101]

As noted above, the implementation of the Treaty into UK law via the Information Society Directive has required amendments to the CDPA. One of two new rights introduced by the 2003 Regulations is the 'making available right' under Section 182CA which enables performers to control on-demand transmission of recordings of their performances. The effect of this is that where a person intends to operate an on-demand music service, for example, they will now require the performer's consent to this.

Rental and Lending rights

Traditionally UK law did not restrict the lending or rental of works. It was not until 1979 that the public lending right scheme was established: this was simply aimed at giving authors some remuneration when their *books* were borrowed from public libraries.[102] The CDPA made some inroads into this area by restricting the rental of sound recordings, films and computer programs.[103] The 1991 Software Directive[104] required a rental right for computer programs but the CDPA had already dealt with this. Then in 1992, the Rental and Lending Right Directive[105] was adopted which required Member States to harmonise their laws in this area.

The Directive was implemented *inter alia* by Section 18A of the CDPA (for copyright works) and Section 182C (for performances), with effect from 1 December 1996.[106] Section 18A provides that the copyright owner can restrict the rental or lending (from an establishment open to the public such as a library) of most types of copyright work. So this right would be infringed if an unauthorised person rented out or a library lent DVDs (which would be classed as films), CDs (ie sound recordings), electronic databases

---

[100] Art 18 and 19.
[101] ss 205C–205N CDPA, inserted by the Performances (Moral Rights etc) Regulations 2006, SI 2006/18. See ch 4.
[102] Public Lending Right Act 1979.
[103] s 18 CDPA.
[104] Council Directive 91/250/EEC on the legal protection of computer programs.
[105] Council Directive 92/100/EEC of 19 November 1992 on rental and lending rights and on certain rights related to copyright in the field of intellectual property [now repealed and replaced by codified and amended version 2006/115/EC].
[106] By the Copyright and Related Rights Regulations 1996 (SI 1996/2967).

(which can be protected by copyright as literary works—see chapter three) or software (eg computer games), for example.

Given the difficulties public libraries and educational establishments would face if Section 18A were rigorously applied, certain exceptions have been built into the legislation permitting activities such as on-the-spot reference and the lending of works by educational establishments.[107] However, digital products such as CDs, DVDs, or software are not classed as 'books' under the Public Lending Right Act 1979. This means that the exception permitting the public lending of books[108] does not currently apply to digital products or analogue sound recordings or videos for that matter.

It is common for authors of literary, dramatic, musical or artistic works and film directors to transfer their rental right to the producer of a sound recording or film—indeed this is presumed in the case of films.[109] Nevertheless authors and directors will remain entitled to 'equitable remuneration' for any rental of the relevant recordings or films. This right cannot be waived or assigned, except to a collecting society. The level of remuneration is to be agreed by the parties or in the absence of agreement the matter may be referred to the Copyright Tribunal.[110] The right to equitable remuneration will clearly apply to the rental of digital works such as CDs or DVDs as well as analogue works. Performers also benefit from similar rights to equitable remuneration.[111]

In the UK it should be noted that broadcasts (including on-demand transmissions) are *not* subject to rental and lending rights. So for example, if I record a live satellite broadcast of a football match or a web cast event and then rent out copies, I will not infringe rental or lending right but may well infringe the reproduction and distribution rights (see below).

Digital Rental and Lending

A difficult area is whether the Directive and the UK implementing Regulations apply to *electronic rental or lending* as opposed to the rental or lending of physical copies of the work. An example of electronic rental is video on demand where the viewer expressly chooses a particular work for delivery from digital storage and viewing (as distinct from pay per view, where the work is broadcast to all subscribers but the viewer has to pay to watch). This could be implemented via Satellite or cable broadcasting or by using the Internet. In essence a digital work is selectively downloaded for viewing (or in the case of an MP3 file, playing) at home.

[107] ss 18A(3), 18(A)(4), 36A and ss 37–44 CDPA; Schedule 2 CDPA, paragraphs 6A and 6B (performer's right).
[108] s 40A CDPA. [NB s 43 Digital Economy Act 2010 now provides for the Public lending of audio books and e-books, but as of June 2013 was not yet in force].
[109] s 93A CDPA.
[110] ss 93B(4) and 93C CDPA.
[111] ss 191F, 191G and 191H CDPA.

Some commentators believe the Directive does apply to these activities[112] but the view of the leading UK commentators[113] was that it does not. The Directive speaks of the 'rental and lending of originals and copies' and rental is defined as the 'making available for use, for a limited period of time and for direct or indirect economic or commercial advantage.'[114] The electronic communication of works in such circumstances and the copying involved in their transmission and use arguably falls more easily into the area of the reproduction right,[115] and the communication to the public right provided for in the Information Society Directive and implemented by the 2003 Regulations.[116] Nevertheless, there is some uncertainty here.

2.3   HOW DIGITAL COPYRIGHT CAN BE INFRINGED

This section looks at how the major economic rights protected by copyright can be infringed. Chapters three and four deal with database rights and moral rights, and related/neighbouring rights such as rights in performances and rental/lending rights are discussed above.

Under UK law the copyright owner has a bundle of exclusive rights which he can prevent others from exercising. These so-called 'restricted acts' include the right to:[117]

(a)   Copy the work (the reproduction right);[118]
(b)   Issue copies to the public (distribution right);[119]
(c)   Perform, show or play the work in public;[120]
(d)   Rent or lend the work to the public (as noted earlier);[121]
(e)   Communicate the work to the public (the communication to the public right, which includes broadcasts and on-demand transmissions).[122] Communication to the public has been held to include connecting a computer to the Internet, where the computer is running P2P software, and in which music files containing copies of copyright works are

---

[112] Reinbothe and von Lewinski, *The EC Directive on Rental and Lending Rights and on Piracy* (London, Sweet & Maxwell, 1993).
[113] Laddie, Prescott and Vitoria, *The Modern Law of Copyright and Designs* (London, Butterworths, 3rd edition, 2000). Their view is now different (4th edition, 2011 at 18.35).
[114] Art 1.
[115] ss 16(2) and 17(6) CDPA.
[116] s 20 CDPA.
[117] s 16 CDPA.
[118] s 17 CDPA.
[119] s 18 CDPA.
[120] s 19 CDPA.
[121] s 18 ACDPA.
[122] s 20 CDPA.

placed in a shared directory—here the works are communicated to the public by the person uploading them;[123]

(f) Make an adaptation of the work or do any of the above in relation to the adaptation.[124]

Copyright in a work is infringed by a person who, without the licence of the copyright owner, does, or authorises another to do, any of the acts restricted by copyright.[125]

It is important to note that infringement in this context involves doing an act restricted by copyright in relation to the work as a whole or any substantial part of it, and either directly or indirectly.[126] The definition of what is meant by 'a substantial part' is not precise. It is a matter of quality not quantity.[127] The House of Lords in *Newspaper Licensing Agency Ltd (NLA) v Marks and Spencer Plc*[128] noted that 'quality' is to be determined by reference to the reason the work is protected by copyright ie the literary or artistic originality, as the case may be, of what has been copied. For example, in another House of Lords case, *Designers Guild Ltd v Russell Williams (Textiles) Ltd*[129] analysed by Lord Hoffmann in the *NLA* case,[130] there had been no photographic or similar exact or literal copying of the claimant's fabric design. Nevertheless, the copying of certain ideas expressed in that design which in their conjoined expression had involved original artistic skill and labour was held to constitute the copying of a substantial part of the artistic work in question. Such non-literal copying often arises in the context of software copyright infringement and is further discussed in chapter six. Note also that whether there can be infringement by the reproduction of small parts of copyright works on a regular basis (none of which by itself amounts to taking a substantial part) is problematic.[131]

In addition to primary copyright infringement noted above, there can also be *secondary* infringement where a person with the requisite knowledge among other things deals in, or enables the making of, infringing copies or performances.[132] This is considered in more detail in chapter seven, section 7.5.1.

---

[123] *Polydor Ltd & Ors v Brown & Ors* [2005] EWHC 3191 (Ch) (28 November 2005), para 7.
[124] s 21 CDPA.
[125] s 16(2) CDPA.
[126] s 16(3) CDPA.
[127] *Ladbroke (Football) v Hill (William) (Football)* [1964] 1 WLR 273.
[128] [2001] 3 WLR 290, para 19 (Lord Hoffmann) (HL).
[129] [2000] 1 WLR 2416.
[130] *Per* Lord Hoffmann at para 19.
[131] *Electronic Techniques (Anglia) Limited v Critchley Components Limited* [1997] FSR 401 at 407–11.
[132] ss 22–7 CDPA.

2.3.1 Digital Aspects

The reproduction right already deals with electronic copying as well as the creation of temporary copies in computer memory when accessing or viewing a work via the Internet and a PC or mobile device:

(a) Copying in relation to a work means reproducing the work in any material form. This includes storing the work in any medium by electronic means.[133] Case law under the 1956 Copyright Act which was concerned with the display of racing information in betting shops suggests that reproduction in 'material form' could include display of a work on a television or for that matter, a computer monitor;[134]

(b) Copying in relation to a film or broadcast includes making a photograph of the whole or any substantial part of any image forming part of the film, or broadcast—this could include a digital photograph;[135]

(c) Copying in relation to any description of work includes making copies which are transient or incidental to some other use of the work.[136]

Internet transmissions can also infringe copyright. Amendments to the CDPA made by the 2003 Regulations mean that in the case of (a) literary, dramatic, musical or artistic works, (b) a sound recording or film, or (c) a broadcast, the 'communication to the public' of the work will be an act restricted by copyright. 'Communication to the public' means communication to the public *by electronic transmission*, and includes (a) the broadcasting of the work and (b) the making of the work available to the public by electronic transmission in such a way that members of the public may access it from a place and at a time individually chosen by them (so-called 'On-Demand Transmission'). As noted earlier, these amendments mean there is no longer any doubt that making copyright works available over the Internet can now infringe this on-demand transmission right.

One of the most difficult areas of copyright law is whether facilitating or enabling copying by others can itself give rise to liability. This is a

---

[133] s 17(2) CDPA.

[134] *Bookmakers' Afternoon Greyhound Services Ltd v Wilf Gilbert (Staffs) Ltd* [1994] FSR 723.

[135] s 17(4) CDPA.

[136] s 17(6) CDPA. In *Kabushiki Kaisha Sony Computer Entertainment Inc v Ball* [2004] EW HC1738 (Ch) at paras 15 and 17 it was held that a transient copy in computer RAM was a reproduction in material form and also (by virtue of s 27 CDPA) the RAM chip itself was an 'article' which was an "infringing copy"'. This was also the view of the Court of Appeal in *R v Higgs*, [2008] EWCA 1324, 24 June 2008 (para 9) (a criminal case under s 296ZB CDPA) where even the playing of a pirate computer game on a console was considered to infringe s 17(6) by virtue of transient copies of the game made in RAM (para 9). Indeed, in this context it was considered by the court that even taking a single frame of a cinematographic film is probably an infringement (see *Spelling Goldberg v BPC Publishing* [1981] RPC 225) (para 9).

particular issue for the Internet where no one person controls the operation of the servers and networks underpinning it. Users have the power to upload infringing works themselves for others to access, or may themselves download infringing materials. Should ISPs or other service providers (such as Google) be liable for hosting infringing content? Should operators of peer-to-peer systems such as Napster be liable if their users swap infringing files? This area is to some extent addressed by the Information Society and Electronic Commerce Directives and is considered further below and in chapter seven.

One principle which also needs to be borne in mind (but which the law now to a large extent expressly addresses through these two Directives) is that where a person has no control over the copying which it is carrying out or facilitating (a classic example is a person who is sent infringing material by fax or e-mail) it must surely be the case that such a person should not be liable for copyright infringement. The same may also be true of an Internet service provider which facilitates the transmission through temporary storage in its network or hardware.[137]

2.3.2   Remedies for Copyright Infringement

Copyright infringement is a statutory tort actionable by the copyright owner.[138] An exclusive licensee has concurrent rights with the copyright owner and can bring an action for copyright infringement in its own name.[139] Traditionally a non-exclusive licensee had no right to take action in its own name. The 2003 Regulations, however, allow a non-exclusive licensee (ie the holder of a licence authorising the licensee to exercise a right which remains exercisable by the copyright owner) to bring an action for copyright infringement where their licence expressly grants this right and certain other conditions apply.[140] It may well be prudent for licensees to take advantage of this right particularly if they are resellers, integrators of technology or distributors and so are likely to suffer financially if there is a third party infringer.

Where copyright is infringed the claimant has available to it all such relief by way of damages, injunctions, accounts or otherwise as is available in respect of the infringement of any other property right.[141]

---

[137] This was accepted by Peter Smith J in *Sony Music Entertainment (UK) Ltd v Easyinternetcafe Ltd* [2003] FSR 48 at 31–5.

[138] s 96(1) CDPA.

[139] ss 101–2 CDPA. An exclusive licence is a licence in writing signed by or on behalf of the copyright owner authorising the licensee to the exclusion of all other persons (including the owner) to exercise a right which would otherwise be exercisable exclusively by the copyright owner (section 92(1)).

[140] The licence must be in writing signed by or on behalf of the copyright owner and the infringing act must be directly connected to a prior licensed act of the licensee (section 101A).

[141] s 96(2) CDPA.

The CDPA also includes criminal sanctions[142] and these have been extended, including by the 2003 Regulations, to bring in new offences of breach of the communication to the public right and the making available right.[143]

2.4   EXCEPTIONS AND DEFENCES TO DIGITAL COPYRIGHT INFRINGEMENT

2.4.1   Statutory Exceptions

There are certain limited statutory exceptions/defences to copyright infringement (or as the CDPA calls them: 'acts permitted in relation to copyright works'[144]). The rationale for these defences includes a desire to preserve some element of the 'public domain': copying is not necessarily wrong—it is how we learn and develop. However, it is clear principle of international copyright law, enshrined in the TRIPS Agreement and the Berne Convention,[145] that any exceptions must (a) be confined to certain special cases which (b) do not conflict with the normal exploitation of the work and (c) do not unreasonably prejudice the legitimate interests of the rights holder (this is the so-called Berne three-step test).

The statutory exceptions to copyright are set out in Part I, Chapter III of the CDPA. There are also similar but not identical provisions for rights in performances in Schedule 2 of the CDPA—these are not commented on here. Changes to certain of these exceptions were made following the implementation by the UK of the Information Society Directive and Electronic Commerce Directive. The more important current exceptions of relevance to digital works or where significant changes have been made by the 2003 Regulations are set out below.

It should be noted that a number of the exceptions only apply where there is 'fair dealing' with the work in question. The CDPA does not provide a definition of 'fair dealing'. The general view is that to benefit from such a fair dealing defence the use must be 'fair' in the circumstances and in assessing fairness, the amount or proportion of the work used and the proportion they bear to the new work will be important, as will be whether usage competes

---

[142] Primarily section 107. There must be knowledge (*mens rea*) on the part of the accused and in the majority of cases the liability only arises where the activity is pursued in the course of a business or otherwise to such an extent as to affect prejudicially the owner of the copyright.

[143] ss 107(2A) and 198(1A) respectively.

[144] Heading of Part I, Ch III CDPA.

[145] Arts 13 and Art 9(2) respectively.

with the copyright owner.[146] In particular, recent case law (in the context of section 30(2) CDPA—reporting current events) sees the most important factor in assessing whether the dealing was 'fair' to be whether the alleged fair dealing was competing commercially with the proprietor's exploitation of the copyright work, the second most important factor was whether the work had already been published prior to the copying in question—so, for example, if the material had been obtained in breach of confidence or underhand dealing, the courts would generally be reluctant to see this as fair dealing, and the third most important factor was the amount and importance of the work taken.[147]

Unlike the USA, the UK currently has no general 'fair use' defence to copyright infringement: Chapter III of Part I of the CDPA codifies the exceptions.[148] However, the UK Gowers Review recommended that there should be an exception for the purpose of caricature, parody or pastiche as well as some limited revisions to current exceptions, and also a more general exception for creative, transformative or derivative works, within the parameters of the Berne three-step test (the latter would require the Information Society Directive to be amended to allow this).[149] The debate here has continued with the Hargreaves Review and follow-up work by the UK Intellectual Property Office including proposals to modernise the copyright exceptions in 2013. At the time of writing this section (21 June 2013) draft legislation had been published for consultation.[150] This covers:

(a)   A new exception for private copying to allow, for example, a lawfully acquired CD to be copied into MP3 format or onto a smartphone or cloud server by an individual but only for non-commercial private use by that individual and provided no hacking of security is required. It would not apply to rented or borrowed works. The exception cannot be overridden by a contract term preventing its application. This would be a new section 28B to the CDPA.

(b)   A new exception to allow fair dealing with a work for the purposes of caricature, parody or pastiche. The exception cannot be overridden by a contract term preventing its application. This would be a new section 30B to the CDPA.

[146] *Hubbard v Vosper* [1972] 2 QB 84 (CA); Flint et al, *A User's Guide to Copyright* (London, Tottel, 6th edn, 2006) at 9.05.
[147] *HRH Prince of Wales v Associated Newspapers Ltd* [2008] EMLR 3 and [2008] EMLR 4 (CA).
[148] However s 171(3) CDPA has kept the door open for a public interest or similar defence—see below.
[149] www.ipo.gov.uk/policy/policy-issues/policy-issues-gowers/policy-issues-gowers-flexibility.htm.
[150] See: UK IPO website (www.ipo.gov.uk) (accessed 21 June 2013).

(c) A new exception for 'quotation'—in fact this will be an amendment to sections 30(1) and 30(1A) CDPA and would replace the present fair dealing exception for criticism and review noted below. It narrows the current exception by permitting use only for the purpose of quotation but widens it by allowing such quotations to be used for purposes other than but similar to criticism and review. The exception cannot be over-ridden by a contract term preventing its application.

(d) Amendments to the CDPA to allow public bodies to make material open to public inspection or on an official register available to the public online.

(e) A new exception for data analysis for non-commercial research—this is to address 'text and data mining'. These are automated analytical techniques which copy electronic information (eg articles in scientific journals and other works) and analyse the data they contain for patterns, trends and other useful information—bulk copying of the 'mined' works is usually required which would otherwise infringe copyright.[151] The exception cannot be overridden by a contract term preventing its application. This would be a new section 29A to the CDPA.

(f) Amendments to modernise the copyright exceptions for education so they apply to all types of copyright work and all types of modern technology. The exception 'fair dealing for the purposes of instruction' cannot be overridden by a contract term preventing its application.

(g) Amendments to modernise the copyright exception for research and private study so it also applies to sound recordings, films and broad-casts. The exception cannot be overridden by a contract term preventing its application. In addition, amendments to deal with the provision of copies of works by librarians and archivists and also amendments to section 42 CDPA to allow certain works to be copied for preservation purposes as well as simplifying and updating the provisions relating to copying by libraries and archives.

Those referring to this section 2.4 in the future will need to check the impact of any such future revisions made to the exceptions noted here.

Transient or Incidental Copies
The making of a temporary copy which is transient or incidental, which is an integral and essential part of a technological process and the sole purpose of which is to enable (a) a transmission of the work in a network between third parties by an intermediary, or (b) a lawful use of the work; and which has

---

[151] See Annex E: Data analytics for non-commercial research in *Modernising Copyright*, IPO, December 2012.

no independent economic significance, will not infringe copyright.[152] This exception applies to literary works (other than computer programs or databases), dramatic, musical or artistic works, the typographical arrangement of a published edition, sound recordings or films.[153] This exception is new and was included in the Information Society Directive to satisfy consumer groups who were concerned that acts of temporary copying such as caching while browsing a website would otherwise infringe copyright.[154] This exception is narrowly drawn: in practice it needs to be read in connection with the broader exceptions to liability (ie for damages and criminal liability—an injunction is still possible[155]) for acting as a 'mere conduit', caching, and hosting set out in the Electronic Commerce Directive as implemented into UK law by the Electronic Commerce Regulations. Note however that the exception was recently revisited by the UK Supreme Court in *Meltwater*,[156] in so far as it can apply to browsing the Internet.

Computer Programs: Lawful Users

The 2003 Regulations tidy up Sections 50A–50C of the CDPA which deal with the rights lawful users of a copy of a *computer program* have to make back-up copies, decompile it, observe, study and test the program, and to copy or adapt it. It is now clear that fair dealing for research and private study does not apply to acts dealt with under Section 50BA of the CDPA (ie to observe, study or test the program to determine the ideas and principles underlying it).[157] Chapter six discusses these exceptions in greater detail.

Research and Private Study

Fair dealing with an artistic, dramatic, musical or literary work for the purposes of research *for a non-commercial purpose* (where the fair dealing is accompanied by sufficient acknowledgement except if this would be impossible for reasons of practicality or otherwise) or private study (there are special rules for software[158] noted above), will not infringe copyright. The limitation that the research must be for a non-commercial purpose is new and was introduced by the 2003 Regulations. This means that any person or organisation (whether commercial or charitable) copying articles or other works *for a commercial purpose* will no longer benefit from this exception.

---

[152] s 28A CDPA.

[153] s 28A CDPA.

[154] See Cook et al, *The Copyright Directive—UK Implementation* (Bristol, Jordans, 2004) at 2.32–2.44, and see also ch 1 of this work.

[155] Regulation 20, Electronic Commerce (EC Directive) Regulations 2002, SI 2002/2013 (Electronic Commerce Regulations).

[156] *Public Relations Consultants Association Ltd v The Newspaper Licensing Agency Ltd* [2013] UKSC 18 (17 April 2013). See section 1.5.1.

[157] s 29(4A) CDPA.

[158] ss 29(4), 29(4A) and ss 50A–50C CDPA.

For example, in the case of *Her Majesty's Stationery Office (HMSO) v Green Amps*[159] the defendants (who were a commercial company involved with renewable energy) had used a student's user account (limited by an on-screen 'click wrap' licence to education and other limited purposes) to copy digital map data from the Ordnance Survey for use in their business. This copying clearly was in breach of the licence and in any event did not benefit from a fair dealing exception. This is not surprising: 'commercial purpose' has a broad interpretation: even copying articles to write a book or article for which the author will be paid can be construed as a commercial purpose. Where a business is concerned, any copying for research purposes is likely to be for a commercial purpose. For example, the Copyright Licensing Agency (CLA) has warned that businesses and others copying works for commercial research will now need a licence from them or an individual licence from the copyright owner.[160]

Criticism or Review
Fair dealing with any work for the purpose of criticism or review provided there is sufficient acknowledgement[161] and provided that the work has been made available to the public *by any means* (but not where this was done through any unauthorised act) (the latter is a new requirement under the 2003 Regulations) will not infringe any copyright in the work. For example, if a literary biographer decided to use extracts from unpublished works in a biography, then it would be prudent for the biographer to clear the rights from the relevant rights owner—this position is different from the position prior to the 2003 Regulations.

News Reporting
Fair dealing with any work (other than a photograph) for the purpose of reporting current events provided there is sufficient acknowledgement does not infringe copyright in the work. No acknowledgement is required in connection with the reporting of current events by means of a sound recording, film or broadcast where this would be impossible for reasons of practicality or otherwise.[162]

---

[159] *Her Majesty's Stationery Office (HMSO) & Anor v Green Amps Ltd* [2007] EWHC 2755 (Ch) (5 November 2007).
[160] Cook et al, *The Copyright Directive UK Implementation*, (Bristol, Jordans, 2004) at 3.80–3.88.
[161] s 30 CDPA.
[162] s 30(3).

Incidental Inclusion

The incidental inclusion of any work in an artistic work, sound recording, film, or broadcast does not infringe copyright.[163] In *IPC Magazines Ltd v MGN Ltd*[164] incidental inclusion was considered to mean that the inclusion was casual, inessential, subordinate or merely background. There are special rules for the inclusion of musical works: a musical work, words spoken or sung with music, or so much of a sound recording or broadcast as includes a musical work or such words, shall not be regarded as incidentally included in another work if it is deliberately included.[165]

Time-shifting

Recording broadcasts for time-shifting purposes does not infringe copyright in the broadcast or any work included in it.[166] The 2003 Regulations have narrowed this exception so that it only applies where the recording is made only for private and domestic purposes and *is made in domestic premises*. If the recording is subsequently sold or let for hire, offered or exposed for sale or hire or communicated to the public then it becomes an infringing copy.[167]

Photographs of Broadcasts

Making photographs of images forming part of a broadcast for private and domestic use does not infringe any copyright in the broadcast or in any film included in it.[168] The 2003 Regulations have also narrowed this exception so that it only applies where the photograph is *made in domestic premises*. If the photograph is subsequently sold or let for hire, offered or exposed for sale or hire or communicated to the public then it becomes an infringing copy.[169]

Free Public Showing or Playing of Broadcasts

The playing or showing of broadcasts in public to an audience which has not paid for admission does not infringe any copyright in the broadcast, any sound recording (except where it is an excepted sound recording[170]) or any

---

[163] s 31 CDPA.

[164] [1998] FSR 43. See also *The Football Association Premier League v Panini UK Ltd* [2004] FSR 1 (CA): 'incidental' was an ordinary descriptive English word—there is no need for the Courts to define it (*per* Mummery LJ at 39). According to Chadwick LJ the question to ask in applying the exception was why, having regard to all the circumstances, had work A been included in work B? In addressing that question consideration could be given to commercial as well as aesthetic reasons (at 26).

[165] s 31(3) CDPA.

[166] s 70 CDPA.

[167] s 70(2) CDPA.

[168] s 71 CDPA.

[169] s 71(2) CDPA.

[170] This is a sound recording (a) whose author is not the author of the broadcast in which it is included, and (b) which is a recording of music with or without words spoken or sung (s 72(1A)).

film included in it.[171] There are specific rules about whether or not the audience shall be treated to have paid for admission—for example, this will be the case if an admission fee is paid or the prices for goods and services supplied on the premises are in some sense attributable to the facilities afforded to see or hear the broadcast.[172] This exception was narrowed by the 2003 Regulations by carving out 'excepted sound recordings' which only benefit from the exception where the showing or playing of the broadcast (a) forms part of the activities of an organisation that is not established or conducted for profit, or (b) is necessary for the purposes relating to the repair of equipment for the reception of broadcasts, or for demonstrating such equipment for sale or hire.[173] The effect of this is that in practice the majority of organisations (pubs, cafés, shops etc) who provide TV sound and pictures, or radio by way of background will now need to get a licence from the relevant collecting society for any music included in the broadcasts.[174]

Education

Certain things done for the purposes of instruction or examination[175] or other stated educational purposes do not infringe copyright.[176] The 2003 Regulations have narrowed a number of the education exceptions down; for example, where copying is permitted in sections 32 and 36 by requiring the instruction concerned to be for a non-commercial purpose although where there is a commercial purpose there is a narrow exception.[177] Also, where copying is permitted there must be sufficient acknowledgement of the source of the work. As has been noted, in today's educational environment the boundary between instruction for commercial and non-commercial purposes is often blurred, not least where professional education is concerned.[178]

Libraries and Archives

Libraries and archives benefit from a range of exceptions.[179] The 2003 Regulations have introduced a requirement that where a librarian is entitled to copy articles or parts of works for users without themselves infringing copyright, the user must satisfy the librarian that they require them for research *for a non-commercial purpose* or private study, and will not use them

---

[171] s 72 CDPA.
[172] ss 72(2) and 72(3) CDPA.
[173] s 72(1B) CDPA.
[174] See sections 128A and 128B CDPA which deal with licensing schemes for excepted sound recordings and Cook et al, *The Copyright Directive UK Implementation*, (Bristol, Jordans, 2004) at 3.102.
[175] s 32 CDPA.
[176] ss 32–36A CDPA.
[177] s 32(2A)—a key condition is that the copying must be 'fair dealing with the work'.
[178] Cook et al, ibid 3.89–3.92.
[179] ss 37–44 CDPA.

for any other purpose. A practical result of this will be that libraries will need to amend their copyright declaration forms which are completed before a copy can be provided.[180] Where the library is prepared to supply commercial users they will need to obtain appropriate licences.

In addition, a statutory scheme has been put in place to allow legal deposit libraries to copy certain works from the Internet without infringing copyright.[181]

Transfers of Copies of Works in Electronic Form

There is express provision in the CDPA permitting the transfer of copies of works in electronic form where this is not restricted by license or otherwise—most software will, of course, contain such a restriction and software and content suppliers are generally advised to ensure such a restriction is included in their licences.[182]

2.4.2   Licences

In addition an express or implied licence (ie a right to use) from the copyright owner or their permitted licensee will be a defence to a claim for infringement of copyright. As noted in chapters one and seven, implied licences appear fundamental to the way the Internet operates.

One hugely important area to the media and publishing industries is whether copyright licences or assignments granted with analogue rights in mind now cover all the possible digital means of exploitation ie how do they deal with what are termed 'electronic rights'? This is a matter of contract interpretation in the UK, although some 'author-friendly' countries such as Germany expressly negate attempts to grant rights to exploit works in some future, as yet unknown format and also limit any grant of rights to the purpose of the contract unless otherwise stated.[183] The Supreme Court in the USA has also ruled on this issue in *Tasini*. This area is discussed in chapter seven.

2.4.3   Public Policy Defences

Finally, in very limited circumstances the courts may permit infringement on public policy grounds including where this is to guarantee the right of freedom of expression under the Human Rights Act 1998.[184] The leading case

---

[180] See Cook et al, ibid 3.86–3.87.
[181] s 44A CDPA; Legal Deposit Libraries Act 2003.
[182] s 56 CDPA. See also section 5.5.10.
[183] Arts 31(4) and 31(5) of the *Urheberrechtsgesetz* (the German Copyright Act).
[184] s 171(3) CDPA; *Ashdown v Telegraph Group Ltd* [2002] RPC 5 (CA).

talks about 'rare circumstances' where freedom of expression will come into conflict with the protections under the CDPA.[185] Having said that, such a defence may well be pleaded with increased frequency. For example, could the disclosure by an academic of a means of decrypting copy-protected content be justified as free expression even if laws such as the DMCA in the USA and the Information Society Directive outlaw this? (See chapter seven).

Finally, as noted earlier and in chapter one, UK courts must also have regard to the idea/expression dichotomy embodied in Article 9.2 of the TRIPS Agreement: 'copyright protection shall extend to expressions and not ideas.'[186]

2.5 WHO OWNS THE DIGITAL COPYRIGHT?

2.5.1 Employees, Directors and Commissioned Works

Under UK law, unless the work is created in the course of employment, where the employer will own the rights (except if otherwise agreed), the copyright in a work will automatically vest in the author.[187] Thus copyright will in general vest with the author, unless a written assignment of copyright is executed by the author.[188] In the case of a commission, the general rule is that the first owner will be the person commissioned (ie the author) so it is important to clarify in writing the ownership position when commissioning copyright works.

It should be noted, however, that ownership by the commissioner in equity may in very limited cases result from the circumstances (for example, on account of the purpose of the commission, that the contractor is creating a derivative work of the client's, or the contractor is part of a team with the client to produce a composite or joint work or it is clear from the circumstances that the commissioner was to have exclusive rights).[189] But often the commissioner may simply have a licence to allow them to use what was

---

[185] Ibid 45. Note also the following statement of principle by the Court of Appeal: 'Freedom of expression protects the right both to publish information and to receive it. There will be occasions when it is in the public interest not merely that information should be published [this may well not infringe copyright at all], but that the public should be told the very words used by a person, notwithstanding that the author enjoys copyright in them. On occasions, indeed, it is the form and not the content of a document which is of interest.' (*Per* Lord Phillips MR ibid 43).
[186] *Designers Guild Ltd v Russell Williams (Textiles) Ltd* [2001] FSR 113 at 120–21 (*per* Lord Hoffmann).
[187] s 11 CDPA.
[188] A written assignment of copyright signed by or on behalf of the assignor is required to transfer legal title: section 90 CDPA.
[189] *R Griggs Group Ltd & Ors v Evans & Ors* [2005] EWCA Civ 11 (25 January 2005).

commissioned as contemplated: ownership then remains with the author.[190] For example, in *John Richardson Computers Ltd v Flanders*[191] it was held that two freelance computer programmers employed to revise and update a computer program held the copyright in the updates and revisions on trust for the commissioner.[192]

In any event, as a practical matter it is always desirable, as noted above, that where work is commissioned the copyright ownership position is clearly spelt out in writing, together with a written assignment from the creator and/ or their employer, depending on the facts. The courts are very reluctant to imply an assignment into a contract where one has been omitted—this will only happen where it is a strict necessity in order to give business efficacy to the arrangement; in other words, it is clear to the court that no other arrangement makes sense from the facts.[193] This was highlighted in the case of *Meridian International Services Ltd v Richardson and others*[194]—where an attempt to imply a term vesting ownership in software in the claimant was rejected both by the High Court and the Court of Appeal. This was despite the fact that the claimant had engaged the defendants to write the software in question as a subcontractor on a major software development project.

From time to time, issues arise in relation to works created by company directors or business partners. If the director was an employee and created the work in the course of their employment, it is clear the company will own the copyright in it. Even if the director was not an employee, if the work was created in the course of the director's duties to benefit the company's business then the director (by virtue of their fiduciary duties to the company) will hold the work on trust for the company.[195]

2.5.2 Authorship and Joint Ownership

As noted earlier, the CDPA recognises works of 'joint authorship'. These are works produced by the collaboration of two or more authors in which the contribution of each author is not distinct from that of the other author or authors.[196] It is also possible for a person who adapts an existing work to claim joint authorship with the author of the earlier work provided the joint

---

[190] *Robin Ray v Classic FM* [1998] EWHC Patents 333.

[191] [1993] FSR 497. See also *Massine v de Basil* [1936–45] Macg Cop Cas 223 and generally Laddie et al, *The Modern Law of Copyright and Designs* at 21.69–21.72.

[192] See also *Cyprotex Discovery Ltd v The University of Sheffield* [2004] RPC 4 where copyright in developed software was also held to vest in the client.

[193] *Robin Ray v Classic FM* [1998] EWHC Patents 333.

[194] [2008] EWCA Civ 609.

[195] *Antocks Lairn Ltd v Bloohn Ltd* [1972] RPC 219; see Laddie et al, *The Modern Law of Copyright and Designs* at 21.73–21.74. See *Coward v Phaestos Ltd* [2013] EWHC 1292 (Ch) for a recent discussion of this whole area in the context of software.

[196] s 10 CDPA.

author has contributed enough by way of skill and independent judgement to the finished work.[197] Claims of joint authorship can often arise in collaborative software development. In assessing whether there is in fact joint authorship the court will determine whether the putative author has contributed the right kind of skill and labour (for example, simply testing software developed by someone else or supplying background information and test data will not be the skill and work of an author and so will not merit joint authorship—this is crucial), and if they have then whether the contribution was big enough.[198]

Joint authors will be joint owners of the copyright in the work as a matter of law and it can also be agreed that a work is jointly owned. Unless agreed otherwise, it appears that joint owners hold as tenants in common. The consent of all owners is required to grant a licence in respect of the work, and each owner cannot exercise the rights in the work personally without the others' consent.[199] It is therefore commercially dangerous to allow a joint ownership arrangement to exist without making clear what rights each of the owners is to have.

2.5.3   Collecting Societies

Often a collecting society will administer and protect the author/performer's copyright and related rights on their behalf. This will become increasingly necessary in the digital environment as rights management becomes much more extensive and complicated. Collective licensing and similar schemes can help content users from having to get consent from each author/performer separately. Instead, they simply deal direct with the relevant collecting society. Chapter nine, section 9.3 considers the role of collecting societies in greater detail.

2.6   THE IMPLEMENTATION OF THE ELECTRONIC COMMERCE AND INFORMATION SOCIETY DIRECTIVES INTO UK LAW

The UK had to implement the Electronic Commerce Directive before 17 January 2002—it was implemented on 21 August 2002 by the Electronic

---

[197] *Brown v Mcasso Music Production Ltd* [2006] EMLR 3. See also: *Fisher v Brooker* [2007] FSR 12 and [2008] FSR 26 (CA).
[198] *Fylde Microsystems Ltd v Key Radio Systems Ltd* [1998] FSR 449 at 456 (*per* Laddie J). See also *Cyprotex* at 84.
[199] See ss 16(2) and 173(2) CDPA; *Ray v Classic FM plc* [1998] FSR 622; *Cescinsky v George Routledge & Sons Ltd* [1916] 2 KB 325; and see generally KM Garnett et al, *Copinger and Skone James on Copyright* (London, Sweet & Maxwell, 14th edn, 1999) 5–165.

Commerce (EC Directive) Regulations 2002.[200] The Information Society Directive had to be implemented before 22 December 2002 and as noted earlier, it was implemented into UK law by the 2003 Regulations.

This section looks at the relevance of the Electronic Commerce Directive for UK copyright law. In particular it looks at the implementation of the so-called 'safe harbours' from liability for service providers. It also discusses how in the end the UK chose to implement the Information Society Directive. The substantive law on digital copyright following the implementation of these two pieces of legislation is discussed elsewhere in this work and in the relevant context.

2.6.1 Implementation of the Electronic Commerce Directive

The Government did not introduce any specific exceptions or limitations into the CDPA to deal with this Directive. Instead the Electronic Commerce Regulations simply set out each safe harbour from liability for damages or for any pecuniary remedy or for any criminal sanction[201] for the service provider, ie a person providing an information society service. Note that this exclusion from liability is not just for copyright, database right or other intellectual property infringement. An information society service is broadly defined as 'any service normally provided for remuneration, at a distance, by means of electronic equipment for the processing (including digital compression) and storage of data, and at the individual request of the recipient of the service'.[202]

Service providers benefit from the exclusion of liability where they are:

(a) **acting as a mere conduit**[203]—ie they simply transmit information provided by a recipient of the service or provide access to a communication network (this may also include automatic, intermediate and transient storage (ie *copying*)[204] taking place *solely to carry out the transmission in the communication network*) provided that:
   (i) any such storage is for no longer than is reasonably necessary for the transmission;
   (ii) the service provider:
   — does not initiate the transmission;
   — does not select the receiver of the transmission; and
   — does not select or modify the information contained in the transmission.

---

[200] SI 2002/2013.
[201] Note that Regulation 21 deals with the burden of proof in such a situation.
[202] Recital 17 of the Electronic Commerce Directive.
[203] Regulation 17 of the Electronic Commerce Regulations.
[204] ss 17(2) and 17(6) CDPA; but see also s 28A CDPA.

(b) **'caching'**[205]—ie the automatic, intermediate and temporary storage of information (as noted above, this would be copying under UK law unless excepted by the transient/incidental copying exception in Section 28A CDPA) performed *solely to make more efficient the information's onward transmission to other recipients of the service upon their request*, provided that the service provider:

   (i)   does not modify the information;

   (ii) complies with conditions on access to the information;

  (iii) complies with any rules regarding the updating of the information, specified in a manner widely recognised and used by industry;

  (iv) does not interfere with the lawful use of technology, widely recognised and used by industry, to obtain data on the use of the information; and

   (v) acts expeditiously to remove or disable access to the information it has stored upon obtaining actual knowledge [as opposed to constructive knowledge where the law deems it ought to have been aware from the circumstances] of the fact that the information at the initial source of the transmission has been removed from the network, or access to it has been disabled, or that a court or an administrative authority has ordered such removal or disablement—this is often termed 'notice and take down'.

(c) **hosting**[206]—ie the storage of information provided by the recipient provided that the service provider:

   (i)   does not have actual knowledge of unlawful activity or information and, where a claim for damages is made, is not aware of facts or circumstances from which it would have been apparent to the service provider that the activity or information was unlawful; or

   (ii) upon obtaining such knowledge or awareness acts expeditiously to remove or to disable access to the information ('notice and takedown').

In addition the recipient of the service must not be acting under the authority or the control of the service provider.

In all cases there is no general obligation on providers when carrying out these activities to monitor the information which they transmit or store or to actively seek facts or circumstances indicating illegal activity.[207] It should be noted that the Electronic Commerce Regulations clarify what is meant

---

[205] Regulation 18 of the Electronic Commerce Regulations.

[206] Regulation 19, Electronic Commerce Regulations.

[207] See Art 15, Electronic Commerce Directive. See also the CJEU decisions *Scarlet Extended SA* Case C-70/10 [2011] ECR I-0000; *Belgische Vereniging van Auteurs, Componisten en Uitgevers CVBA (SABAM)* Case C-360/10, 16 February 2012. In the latter case the CJEU ruled that an injunction requiring a social network service provider Netlog to implement a system to filter

by notice for the purposes of actual knowledge in the context of 'notice and take down'.[208]

Nothing in these 'safe harbours' prevents a person agreeing different contractual terms or affects the rights of any party to apply to court for relief to prevent or stop infringement of any rights.[209] In fact, the 2003 Regulations also give the High Court (in Scotland, the Court of Session) the power to grant an injunction against a service provider where that service provider has actual knowledge of another person using their service to infringe copyright or a performer's property right.[210] In determining whether a service provider has actual knowledge, similar principles apply to those relevant to 'notice and takedown.'[211]

These exclusions from liability remain of fundamental importance, in particular given the increased hosting by sites of user-generated content. The scope of the exclusions are also increasingly being examined by the courts—for example, in a case relating to trade mark infringement (rather than copyright) the CJEU ruled that to benefit from the liability exclusion, a service provider must not play an active role allowing it to have knowledge or control of the data stored through its service.[212]

International Aspects[213]

The approach of the Directive is broadly similar to the equivalent US legislation, the (earlier) Digital Millennium Copyright Act 1998 (DMCA), which was designed to implement the WIPO Treaties, amongst other things. Indeed, one would want a consistent approach across states to these issues given the international nature of the Internet. However the 'notice and take down' provisions of the DMCA are more involved and designed to balance the interests

---

information in order to block allegedly infringing files part of the 'repertoire' of the collecting society SABAM was contrary to Article 15(1).

[208] Regulation 22 states that in determining whether a service provider has actual knowledge, a court shall take into account all matters which appear to it to be relevant and, among other things, shall have regard to: (a) whether a service provider has received a notice through a means of contact made available in accordance with regulation 6(1)(c) [ie their e-mail address] and (b) the extent to which any notice includes (i) the full name and address of the sender of the notice; (ii) details of the location of the information in question; and (iii) details of the unlawful nature of the activity or information in question.

[209] Regulation 20(1). The power of an administrative authority to prevent or stop infringement of any rights is also preserved (Regulation 20(2)).

[210] ss 97A and 191JA CDPA: this reflects Art 8(3) of the Information Society Directive.

[211] ss 97A(2) and 191JA(2); for actual knowledge in the context of 'notice and take down' see in 196 above. See also the discussion in section 8.3.4 below.

[212] See *L'Oreal SA and Others v eBay International AG and Others*, Case C-324/09, 12 July 2011.

[213] See for example: Yakobson, 'Copyright Liability of Online Service Providers after the Adoption of the E.C. Electronic Commerce Directive: A Comparison to U.S. Law' [2000] *ENTLR* 144.

of providers and users of hosting services. These include the designation of an agent to receive notifications who must be notified to the US Copyright Office,[214] and that the party claiming infringement must provide a statement that they have a good faith belief that use of the material in the manner complained of is not authorised by the copyright owner, its agent, or the law.[215] For example, in a US case a woman (Stephanie Lenz) who had posted a short video of her baby dancing to a song by Prince on YouTube challenged Universal Music's attempt to have YouTube take down the allegedly infringing video content on the grounds that her use was clearly protected as 'fair use'. Universal Music had required YouTube to take down the video pursuant to the DMCA but Ms Lenz objected and the video was reinstated. Ms Lenz sued Universal Music for misrepresentation under the DMCA.[216]

The DMCA also specifically addresses issues such as those providing links to infringing material,[217] clarifying the liability of providers to users/recipients when they take down allegedly infringing material in good faith,[218] and the protection of educational institutions,[219] which the Directive does not. However Article 21 of the Directive leaves open the door for the EU to revisit this area. In 2005, the UK Government consulted on this area with specific reference to the liability of hyperlinkers, location tool and content aggregators, but in the end decided that there was insufficient evidence to justify extending the provisions of the Electronic Commerce Directive into these areas, pending a more general review of this area by the European Commission in 2007, although so far there seem to be no further developments in this area.[220]

The UK government has in the past indicated that it sees self-regulation, through industry codes of conduct, such as 'RightsWatch' (see Glossary), being necessary to clarify the operation of 'notice and take down' in practice.[221] This needs to be done at a pan-European level and it is argued this would avoid the need for prescriptive Regulations dealing with this akin to the DMCA.

For example, take a Belgian case which pre-dates the implementation of the Electronic Commerce Directive, *Belgacom Skynet v IFPI Belgium &*

[214] s 512.
[215] s 512 (c) (3).
[216] www.eff.org/cases/lenz-v-universal.
[217] s 512(d) (so-called information location tools).
[218] ss 512(f) and (g).
[219] s 512(e).
[220] Consultation Document on the Electronic Commerce Directive: the liability of hyperlinkers, location tool and content aggregators: Starting Date: 08-06-05; Closing Date: 23-09-05; Consultation Document on the Electronic Commerce Directive: the liability of hyperlinkers, location tool services and content aggregators; Government response and summary of responses—December 2006.
[221] Consultation Document on Implementation of the Electronic Commerce Directive DTI (10 August 2001).

Polygram Records.[222] The appellant, Belgacom Skynet, was accused of hosting websites containing lists of hyperlinks to illegal MP3 music files; Belgacom did not itself host the MP3 files. Belgacom refused to disable access to the websites it was hosting. At first instance, the court ruled against Belgacom on the basis that its refusal to disable access amounted to an unfair trade practice. But the Appeal Court effectively reversed this decision and set out detailed conditions similar in certain respects to those in the DMCA and the Electronic Commerce Directive for when an ISP such as Belgacom had to disable/take down allegedly infringing content or links to such material. This case highlights the need for a consistent implementation of the Electronic Commerce Directive across Europe to ensure legal certainty for ISPs. This area is discussed further in chapter seven, section 7.6.

2.6.2   Implementation and Effect of the Information Society Directive

Overview and CJEU Case Law
The Directive aims to harmonise the legal protection for copyright owners across Europe, especially over the Internet and to provide adequate legal measures to enable effective electronic rights management (such as digital watermarking) and electronic protection (such as encryption) in relation to copyright works. It also enables the EU to ratify the two WIPO Treaties.

Prior to the 2003 Regulations UK law (CDPA) already dealt with a number of aspects of this Directive. But some significant amendments to the CDPA were required to implement it. By way of conclusion to this overview of UK digital copyright law, the more important changes made to UK copyright law by the Information Society Directive which are discussed in more detail elsewhere in this work are summarised below. The changes dealing with technical measures are discussed more fully in chapter seven, section 7.9.

It is also important to understand that the impact and effect of the Information Society Directive on UK copyright law are starting to be far reaching. This is because of the increasing number of questions on the interpretation of the Directive referred by the courts of EU Member states to the CJEU, which is creating a European copyright jurisprudence of which the courts of the UK increasingly need to take regard. Some developing themes that are relevant to this book and the discussion of UK law in this chapter are as follows:

(a)   The communication to the public right in Article 3 of the Directive should be interpreted broadly to ensure the Directive's aims of ensuring

---

[222] Brussels Court of Appeal, 13 February 2001; [2001] *CTLR* N-122.

a high level protection for authors.[223] So, for example, in a recent CJEU decision retransmission of copyright works included in a terrestrial TV broadcast through a website streaming service was a new 'communication to the public' separate from the initial broadcast.[224] However, it clearly does not cover a direct representation or performance ie to public physically present at the time of the representation or performance—so the right does not apply to circus or cabaret performances or indeed other conventional performances; the right is aimed at online transmission and broadcasting.[225] So, for example, the transmission of broadcasts of football games to customers in a pub would be a 'communication to the public' of any copyright works in the broadcast.[226]

(b) Exceptions to copyright must be interpreted strictly.[227]

(c) The reproduction right set out in Article 2 of the Directive is a Community concept to be interpreted uniformly across the EU—so this covers direct or indirect, temporary or permanent reproduction by any means and in any form, in whole or part of author's 'works' (and also films etc) and should also be interpreted broadly.[228]

(d) 'Works' must be 'intellectual creations'[229] (so it could be argued that the concept of what a work is should be broader than the specifically defined categories in UK law).

(e) The test for the originality of the work is that it is the author's own intellectual creation.[230] In a recent CJEU case even short works can potentially be protected by copyright eg as short as 11 words from a newspaper article (*Infopaq*) and in the UK in a recent case (*Meltwater*), applying *Infopaq* newspaper headlines were held to be potentially protected by copyright.[231] So this case law also suggests some book and

---

[223] See eg: *Sociedad General de Autores v Editores de España (SGAE) v Rafael Hoteles SA* [2006] ECR I-11519; *ITV Broadcasting Ltd and Others v TV Catchup Ltd*, Case C-607/11, 7 March 2013. See also Recital 23 of Information Society Directive: '[t]his right should be understood in a broad sense covering all communication to the public not present at the place where the communication originates.'

[224] *ITV Broadcasting Ltd*—see above.

[225] See eg: *Circul Globus Bucuresti* Case C-283/10, 24 November 2011.

[226] *Football Association Premier League Ltd and Others v QC Leisure and Others*; *Karen Murphy v Media Production Services Ltd* Joined Cases C-403/08 and C-429/08 (4 October 2011).

[227] *Infopaq International* (Intellectual property) [2009] EUECJ C-5/08 (16 July 2009) at para 56. See also the UK case *The Newspaper Licensing Agency Ltd & Ors v Meltwater Holding BV & Ors* [2010] EWHC 3099 (Ch) (26 November 2011).

[228] *Infopaq* paras 27–9 and 41–3.

[229] *Infopaq* at para 34.

[230] *Infopaq* paras 30–51. In other words, the author's 'creativity' not the traditional UK law concept of 'sweat of the brow' is what counts.

[231] *The Newspaper Licensing Agency Ltd & Ors v Meltwater Holding BV & Ors* [2010] EWHC 3099 (Ch) (26 November 2010). However, the Court of Appeal in this case saw no change to the UK law on originality (see [2011] EWCA Civ 890 at para 20).

article titles, for example, might conceivably be protected by copyright (overturning the long-held view against this[232]). Also, if the test for infringement in light of *Infopaq* is changed from the UK test of taking all or a *substantial* part of the copyright work to that in *Infopaq*, where there was infringement where even limited parts of a work were taken, as long as these parts were the author's intellectual creation, query what impact this will have.[233]

A New Communication to the Public Right[234]

This has clarified that uploading films, broadcasts, music, text and/or images onto a website can be controlled by the rights owner. This will be regardless of whether other infringing acts (such as copying) are taking place. Also as noted earlier, performers as well as phonogram producers will now have clear rights to prevent the circulation and transmission of their recordings in MP3 format over the Internet.

A New Exception to Copyright for Temporary Acts of Reproduction[235]

These are transient or incidental and an integral and essential part of a technological process and whose sole purpose is to enable:

(a)   a transmission in a network between third parties by an intermediary; or

(b)   a lawful use of a work or other subject matter to be made, and which have no independent economic significance. This compliments the Electronic Commerce Directive exceptions and is broader as it does not just apply to service providers eg if I browse a website on my home PC, I may well have the benefit of this exception to the extent needed for my lawful use of the site. Indeed, the Supreme Court in *Meltwater* has recently given a broad interpretation to this exception but referred the matter to the CJEU.[236]

Changes to the Permitted Exceptions to Copyright[237]

Only those exceptions listed in the Directive which the UK has chosen to retain are permitted. In particular the UK has in the past resisted permitting the private copying of copyright works except in narrow circumstances. Other EU states tolerate this provided fair compensation is paid to rights holders

---

[232] See eg: *Francis Day & Hunter v 20th Century Fox* [1940] AC 112; and *Exxon v Exxon Insurance* [1982] RPC 69.

[233] For a recent discussion of 'substantial part' which applies existing UK law see: *Coward v Phaestos Ltd* [2013] EWHC 1292 (Ch) at paras 24–6.

[234] Art 3; section 20 CDPA (copyright).

[235] Art 5(1).

[236] See section 1.5.1 above.

[237] Arts 5 (2)–5(5).

eg by levies on blank tapes. The UK has decided not to go down the route of fair compensation. Instead, a number of the exceptions have been narrowed to reflect the Information Society Directive (and the Berne Three Step Test). The most significant change is removing commercial research from the ambit of fair dealing for the purposes of research and private study.

Protection against Circumventing Technological Measures (Such as Encryption) Designed to Prevent Copying or Unauthorised Performance or Viewing[238]

So simply using say a 'cloned' digital broadcasting access card to watch scrambled transmissions could potentially infringe this new right. However, this right *cannot* be used to override the exceptions to copyright (eg right to decompile and observe/test) in the Software Directive.[239] It is also stated that it should not hinder research in cryptography.[240]

Electronic Rights Management Information (ERMI)

There is now protection against: (a) the removal or alteration of electronic rights management information (*ERMI*), or (b) the distribution, broadcasting, importation for distribution, communication or making available to the public of works where the *ERMI* has been removed or altered without authority,[241] where in each case the person committing the act knows or has reason to believe that by doing so he is inducing, enabling, facilitating or concealing an infringement of copyright or any similar rights including database right.[242]

So for example, removing an electronic copyright notice from an electronic image or a piece of software or removing a digital watermark would infringe this new right. In fact, this right is potentially of broad scope and also protects the distribution of software with an on-screen copyright licence. 'Rights management information' in this context includes any information provided by right-holders which identifies the work, the author or any other right-holder, or information about the terms and conditions of use of the work, and any numbers or codes that represent such information, which is associated with a copy of, or communication to the public of, a work.

When Did these Changes Take Effect?

The 2003 Regulations came into effect on 31 October 2003 ('Commencement'). The changes made apply to copyright works made, performances given, databases (in which database right vests) made, and works in which publication

---

[238] Art 6(1); sections 296ZA–ZF CDPA.
[239] Recital 50.
[240] Recital 48; section 296ZA (2) CDPA.
[241] Art 7; section 296ZG CDPA.
[242] s 296ZG (8).

right vests first published, before or after Commencement.[243] But no act done before commencement shall be regarded as an infringement of any new or extended right arising by virtue of the 2003 Regulations.[244]

The 2003 Regulations do not affect any agreement made before 22 December 2002 (this was the date the Information Society Directive had to be implemented). Also, no act done after Commencement in pursuance of an agreement made before 22 December 2002 shall be regarded as an infringement of any new or extended right arising by virtue of the Regulations.[245]

Other 'transitional provisions' are set out in Part 3 of the 2003 Regulations. The majority of these deal with any extended copyright in sound recordings.[246]

SUMMARY

(a) The sources of law for Digital Copyright are the Copyright, Designs and Patents Act 1988 (CDPA), a number of European Directives dealing with a range of copyright matters and the Statutory Instruments implementing these Directives and accordingly amending the CDPA.

(b) The principles developed over the years for analogue copyright: classes of work protected by copyright, qualifying factors for protection, originality, authorship, ownership, infringement, related and neighbouring rights, exceptions to copyright, are all relevant to digital copyright. However, there remain a number of issues and problem areas including:

   (i)   to what extent linking to or including content on a website infringes copyright beyond any infringement of the reproduction right or communication to the public right;

   (ii) how effective are performers' rights in the digital environment?

   (iii) service provider liability for innocently transmitting, storing (caching) or hosting infringing content, or operating a peer-to-peer service such as Napster or hosting user-generated content;

---

[243] Regulation 31(1).
[244] Regulation 31(2).
[245] Regulation 32.
[246] Changes to section 13A of the CDPA potentially extend copyright in certain sound recordings eg, those that are first made available over the Internet via an on-demand service.

(iv) determining whether old, analogue rights contracts allow the use of licensed content in digital works eg converting films into DVD format, recordings into MP3 files, newspaper articles into websites, etc;

(v) the sheer complexity of categorising and dealing with multimedia works including collective rights management issues for digital exploitation of works;

(vi) the Electronic Commerce and Information Society Directives address some but not all of the above concerns.

(c) The 2003 Regulations strengthen the protection of 'technological measures' such as copy-protection systems and also introduce new rules protecting electronic rights management information.

3

Digital Database Law and the Internet

3.1 THE RELATIONSHIP BETWEEN COPYRIGHT AND DATABASE RIGHT[1]

3.1.1 Position Before 1 January 1998

As noted earlier, UK copyright law has traditionally applied a low standard of originality when assessing whether a work is protected by copyright. Some independent skill and labour, some 'sweat of the brow', is enough either in collecting and/or verifying the information. So in the analogue world, collections of information in material form, such as timetables, telephone books, directories, betting coupons, etc, were all potentially protected by copyright. Traditionally such works were viewed as a class of *literary work* ie as a table or compilation.[2]

Also, UK law has been more favourable to protecting compilations of factual information than many other countries in Europe and also the USA. For example, in the landmark US Supreme Court case *Feist Publications Inc v Rural Telephone Service Co*,[3] the court held that a telephone directory was not protected by copyright; it lacked sufficient originality—'some minimal degree of creativity' was required.[4]

UK law has also traditionally been quite clear that databases as a whole (whether electronic or otherwise) benefit from copyright protection as compilations. What is protected is the structure and organisation (including its selection and arrangement) of the database. This is in addition to any copyright in the contents of the database or compilation—but if this is merely

---

[1] See generally: Chalton, 'Database Right: Stronger Than It Looks?' [2001] *EIPR* 296; Hugenholtz, 'The New Database Right: Early Case Law from Europe', paper presented at Ninth Annual Conference on International IP Law & Policy, Fordham University School of Law, New York, 19–20 April 2001; and Laddie, Prescott and Vitoria, *The Modern Law of Copyright and Designs* (London, Butterworths, 4th edn, 2011) ch 32 (Rights in Databases).
[2] s 3(1) CDPA.
[3] 499 US 340 (1991).
[4] Ibid 345.

factual information the protection is likely to be limited. So despite 'sweat of the brow', there was considerable uncertainty as to how the copyright in the database could be infringed and in particular how much had to be copied for infringement to occur.

Database owners and creators therefore welcomed the 1996 Database Directive,[5] which harmonised database law across Europe. The key innovation of the Directive was to create a new so-called *sui generis* intellectual property right, database right, to protect against the extraction or reutilisation of all or the substantial part of the contents of a database. This is in addition to any copyright in the database either as a whole or in its contents. So even if the database contents are not themselves protected by copyright, database owners now have protection against the piracy of their databases.

3.1.2   Position from 1 January 1998

The Database Directive was implemented into UK law by the Copyright and Rights in Databases Regulations 1997.[6] The Regulations took effect on 1 January 1998.

The effect of the Regulations was to amend existing copyright law (the Copyright, Designs and Patents Act 1988 (CDPA)) to introduce the new database right. Also crucial to the new scheme is that a higher standard was introduced into UK law for the originality required in order for databases to be protected by copyright, as opposed to database right. This reflects the Directive, which in turn is consistent with the treatment of databases and compilations in the international copyright treaties—the Agreement on Trade-Related Aspects of Intellectual Property Rights (TRIPS Agreement 1994),[7] the WIPO Copyright Treaty 1996[8] and the Berne Convention[9]—referred to in chapter 1.

3.2   DIGITAL COPYRIGHT PROTECTION FOR DATABASES

The CDPA defines a database as a collection of independent works, data or other materials which:

(a)   are arranged in a systematic or methodical way; and
(b)   are individually accessible by electronic or other means.[10]

---

[5]   Directive 96/9/EC on the legal protection of databases.
[6]   SI 1997/3032 (Regulations).
[7]   Art 10(2).
[8]   Art 5.
[9]   Art 2(5).
[10]   s 3A CDPA (as amended by the Regulations).

Databases are accordingly protected by copyright as literary works in addition to tables or compilations (which are not themselves databases).[11] It will be clear from the definition that databases can be in analogue form as well as being electronic—a printed telephone directory would also be a 'database'. The material which enables the database to be used, such as the index, is also part of the database,[12] although any computer program used in connection with the database is not part of it.[13] The definition of 'database' is broad and so could include the following (whether in analogue or digital form), although as noted, there are question marks over whether some of these are databases, depending on the precise circumstances at issue:

(a)   a magazine or newspaper
(b)   an encyclopaedia
(c)   a web page (?)
(d)   a music album CD (?)[14]
(e)   law reports
(f)   more typical databases (eg directories, catalogues, etc)
(g)   textbooks containing a selection of different materials (?)—some publishers now identify the 'maker' of the book (database) on their printed publications in addition to the typical copyright notice
(h)   multi-media works (?)
(i)   a library (?)

'Sweat of the brow' remains the test of originality for copyright protection for databases created on or before 27 March 1996 and which were in copyright immediately before 1 January 1998.[15] For databases created after 27 March 1996, copyright can only subsist in the database if it is original in a new, higher sense than simply because of the 'sweat of the brow' of the author. Instead of 'sweat of the brow', the test of originality is that 'by reason of the selection or arrangement of the contents of the database the database constitutes the author's own intellectual creation.'[16] So copyright can protect the structure and arrangement of the database if this is sufficiently original. So merely ordering a database in alphabetical order is unlikely to satisfy this threshold. In *Football Dataco Ltd v Brittens Pools Ltd*[17] the High Court found that football fixture lists were the subject of copyright protection as a database but not protected by database right. The Court of Appeal upheld

---

[11] s 3, CDPA.
[12] Directive, Recital 20.
[13] Directive, Recital 23.
[14] See Directive, Recital 19.
[15] Regulation 29(1).
[16] s 3A(2).
[17] [2010] RPC 17.

the decision as to the lack of database right protection[18] but the copyright protection of the lists was referred to the CJEU. The CJEU made clear that what is important for database copyright to subsist is not the intellectual effort and skill of creating the data in the database—this is irrelevant. A database is protected by database copyright under the Directive only 'provided that the selection or arrangement of the data which it contains amounts to an original expression of the creative freedom of its author ...'[19]

3.3   DATABASE RIGHT PROTECTION

There are no formalities for database right protection; there is no need to register your rights—they come into existence automatically upon creating the database. To benefit from database right protection there must have been a *substantial investment* in obtaining, verifying or presenting the contents of the database.[20] Substantiality is to be assessed in terms of quantity or quality or both.[21]

It is important to note that database rights only apply within the EU/EEA and also the maker of the database must have an ongoing connection with an EEA state, such as having its principal place of business in the EEA and being incorporated in the EEA.[22] Or in the case of an individual, being an EEA national or resident. For example, a US corporation will not benefit from database right unless the relevant connection with the EU/EEA can be demonstrated.

The maker of the database is the person who qualifies for database right protection. Except in the case of works created during the course of employment (where the maker is the employer—critical here is whether the database is made in the course of employment and not privately and for personal purposes[23]), or where the parties agree otherwise, the first owner of database right will be the maker of the database.[24] The maker of the database is in general the person who takes the initiative in obtaining, verifying or presenting the contents of a database and assumes the risk of investing in that

---

[18] [2011] RPC 9.
[19] *Football Dataco Ld v Yahoo! UK Ltd* (Case C-604/10) (1 March 2012) [2013] FSR 1 at 23.
[20] Regulation 13(1).
[21] Regulation 12.
[22] Regulation 18.
[23] So, for example, address lists maintained by an employee on their employer's email system will potentially be a database belonging to their employer, although purely personal contacts kept or marked separately from business contacts are likely to belong to the employee (depending on what the firm's e-mail policy is)—see *Penwell Publishing (UK) Ltd v Ornstien* [2007] EWHC 1570 (QB) (18 June 2007).
[24] Regulations 14(2) and 15.

obtaining, verification or presentation.[25] Note that the maker of the database and the author (for copyright purposes) could well be different persons. Where a third party is creating and/or maintaining a database on your behalf it is important to agree who will own the database. For example, if a business appoints an agent and the agent creates and maintains a customer database, this database will belong to the agent on the basis they will be deemed to be the maker unless there is an agreement to the contrary.[26]

Database right lasts for 15 years from the end of the calendar year of completing the database or making it available to the public, whichever is longer.[27] It applies retrospectively so that databases created between 1 January 1983 and 31 December 1997 will have 15 years' protection from 1 January 1998.[28] Also, a substantial change to the contents of a database (eg updating) can also effectively extend the term of protection to a further 15 years from the date of the change.[29] This is important as many databases are constantly updated— the effect of this is that many of these will continue to benefit from database right protection for an indefinite period.

As noted above, database right protects against the extraction or re-utilisation of all or the substantial part of the contents of a database:[30]

Extraction means the permanent or temporary transfer of the contents to another medium by any means, eg by viewing the data on-screen or printing them out. Extraction can be done directly or indirectly—you do not need to have access to the original database, nor does it necessarily just include the physical/electronic copying or removal of data (eg copying and pasting)— extraction can occur when the data is referred to as a source of information and then copied manually or retyped.[31] It is a broad concept—'[it must] be given a broad interpretation as referring to any unauthorised act of appropriation of the whole or a part of the contents of a database, the nature and form of the process used being immaterial.'[32] It is also clear from CJEU jurisprudence that a database accessible via a website located outside the UK can nevertheless be infringing under UK law if the website operator targets

---

[25] Regulation 14.

[26] These were the facts in *Cureton v Mark Insulations Ltd* [2006] EWHC 2279 (QB) (7 March 2006).

[27] Regulations 16 and 17, subject to the transitional provisions in Regulation 30.

[28] Regulation 30.

[29] Regulation 17(3).

[30] Regulation 16.

[31] See *Directmedia Publishing GmbH v Albert-Ludwigs-Universität Freiburg* [2008] EUECJt C-304/07_O (10 July 2008) (Opinion of Advocate General Sharpston) and also the decision of the Court—9 October 2008. Note that in *British Horseracing Board & Ors (Approximation of laws)* [2004] EUECJ C-203/02 (9 November 2004), para 54, the ECJ said that the 'consultation' of a database (as opposed to 'extraction' and reutilisation') was not within the scope of the right.

[32] *Apis-Hristovich EOOD v Lakorda AD* (CJEU Case C-545/07, 5 March 2009) 40.

the UK public—the extraction by the UK users is an infringement by those users, and there is also primary infringement of the right by the targeting by the website operator of the infringing database to them.[33]

Re-utilisation means making the data available to the public by any means, eg by online transmission or possibly even hyperlinking—it must also be understood broadly.[34]

Substantial in the context of infringement means substantial in terms of quality or quantity or a combination of both.[35] Repeated and systematic extraction or re-utilisation of insubstantial amounts of the database can also infringe if this conflicts with a normal exploitation of the database or unreasonably prejudices the legitimate interests of the maker of the database.[36]

The fair dealing and moral rights provisions in the CDPA do not apply to database right. There are only very limited exceptions to database right as compared to copyright. These are limited, 'fair dealing' type restrictions.[37]

At present database right remains a strictly European IP right. Attempts to introduce similar legislation in the USA have so far failed. To illustrate the scope of the right and its application, it is instructive to consider some of the European Court of Justice/CJEU decisions in this area, in particular one which considers a UK database, that developed by the British Horseracing Board listing fixtures and runners and other racing information.

3.3.1 *British Horseracing Board Limited v William Hill (2001)*[38]

In February 2001, the High Court in London gave its first full decision on database rights. It was a remarkable decision, not least as the judge, with the agreement of Counsel, simply applied the text of the Directive as opposed to the Regulations to the matters in issue, thus side-stepping any inconsistencies between the two. As the Directive governs, this was a sensible approach and highlights that database rights are purely European in origin. The judge went back to the Directive and to its underlying purpose to determine its proper scope and application.

---

[33] [2012] EUECJ C-173/1; *Football Dataco Ltd & Ors v Stan James Plc & Ors* [2013] EWCA Civ 27 (6 February 2013).
[34] *Football Dataco Ltd v Sportradar GmbH* (CJEU Case C-173/11) [2013] FSR 4. See also: 3.4 below.
[35] Regulation 12(1); Directive, Art 7(1). For a relatively recent CJEU case examining what is meant by 'substantial' here see *Apis-Hristovich EOOD v Lakorda AD* (CJEU Case C-545/07); 5 March 2009.
[36] See Regulation 16(2) and Directive, Art 7(5).
[37] Regulation 20 and Schedule 1.
[38] Laddie J, Ch D 9 February 2001.

The case concerned the extraction and/or re-use by the defendants of the claimants' data on the defendant's Internet betting site. The claimants had invested significant sums (£4 million per annum) to obtain, verify, maintain and develop their database of horse racing fixtures and runners and other racing information (BHB Database). The judge had no problem in categorising the BHB Database as a 'database': 'it seems ... that the expression "database" has a very wide meaning covering virtually all collections of data in searchable form.'[39] It was also clear to the judge that there was substantial investment in obtaining, verifying or presenting its contents.

What database right protects, according to the judge, is not the *form* of the data (its order, structure and 'searchability') but the *investment* put into making the database. So taking the contents of a database and re-arranging them will still infringe database right—the investment in the database is still misappropriated. As far as substantial taking was concerned, on a quantitative analysis only a small amount of data was being taken. However, the judge held that there was infringement. What was taken was the most recent and core information in the BHB Database (ie current runners in a particular race for inclusion on William Hill's website). Qualitatively, this was a substantial part of the database.

Also, as the database was being continuously updated it should be viewed as a *single* database in a constant state of revision and not a sequence of separate databases. So William Hill's daily borrowings from it also fell within Article 7(5) of the Directive ie repeated and systematic extraction and re-utilisation of part of its contents.

William Hill appealed and on 31 July 2001, the Court of Appeal agreed to refer 11 questions to the European Court of Justice for determination under Article 234 of the EC Treaty, before giving judgment.[40] The areas the questions touched on included the following:

(a)   Where there is a constantly updated database, is there a new database separate from the previous database whenever any substantial change has occurred? *As noted above BHB argued this was not the case.*

(b)   Do you have to have access to the actual database in order to extract or re-utilise the information in it? *Here William Hill only had access to the 'data feeds' from the database and not the actual database itself.*

(c)   Does database right essentially protect the information in a database from direct or indirect extraction or re-utilisation *(which is in essence what the judge found by focusing on the protection of the investment by*

---

[39] Paragraph 30.

[40] *British Horseracing Board (BHB) v William Hill*, Court of Appeal judgment of 31 July 2001; for the questions referred see ECJ, Opinion of Advocate General Stix-Hackl, Reference for a preliminary ruling from the UK Court of Appeal, Case C-203/02 (8 June 2004) 27.

the maker of the database). Or does it just protect 'database-ness' ie the manner in which the materials in a database are arranged. So in this interpretation (*as argued by William Hill*) any acts which do not make any use of the arrangement of the contents of the database nor take advantage of the way in which the maker has rendered the contents individually accessible cannot infringe the database right.

Indeed, there are now a number of European cases which apply the Database Directive and the decisions often conflict on these and other fundamental issues, such as what is meant by 'substantial investment' and 'substantial' in the case of infringement.

On 8 June 2004, the Advocate General (AG) delivered her opinion in the *BHB* case, and three other parallel database rights cases.[41] The ECJ issued judgment on 9 November 2004. The ECJ decisions effectively narrow the scope of database right protection from the position reached in the High Court in *William Hill*.

3.3.2 The ECJ Decision

The ECJ in the *OPAP* case[42] said that the whole purpose of database right is to promote the establishment of storage and processing systems for *existing information* and *not* the creation of materials capable of being collected subsequently in a database.[43]

However, before the decision of the ECJ in *William Hill* (and the related cases such as *OPAP* involving football fixtures lists)[44] the view in the UK was that the level of investment required was fairly low and it was permissible to focus both on the effort put in to gathering the data in question and also that spent on verifying it and presenting it (presentation included effort put in to making the data accessible to users).[45] Unlike other EU courts (eg The Netherlands), the UK courts had not clearly formulated the so-called 'spin-off' doctrine where databases (such as a list of sporting fixtures) which are by-products ('spin-offs') of the main or other activity of the producer

---

[41] *BHB:* ECJ, Opinion of Advocate General Stix-Hackl, Reference for a preliminary ruling from the UK Court of Appeal, Case C-203/02 (8 June 2004); see also references for a preliminary ruling in cases C-46/02 (*Fixtures Marketing Ltd v Oy Veikkaus Ab* (from Finland)), C-338/02 (*Fixtures Marketing Ltd v Svenska Spel AB* (from Sweden)), and C-444/02 (*Fixtures Marketing Ltd v OPAP* (from Greece)). The latter three cases relate to football fixtures lists relating to English and Scottish football.

[42] *Fixtures Marketing v OPAP* (Case C-444/02).

[43] Ibid 40.

[44] Judgment was given on 9 November 2004 in: *BHB v William Hill* (Case C-203/02), *Fixtures Marketing v Svenska Spell* (Case C-338/02), *Fixtures Marketing v OPAP* (Case C-444/02), and *Fixtures Marketing v Oy Veikkus Ab* (Case C-46/02).

[45] *BHB v William Hill* (High Court) [2001] 2 CMLR 12 at paras 32–7.

(eg, football or horseracing fixtures, stock prices, telephone subscriber data) are excluded from database right protection.[46]

The ECJ in *William Hill* narrowed the types of databases which can benefit from database right. In particular 'investment in … the obtaining … of the contents' of a database refers to the resources used to seek out existing independent materials and collect them in the database. It does not cover the resources used for the creation of materials that make up the contents of a database.[47] Also 'investment in … the … verification … of the contents' of a database refers to the resources used, with a view to ensuring the reliability of the information contained in the database, to monitor the accuracy of the materials collected when the database was created and during its operation. The resources used for verification during the stage of *creation* of materials, which are subsequently collected in a database, do not fall within that definition.[48]

The ECJ also effectively restricted the scope of infringement of database right, focusing on the need for there to be a substantial part appropriated of the investment made by the maker that database right protects.[49]

Also, where the maker is trying to prevent the repeated and systematic extraction or reutilisation of *insubstantial* parts of a database, they will now only succeed if they can show that their cumulative effort was to reconstitute or make available to the public *the whole or a substantial part* of the contents of the database and thereby seriously prejudice the maker's investment.[50]

However, the ECJ did clarify that the terms 'extraction' and 're-utilisation' as defined in Article 7 of the Directive must be interpreted as referring to any unauthorised act of appropriation and distribution to the public of the whole or part of the contents of a database. Those terms do *not* imply direct access to the database concerned. It is also irrelevant that the database has been made accessible to the public.[51]

3.3.3   Impact of the ECJ Decision in the UK Courts

On 13 July 2005, the Court of Appeal applied the ECJ's decision and upheld William Hill's appeal, effectively denying BHB database right protection for their database.[52] The Court applied the ECJ's reasoning and came to the

---

[46] See Estelle Derclaye, 'Databases "Sui Generis" Right: Should We Adopt the Spin-off Theory?' [2004] *EIPR* 402.

[47] Paragraph 1 of the ECJ's ruling.

[48] Ibid.

[49] This is either based on the sheer volume taken (quantitatively) or (qualitatively) based on the scale of the investment made and what was misappropriated.

[50] Paragraph 4 of ECJ ruling in *William Hill*.

[51] Paragraph 2 of ECJ ruling.

[52] [2005] EWCA Civ 863.

conclusion that, '[s]o far as BHB's database consists of the officially identified names of riders and runners, it is not within the sui generis right of Art.7(1) of the Directive.'[53] This was despite an ingenious argument by counsel for BHB that the BHB do not 'create' the information in its database, but they 'gather it in' and check it—in other words, there was investment in obtaining the contents of the database, not least as data had to be collected from owners about entries for specific races which owners tell the BHB their horses intend to run. This data was then analysed and verified and a list of runners produced, so the database was protected by the *sui generis* database right. This argument was rejected by the court as the database contained unique information; the official list of riders and runners which BHB had created. The nature of the information held in the database had changed with the stamp of official approval. It had become something different from a mere database of existing material and so was not protected by database right.[54]

The effect of the Court of Appeal's decision is to significantly narrow the scope of database right protection in the UK from what had been thought to have been the position, in order to follow European law. Not surprisingly, some commercial organisations receiving data from BHB decided in light of the ECJ ruling to revisit their commercial arrangements with BHB on the basis they were in effect paying for the right to use data no longer protected by intellectual property rights. This argument has not found favour with the courts—indeed the Court of Appeal was clear that:

> [C]ontractual control of the supply of pre-race data was still possible in respect of pre-race data provided directly or indirectly under contract by BHB. The ruling [ie of the European Court of Justice as applied by the Court of Appeal] did not mean that, if someone wished to obtain a reliable supply of pre-race data from BHB or its authorised suppliers, he could do so without charge. Valid contractual arrangements could be made relating to the supply of reliable pre-race data by BHB's authorised suppliers. BHB was entitled to charge contractually for access to its pre-race data product, even if the product itself was not protected by database rights from use by third parties to the extent asserted by BHB prior to the ruling of the Court of Justice.[55]

This highlights the role of contract law in regulating the supply and access to data: where access to data is valuable and can be controlled, data can still be licensed and charged for even if the data itself is not protected by copyright or database right.

---

[53] *Per* Jacob LJ at para 35.
[54] *Per* Jacob LJ at, s 30 and 35. For a further discussion see: Beunen, *Protection for Databases* (Nijmegen, Wolf Legal Publishers, 2007) 129–30.
[55] *Attheraces Ltd & Anor v The British Horseracing Board Ltd & Anor Rev 2* [2007] EWCA Civ 38 (2 February 2007), para 20 (*per* Mummery LJ). See also *Attheraces Ltd & Anor v The British Horseracing Board Ltd & Anor* [2005] EWHC 1553 (Ch) (15 July 2005), and *BHB Enterprises plc v Victor Chandler (International) Ltd* [2005] EWHC 1074 (Ch) (27 May 2005).

Finally, some interesting competition law arguments were also raised in these cases (abuse of a dominant position through excessive and discriminatory pricing by BHB) which are discussed in chapter 5, section 5.5.8.

In addition to the BHB case another important UK case raising issues of EU database rights law is *Football Dataco Ltd v Sportradar Gmbh.*[56] This concerned alleged database right infringement in relation to a database of live football data. This data included live scores—were these created or obtained data? The judge (Floyd J) followed the approach adopted by the CJEU previously in finding that created data was not protected but obtained data was. The live scores were protected as obtained data—this was upheld by the Court of Appeal who also discussed scientific data in the same light—a scientist does not create data as such, they obtain it. It is absurd to suggest that databases of factual information such as live sporting results or scientific data should not be protected through a specious argument that somehow this data is created—this is quite different from the BHB fixture list data, which was clearly the result of human creation rather than the reporting of factual events, whether sporting or scientific.[57] Floyd J's analysis is worth repeating:

> Although not expressed by the CJEU in exactly these terms, it seems to me that a reason which supports the approach adopted by the CJEU in relation to the distinction between created data and obtained data is the following. Data which is created by an individual or organisation is, in most cases at least, not available to others until it is created. There is, accordingly, no alternative source for such data. If one allows a database right to attach to data which is created by the maker of the database, the creator obtains a true monopoly in that data. Such a result would be inconsistent with the objectives of the [Database] Directive. The Directive should not be construed in a way which gives a party a monopoly in facts, such as the runners and riders or the fixture lists. On the other hand where a database consists of data obtained from sources available to the public, such as existing published data, the balance of policy considerations is different. There is (or should be) nothing to prevent the public from investing in obtaining those data themselves. The owner of a database right in data which is obtained in this way does not achieve a stranglehold on the facts. The objectives of the Directive are therefore furthered by encouraging investment in the obtaining, verification and presentation of data, without creating monopolies in facts.[58]

3.3.4   Future Development of the Database Directive

On 12 December 2005, the European Commission published its first evaluation of the Database Directive.[59] This document looks at the operation of the

[56] [2012] EWHC 1185 (Ch); [2013] FSR 3.
[57] *Football Dataco Ltd & Ors v Stan James Plc & Ors* [2013] EWCA Civ 27 (6 February 2013) 33–69.
[58] [2012] EWHC 1185 (Ch) 19.
[59] DG Internal Market and Services Working Paper, 'First Evaluation of Directive 96/9/EC on the Legal Protection of Databases' (Brussels, 12 December 2005). See also Bitton, 'Exploring

right since its introduction and controversially it concluded that the Directive has had no proven impact on stimulating the production of databases in Europe. This was despite strong representations from the European publishing industry that database right protection was crucial to the continued success of these activities. There was a period of stakeholder consultation following the publication of the evaluation which ended on 12 March 2006. The impression that the evaluation gives is that the Commission do not appear to want a radical reform or repeal of the Directive but that 'maintaining the status quo' is perhaps their preferred option, although the evaluation leaves this point open for debate.

What is clear is that the Commission see the four judgements of the European Court of Justice (ECJ) in November 2004[60] as arguably limiting the scope of database right to 'primary' producers of databases (ie those who obtain data from others and then assemble the database, such as the publishers of directories, listings and maps) and not to those for whom databases are a 'secondary' activity (eg broadcasters producing programme schedules, sports bodies producing fixtures lists, and others who 'create' the data that makes up their databases). Certainly more recent CJEU decisions follow this approach, as discussed above.

There is also the suggestion by the Commission that in light of the ECJ judgements, websites which contain certain sorts of data such as real estate or job advertisement databases might not be protected by database right as they are at risk of failing to satisfy the criteria that there must be 'substantial investment' of the right kind (ie in the obtaining, verification or presentation of the contents of the database).[61] The Commission also highlighted the differences of interpretation given to the phrase 'substantial investment' by the various national courts in the EU which has given rise to some legal uncertainty.

3.4   SOME PRACTICAL SUGGESTIONS

As well as digital copyright, database right can be a powerful tool in protecting digital information. Because of the breadth of how 'database' is defined, and the limited guidance in the Database Directive on this point, many information products not typically viewed as databases, such as websites and

---

European Union Copyright Policy Through the Lens of the Database Directive' (4 April 2009). *Berkeley Technology Law Journal*, Vol 23, 1411, Fall 2008. Available at SSRN: http://ssrn.com/abstract=1802779 or http://dx.doi.org/10.2139/ssrn.1802779.

[60]   *BHB v William Hill* (Case C-203/02), *Fixtures Marketing v Svenska Spell* (Case C-338/02), *Fixtures Marketing v OPAP* (Case C-444/02), and *Fixtures Marketing v Oy Veikkus Ab* (Case C-46/02).

[61]   Article 7(1), Database Directive.

possibly even some music CDs, may fall within its ambit, although it is fair to say that the 2004 ECJ decisions have narrowed the protection of certain types of database. So persons exploiting digital products should always bear copyright and database right in mind, as well as the use of contractual licence terms that ensure an income stream even if there are doubts about the protection of the underlying data in the light of the ECJ decisions. These licences will require careful drafting if they are not to fall foul of some of the issues raised in recent UK cases, in particular as regards any representations or warranties about the extent of database right protection and also making clear that payment is in respect of the provision of services, as well as in respect of an IP licence where applicable.[62]

Some continental cases have suggested that hyper-linking to websites can infringe database right although the cases conflict from country to country. In Germany, Stepstone obtained an injunction preventing a rival recruitment group OFIR from hyper-linking to its website pages on the basis of database and copyright infringement.[63] However in France, Stepstone were unable to prevent this, as among other things there was no substantial taking from the database/website.[64] A similar result was also reached in *Cadremploi v Keljob.*[65] This area is considered in greater detail in chapter seven, section 7.2.

In any event, persons making or commissioning databases need to take care to ensure their investment in the product is fully documented and in light of the 2004 ECJ decisions that it is of the right 'type'. This will assist in arguing that there has been 'substantial' investment in the product concerned. Any updating should also be documented. Also wherever possible, databases should be subject to binding licence terms (whether on-screen, shrink wrap or otherwise) to restrict the rights granted to users to what is commercially desirable and to seek to prevent any re-use or resale of the data or the database.

Finally, to help ensure they benefit from database right, the maker of a database is also well advised to ensure they are identified as maker with the date of publication on copies of the database: by doing this it is presumed this information is correct unless the contrary is proved.[66] In addition, this information should appear on-screen where appropriate.

---

[62] *Attheraces Ltd & Anor v The British Horseracing Board Ltd & Anor Rev 2* [2007] EWCA Civ 38 (2 February 2007), *Attheraces Ltd & Anor v The British Horseracing Board Ltd & Anor* [2005] EWHC 1553 (Ch) (15 July 2005), and *BHB Enterprises plc v Victor Chandler (International) Ltd* [2005] EWHC 1074 (Ch) (27 May 2005). See in particular: the discussion in *Attheraces Ltd & Anor v The British Horseracing Board Ltd & Anor Rev 2* [2007] EWCA Civ 38 (2 February 2007) at paras 92, 224, and 252–8.

[63] *Financial Times*, 17 January 2001.

[64] *Sarl Stepstone France v Sarl Ofir France*, Judgment by the Commercial Tribunal of Nanterre, 8 November 2000.

[65] Judgment by the Appeal Court of Paris (Cour d'appel de Paris, 14th Chambre, s B) (25 May 2001).

[66] Regulation 22.

SUMMARY

(a) Databases can benefit from both copyright and database right protection.

(b) The copyright and database right could well be owned by different persons, unless contracts are put in place to deal with this.

(c) The date the database was created and/or updated is crucial in assessing which form(s) of protection will apply.

(d) Database right is aimed at protecting the *investment* made in obtaining, verifying or presenting *existing* data in a database (and not the creation of data by itself) and it protects against the extraction or re-use of data, even if this would not be copyright infringement.

(e) Many digital information products are potentially 'databases' for database right protection: websites, multimedia products, online databases, CD ROM directories, etc.

(f) Database owners will want to use a mixture of copyright, database law, technical measures (eg encryption—see chapter seven), confidentiality (if appropriate) *and* licences (ie contract law) to protect their databases wherever possible.

(g) Database owners should ensure they are identified as copyright owner and maker (as appropriate) on all copies of the database and on-screen.

(h) Non EU/EEA database makers (eg those in the USA) need to look at basing their operations in the EU/EEA or otherwise taking steps to qualify for database right protection.

4

Digital Moral Rights:
The Basics

4.1 WHAT ARE DIGITAL MORAL RIGHTS?

4.1.1 Background[1]

Copyright systems based on the concept of authors' rights (*droit d'auteur*), such as those in France and Germany, ensure that the *personality* of authors, as expressed in their creations, benefits from a form of copyright or *moral rights* protection. Accordingly, authors' works should not be altered or distorted in a manner prejudicial to the author. To mistreat the work is to mistreat the author, to invade his privacy and impair his personality. Also the author has the right to be identified whenever their works are published or exploited. These *moral rights* are in addition to the *economic rights* of authors in their works, in particular the right to control their copying and distribution.

Moral rights can also be justified on economic and public policy grounds. The European Commission has stated that by protecting the authorship and authenticity of a work, moral rights also serve consumer interests as they can assist consumers in verifying they have received the authentic product they are seeking and not any different or pirated goods.[2]

The first country to protect moral rights was France, although it was not until the early part of the last century that the French courts began to speak about a *droit moral* or moral right as such. Both France and Germany give at least equal recognition to the moral rights and economic rights in a work,

---

[1] See generally: Laddie, Prescott and Vitoria, *The Modern Law of Copyright and Designs* (London, LexisNexis 4th edn, 2011), ch 13 (Moral Rights); Stokes, *Art and Copyright* (Oxford, Hart Publishing, 2nd edn, 2012).

[2] See: 'Follow-Up to the Green Paper on Copyright and Related Rights in the Information Society' COM(96), 568 final (20 November 1996) 27.

although the basic assumptions in each case are different. French law renders moral rights perpetual as well as (in some sense) inalienable (ie they cannot be transferred); German law gives the moral rights and economic rights in a work the same duration. Common law countries such as the UK and the USA have traditionally viewed moral rights as quite alien.

The Berne Convention[3] establishes two key moral rights:

(a) the right to be identified as author (right of paternity—sometimes also termed the right to attribution); and

(b) the right to object to certain types of derogatory acts in relation to one's work (right of integrity), what the Berne Convention describes as 'the right ... to object to any distortion, mutilation or other modification of, or other derogatory action in relation to, the ... work, which would be prejudicial to [the author's] honour or reputation.'[4]

In fact, authors' rights in countries such as France and Germany tend to go further and in addition to these two rights, moral rights in these countries may well include some or all of the following:

(a) the right to decide upon first publication or other release (the so called 'right of disclosure' in French law), including the right to refuse to supply the original of a work;

(b) the right of the author to insist on completion of the original where that depends on the execution of others;

(c) the right to correct or withdraw works of which the author no longer approves; and

(d) the right to object to the destruction or removal of the original work. This goes further than the Berne Convention where the general view is that the right of integrity does not extend to preventing the destruction of works.

In recent years the concept of moral rights has been expanded beyond protecting authors, and performers also now have moral rights. The motivation for this development was to prevent performers being damaged by the digital manipulation and alteration of their performances.[5] As moral rights for performers are a new concept in UK law (having only been in effect since 1 February 2006), they are discussed at the end of this chapter—the discussion which follows focuses on the moral rights of authors and not performers.

---

[3] Art 6 *bis.*

[4] Art 6 *bis.*

[5] See Davies and Harbottle, *Copinger and Skone James on Copyright—Second Cumulative Supplement to the Fifteenth Edition*, (Oxford, Sweet & Maxwell, 2007) 88–92.

4.1.2   UK Law

Until 1 August 1989, when the Copyright, Designs and Patents Act 1988 (CDPA) came into force, moral rights as such were not expressly recognised by UK copyright law. However, limited protection was afforded by the law of defamation, passing off, contract and section 43 of the Copyright Act 1956 (false attribution of authorship). The CDPA incorporated the rights of paternity and integrity into UK law, and also added the right to object to false attribution and the right to privacy of certain photographs and films.[6]

Unlike copyright, *moral rights cannot be assigned by the author*,[7] but under UK law they may be *waived* by an instrument in writing signed by the person giving up the right.[8] They are also (in most cases) transmissible on death.[9] Also, infringement of the moral right of paternity can only arise after the right has been *asserted* by the author.[10] In general terms employees have no or very limited moral rights in works created during the course of their employment.[11]

All the moral rights except that of false attribution continue to subsist for as long as copyright subsists in the work. The right in relation to false attribution subsists for 20 years after a person's death.[12] No moral rights apply if the author died before 1 August 1989 (date of commencement of the CDPA) or in respect of films made before that date and there are transitional provisions in respect of 'existing' works (ie works made before 1 August 1989).[13] Breach of moral rights is actionable as a breach of statutory duty.[14]

In summary, the following moral rights are of relevance in the UK:

(a)   **Right of paternity:** the author of a copyright literary, dramatic, musical or artistic work and directors of copyright films have the right to be identified whenever the work is *inter alia*: published commercially (for films and sound recordings), copies of it are issued to the public, or the work is exhibited (in the case of artistic works) or performed or shown in public, or the work is communicated to the public.[15] This right must be asserted to be effective. This must be done in writing (although there are special rules for artistic works).[16]

---

[6] Ch IV CDPA.
[7] s 94 CDPA.
[8] s 87(2) CDPA.
[9] s 95 CDPA.
[10] s 78 CDPA.
[11] ss 79(3) and 82 CDPA.
[12] s 86 CDPA.
[13] Sch I, para 23 CDPA.
[14] s 103 CDPA.
[15] s 77 CDPA. The inclusion of 'communicated to the public' was included by the 2003 Regulations and removes any doubt (if there was any) that websites are subject to moral rights.
[16] s 78 CDPA.

(b) **Right to object to derogatory treatment of a work** (right of integrity): derogatory treatment is where the *treatment* (which is a broad, general concept[17]) amounts to distortion or mutilation of the work or is otherwise prejudicial to the honour or reputation of the author or director. The right is infringed by a person who, in a similar manner to the paternity right, *inter alia* exploits a derogatory treatment of the work.[18] *Treatment* means any addition to, deletion from, or alteration to or adaptation of the work (subject to certain limited exceptions[19]).

(c) **Right not to have a work falsely attributed to a person as author or director:** this is infringed eg if a person were to exhibit in public, perform, communicate to the public, or issue copies to the public of, a work in respect of which there is a false attribution.[20] It can also be infringed by dealing with an altered artistic work as if it were unaltered.[21] An example of this right being used was *Clark v Associated Newspapers Ltd*[22] where the politician and author Alan Clark prevented publication of spoof diaries entitled *Alan Clark's Secret Political Diaries.*

(d) **Right of privacy in certain photographs and films:** a person who for private and domestic purposes commissions the taking of a photograph or the making of a film has, where copyright subsists in the work, the right not to have copies of the work issued to the public, the work exhibited or shown in public, or the work communicated to the public.[23]

4.2 HOW ARE DIGITAL MORAL RIGHTS INFRINGED?

4.2.1 Right of Paternity

Provided the author has *asserted* their right of paternity, then any commercial publication, public performance or (in general) other exploitation of the work including via the Internet must identify the author (or director of a film) otherwise this right will be infringed.[24] *Commercial publication* includes making the work available to the public by means of an electronic retrieval system.[25] One might consider the Internet to be one enormous electronic

---

[17] *Harrison v Harrison* [2010] FSR 25.
[18] s 80(3) and section 80(4).
[19] s 80(2)(a) CDPA.
[20] s 84 CDPA.
[21] s 84(6) CDPA.
[22] [1998] 1 All ER 959.
[23] s 85 CDPA.
[24] s 77(1) CDPA.
[25] s 175 (2) CDPA.

retrieval system. Also, the inclusion in the CDPA by the 2003 Regulations of the act of 'communication to the public' as an act potentially infringing moral rights in a work means that it is now clear (if there was any doubt) that moral rights apply to websites.

The right of paternity does not apply to certain digital works namely computer programs or computer-generated works. There are also other limited exceptions for both digital and analogue works.[26]

The UK case law on the right of paternity is very limited but some guidance is given in *Hawkins v Hyperion Records Ltd.*[27] In this case the author of a musical work was given the following attribution—'With thanks to Dr Lionel Sawkins for his preparation of performance materials for this recording'—the Court of Appeal regarded this as insufficient under s 77(1) CDPA (right to be identified as the author or director), as Dr Sawkins should have been named as author eg through the use of a copyright notice such as '© Copyright 2002 by Lionel Sawkins'.

4.2.2   Derogatory Treatment

It is difficult to provide clear guidance as to what might amount to derogatory treatment of a work. As there is no decision on this point after full trial in the UK, or indeed in the higher courts at all, there remains uncertainty as to what might amount to derogatory treatment. Is it *subjective*—is it enough that the author feels that his reputation has been prejudiced, or is there an *objective* element akin to defamation law: 'would right thinking members of the public think less of him because of the treatment?' The cases to date certainly suggest an objective, rather than a subjective, test. But the scope of derogatory treatment remains uncertain in UK law. Certainly, it must be more than a trivial complaint.[28]

If the interpretation of article 6 *bis* of the Berne Convention is also considered, the stress is on *derogatory* action which would be prejudicial to the author's honour or reputation. The adjective *derogatory* appears to imply a subjective standard but this is made subject to the more objective criterion of prejudice to honour or reputation. Indeed, it has been argued that 'honour' and 'reputation' are more objective concepts, being analogous to the personal interests protected by the law of defamation, as noted above.

In any event, the right of integrity does not apply to computer programs or computer-generated works. There are also further limited exceptions.[29]

---

[26] s 79 CDPA.
[27] [2005] 3 All ER 636 at 651.
[28] *Harrison v Harrison* [2010] FSR 25.
[29] s 81 CDPA.

The reported cases on derogatory treatment include:

Morrison Leahy Music and Another v Lightbond Limited and Others[30]

The defendants had produced a sound recording which was a medley or 'megamix' of words and music from five compositions of which the second plaintiff (the singer and composer George Michael) was the author and the first plaintiff the copyright owner. These were interspersed with fill-in music composed by others. The plaintiffs sued for infringement of copyright, and they also claimed that the defendants' actions infringed their moral rights under section 80(2) CDPA.

The judge (Morritt J) held that what the defendants had done clearly amounted to 'treatment' within the meaning of section 80(2)(a) of the CDPA. He also thought it was arguable that such 'treatment' amounted to distortion or mutilation within section 80(2)(b). However, as this was an interlocutory decision for an injunction pending full trial, the matter as to whether there was in fact derogatory treatment was left by the judge as a question of fact at trial.

Tidy v The Trustees of the Natural History Museum and Another[31]

In this case, an application for summary judgment rather than a full trial, Bill Tidy, the well-known cartoonist, had drawn some cartoons of dinosaurs to be displayed at the Natural History Museum. In May 1993 a book was published. It reproduced Tidy's drawings in smaller dimensions (from 420mm by 297mm to 67mm by 42mm). Tidy made an application for summary judgment on the grounds that the reduced size amounted to a distortion (as opposed to a mutilation) of the drawings or was in any event prejudicial to his honour or reputation ie it was derogatory treatment under section 80 of the CDPA. The plaintiff contended that the reduction in size detracted from the visual impact of the cartoons; it would also lead people to believe he could not be bothered to redraw the cartoons for the book, especially since he was given credit in the book for the drawings.

In fact the judge (Rattee J) was not prepared to grant summary judgment in Tidy's favour in the absence of evidence as to whether the public considered the reproduction as affecting Tidy's reputation. Nor was it clear beyond argument that the reduction in size was distortion of the original drawings.

Counsel for Tidy had referred to the Canadian Ontario High Court decision *Snow v The Eaton Centre*:[32] in that case legislative language comparable to the CDPA was considered and the judge in that case held that the words 'prejudicial to his honour or reputation' involved a 'certain subjective element

---

[30] [1993] *EMLR* 144.
[31] Ch D Rattee J, 29 March 1995; [1996] 3 *EIPR* D-81.
[32] 70 CPR (2d) 105.

or judgment on the part of the author so long as it is reasonably arrived at.' Rattee J held that even if he accepted the Canadian principle, he would still have to be satisfied that the view held by the artist was a reasonable one—this inevitably involved applying an objective test of reasonableness. So evidence from the public as to how the reproduction affected Tidy's reputation in their minds was required. More recent cases also suggest an objective test (see for example *Confetti Records v Warner Music*,[33] where a rap line and parts of another track were added to an existing recording).

Pasterfield v Denham and Another[34]

Here (a County Court decision concerning artistic works) the judge held that to find an infringement of the right of integrity, the artist must establish that the treatment accorded to his work is either a distortion or a mutilation that prejudices his honour or reputation as an artist. It is not sufficient that the artist is himself aggrieved by what has occurred. Nor is distortion or mutilation alone enough—it must be prejudicial to the artist's honour or reputation.

4.2.3   Moral Rights in the USA

Until 1990, the USA (at least at Federal level) had no express enactment dealing with moral rights, although the US courts had at times offered protection for interests analogous to moral rights through the extension of common law rights or trademark laws. Following the Visual Artists Rights Act 1990 (VARA), US copyright law was amended to give authors of certain specified *art* works (as opposed eg to musical or literary works) the rights of attribution (ie to claim authorship and to prevent false attribution to an artist) and integrity (which extends both to *intentional* distortion, mutilation or modification of a work which would be prejudicial to the artist's honour or reputation *and* to any intentional or grossly negligent destruction *of the work*). Also, a number of US state laws also recognise moral rights in a greater or lesser degree to VARA.

Because of the way VARA is drafted it appears to have little relevance to where a work is digitised or put on a website. So for the moment digital moral rights are primarily a European issue.

4.2.4   Performers' Moral Rights

The Performances (Moral Rights, etc) Regulations 2006 (SI 2006/18) created two new moral rights for performers of qualifying performances. The first right (granted by section 205C CDPA) is the right to be identified as the

---

[33] [2003] EWCH 1274 (Ch).
[34] Plymouth County Court, His Honour Judge Overend, 9 and 10 March 1998; [1999] FSR 168.

performer, the second right (granted by section 205F CDPA) is the right to object to derogatory treatment. These rights came into effect on 1 February 2006 and do not apply in relation to any performance that took place before 1 February 2006. They apply to any type of live performance and to sound recordings of any such performance but they do not apply to fixations of audiovisual performances (e.g. films).[35]

Right to be Identified as Performer[36]
Whenever a person:

(a)   produces or puts on a qualifying performance that is given in public (ie live performance),
(b)   broadcasts live a qualifying performance,
(c)   communicates to the public a sound recording of a qualifying performance, or
(d)   issues to the public copies of such a recording,

then the performer has the right to be identified as such. The right of the performer to be identified is as follows:

(a)   in the case of a performance that is given in public, to be identified in any programme accompanying the performance or in some other manner likely to bring his identity to the notice of a person seeing or hearing the performance,
(b)   in the case of a performance that is broadcast, to be identified in a manner likely to bring his identity to the notice of a person seeing or hearing the broadcast,
(c)   in the case of a sound recording that is communicated to the public, to be identified in a manner likely to bring his identity to the notice of a person hearing the communication,
(d)   in the case of a sound recording that is issued to the public, to be identified in or on each copy or, if that is not appropriate, in some other manner likely to bring his identity to the notice of a person acquiring a copy,

or (in any of the above cases) to be identified in such other manner as may be agreed between the performer and the person mentioned.

Where the performers are part of a group and the group is identified then the requirement to identify all the individual performers is less strictly applied (s 205C(3)).

For the right to apply it must be asserted (s 205D) (this requirement is similar to that which applies to authors and film directors (see 4.2.1 above)) and

[35] Davies and Harbottle, *Copinger and Skone James on Copyright: Second Cumulative Supplement to the Fifteenth Edition* (London, Sweet & Maxwell, 2007) 88.
[36] S 205C CDPA.

there are certain exceptions to the right (s 205E), which include performances given for the purposes of reporting current events and for the purposes of advertising any goods or services or where it is not reasonably practicable to identify the performer. The right applies in relation to the whole or any substantial part of a performance (s 205K).

Right to Object to Derogatory Treatment of Performance
The performer of a qualifying performance has a right which is infringed if:

(a)   the performance is broadcast live, or
(b)   by means of a sound recording the performance is played in public or communicated to the public,

> with any distortion, mutilation or other modification that is prejudicial to the reputation of the performer (this is similar to the right of integrity discussed at 4.2.2 and similar principles will apply to assessing this although unlike for authors or directors, only 'reputation' is mentioned and not 'honour or reputation').[37]

The right need not be asserted first in order for it to apply but there are certain exceptions to it (s 205G). The right applies in relation to the whole or any part of a performance.

Duration; Waiver; Assignment
As is the case for moral rights for authors, moral rights for performers cannot be assigned but can be transmitted on death. They last for the same duration as the performers right (ie the performer's economic rights) in the work. They can also be waived.

4.2.5   Implications of Moral Rights for the Digital Environment

As noted earlier, moral rights apply equally to digital copyright works (apart from computer programs and computer-generated works) and the Internet, as well as to analogue works and to performances. For example:

(a)   A digitised copy of an artistic work in which the right of paternity has been asserted is put on a server available for browsing over the Internet. The artist is not identified in relation to the image made available over the Internet: this would be an infringement of the artist's right of paternity as well as any copyright infringement.
(b)   The digitised copy referred to above is manipulated electronically, for example, the colour tones are altered: this may amount to derogatory treatment. There is a dearth of case law in this area: as discussed earlier,

---

[37] Compare s 80 with s 205F.

a treatment is derogatory if it amounts to distortion or mutilation of the work or is otherwise prejudicial to the honour or reputation of the author.

(c)   A derogatory hypertext link is placed on one website linking to an image of an artistic work on another website: could this be derogatory treatment?

(d)   Digitally sampling a work, for example, could infringe the author's and performers' moral rights even if the copyright owner (the record company) had consented to this.

(e)   In France it has even been discussed whether simply digitising a work could be derogatory treatment of the work.

Moral rights pose difficult challenges for the Internet and the digital exploitation of works. Moral rights laws vary substantially in scope from country to country, in particular as to who possesses such rights and their scope. This has led to arguments that the global nature of the Internet requires a harmonisation of moral rights laws. Indeed, the 'strong' inalienable nature of moral rights (especially in authors' rights systems) means that an aggressive assertion of moral rights could stifle the exploitation of artistic and other copyright works on the Internet. This has led to calls for a more flexible moral rights system internationally, together with collective schemes for moral rights management.

However, it has also been argued that the very notion of moral rights is under threat from digitisation. The possibility of both perfect and distorted copies seems to fly in the face of the copyright work being forever viewed as an extension of the author's personality

It is possible that at some point in the future the European Commission may propose a Directive to harmonise moral rights protection across Europe. But this appears to be on the back burner at present.[38]

4.3   DEALING WITH MORAL RIGHTS IN PRACTICE

As a practical matter anyone commissioning copyright works needs to consider acquiring a waiver of moral rights in order to avoid problems later on, for example, if the work is edited or poorly reproduced; such waivers may not necessarily be effective for all territories. This is in addition to getting a

---

[38] For example, '… there is no apparent need to harmonise moral rights protection in the Community …' (European Commission Staff Working Paper on the review of the EC legal framework in the field of copyright and related rights, SEC (2004) 995, 19.7.2004). Nor were they a key policy initiative in a more recent Communication on 'A Single Market for Intellectual Property Rights' (Brussels 24.5.2011 COM(2011) 287 final).

copyright licence or assignment. Also, persons acquiring rights should consider adding warranties dealing with whether or not moral rights have been asserted or the appropriate waivers obtained, etc.

SUMMARY

(a)   Moral rights are designed to protect the authors' and performers' reputation, rather than giving authors the right to benefit commercially from their works.

(b)   Moral rights are distinct from the copyright in a work; copyright can be assigned or licensed; moral rights cannot.

(c)   The two main moral rights are the right of paternity (attribution) and the right to prevent the derogatory treatment of an author's work or a performance.

(d)   Moral rights generally apply to digital works and the Internet with the exception of computer programs and computer-generated works.

(e)   At present moral rights laws are not harmonised across Europe.

(f)   Anyone commissioning copyright works or performances needs to consider acquiring a waiver of moral rights in order to avoid problems later on eg if the work is edited or poorly reproduced; such waivers may not, however, be effective for all territories.

5

Digital Rights and Competition Law

5.1 OVERVIEW: COMPETITION LAW AND DIGITAL COPYRIGHT[1]

As discussed earlier in this book, there are various statutory exceptions to copyright: for example, fair dealing for the purposes of private study or research, etc. Those who need to access and use copyright-protected works may also be able to use competition law to their advantage.

Competition law is designed to ensure the efficient functioning of the free market economy. Monopolies may not necessarily be outlawed but the way in which monopolists can behave is constrained. In the European context competition law also seeks to ensure the free movement of goods and services within the EU. Digital copyright and competition law can come into conflict in a number of ways, for example:

(a) A software licence obliges the licensee to acquire maintenance and/or hardware exclusively from the licensor (a 'tie-in');

(b) A software licensor refuses to give users and third party maintainers the right to maintain their software;

(c) A database provider has obtained data not available from other sources and either refuses to allow access to this data or only allows access at inflated prices;

(d) A market leading computer operating system has a proprietary web browser bundled with it;

(e) A distributor of CDs in the UK is prevented by its supplier from selling the CDs outside the UK on the basis this would infringe foreign copyrights;

(f) A publisher of eBooks requires its online distributors to resell above a minimum price.

---

[1] For background see: eg Slot and Johnston, *An Introduction to Competition Law* (Oxford, Hart Publishing 2006).

There is a potential competition law issue in each of the above scenarios. Before further exploring this area it is necessary to set out the basics of competition law. Businesses operating in the UK need to be aware of both UK and EC competition law. Where the activities in question have no EU dimension and take effect just in the UK, then only UK competition law will be relevant. Where trade between member states of the EU may be affected then it is likely that EU competition law will also apply. As UK competition law is now modelled on EU competition law the UK system will be considered first.

5.2   UK COMPETITION LAW

5.2.1   The Competition Act 1998

This is the most relevant UK competition law statute. It is divided into two chapters which seek to curb anti-competitive behaviour on the part of companies and businesses of all types and sizes (even sole traders) by imposing specific prohibitions.

The 'Chapter I' Prohibition: Anti-competitive Agreements
This mirrors for UK purposes Article 101 of the Treaty on European Union (TFEU) (formerly Article 81 (in turn formerly Article 85) of the EU Treaty) (ie existing European competition law). It prohibits:

(a)   agreements between undertakings (ie persons, partnerships, companies), decisions by associations of undertakings and concerted practices (ie any informal or formal arrangements);
(b)   which may affect trade within the United Kingdom; and
(c)   which have the 'object or effect' of preventing, restricting or distorting competition within the UK.

This could catch more or less *any* agreement granting exclusivity, carving up markets or fixing prices, for example. However, the Office of Fair Trading (OFT), which enforces the Act,[2] has indicated that only arrangements with an *appreciable effect on trade* will be caught by the Act (in other words in line with European Commission (Commission)) practice agreements with *de minimis* effects are not subject to the Chapter I prohibition). The OFT takes the view that an agreement will generally have no appreciable effect on competition if the parties' combined share of the relevant market does

---

[2] Note the UK's sectoral regulators (eg in relation to electronic communications, OFCOM) have concurrent powers to investigate breaches in their sector.

not exceed 25%. 'Small agreements' between undertakings which have a combined turnover of less than £20 million are also potentially immune from fines.[3] However, serious anti-competitive practices such as price fixing will always be an issue.

Some examples of offending clauses are those which:

(a)   directly (eg by agreement with competitors) or indirectly fix prices or any other unfair trading conditions;

(b)   agree with competitors or trading partners to limit or control production, markets, technical development or investment;

(c)   agree with competitors or trading partners to share markets or sources of supply;

(d)   apply price or other discrimination: ie they apply dissimilar conditions to different trading parties placing persons at a competitive disadvantage;

(e)   make contracts subject to acceptance of supplementary obligations which have no proper connection with the contract in question (eg 'tying' arrangements).

However, companies may be able to avoid the 'Chapter I' Prohibition by seeking to rely on an exemption.[4] In practice, the two most important avenues are: (a) a specific and pre-existing block exemption or exclusion issued by the OFT or through an EU Regulation: subject to certain criteria (eg market shares of relevant parties not exceeding a certain threshold) this will set out a list of contractual terms which are acceptable even though they may be restrictive of competition. This gives the greatest degree of legal certainty generally available and leads to automatic exemption from the 'Chapter I' Prohibition. In particular certain classes of agreements, including especially 'vertical agreements', may well be pro-competitive even if they contain prima facie restrictions on competition. Vertical agreements are agreements between businesses at different levels in the production or distribution chain, such as software or CD distribution agreements which do not restrict the buyer from setting their sale price. At EU level a number of block exemptions exist (which also apply directly to the Competition Act) and these automatically exempt agreements from the Chapter I Prohibition/Article 101 TFEU by applying

---

[3] s 39 Competition Act 1998: Competition Act 1998 (Small Agreements and Conduct of Minor Significance) Regulations 2000. Note also the European Commission's *de minimis* notice (OJ 2001 C368/07) discussed below.

[4] From 1 May 2004 the OFT no longer accepted notifications for a decision or guidance under the Competition Act, and under EC law notification to the Commission in Brussels is also no longer available as a result of Council Regulation 1/2003/EC which gave domestic competition authorities and the national courts the power to apply the benefit of Art 81(3) to agreements, decisions and concerted practices which would otherwise infringe Art 81(1). In other words, the regime is one of self-assessment in light of the law.

the exemption available under Article 101(3) TFEU. There are a number of existing EU Regulations providing for block exemptions including:

(i)   exclusive distribution, purchasing and franchise agreements and other similar 'vertical agreements'[5]

(ii) technology licensing[6]

(b) An agreement that does not benefit from a block exemption may still not be prohibited if it falls under the so-called 'legal exception regime', introduced by the Modernisation Regulation.[7] The 'legal exception regime' means that an agreement that falls within Article 101(1)/Chapter I Prohibition but which satisfies the conditions set out in Article 101(3) shall not be prohibited, no prior decision to that effect being required.[8] Such an agreement is valid and enforceable from the moment that the conditions in Article 101(3) are satisfied and for as long as that remains the case. So absent any block exemption or a court, OFT or European Commission decision on the matter, the parties to an agreement that infringes Article 101(1)/Chapter I Prohibition can seek to rely on the automatic exemption under Article 101(3) as long as they and their legal advisers are confident the conditions in Article 101(3) apply. These conditions are the agreement must:

> Contribute to improving the production or distribution of goods[9] or to promoting technical or economic progress, while allowing consumers a fair share of the resulting benefit, and which does not: (a) impose on the undertakings concerned restrictions which are not indispensable to the attainment of these objectives and (b) afford such undertakings the possibility of eliminating competition in respect of a substantial part of the products in question.

The Commission has issued guidelines on how Article 101(3) (formerly Article 81(3)) is to be applied.[10] In effect what Article 101(3) is seeking to permit is where the pro-competitive effects of the agreement outweigh any anti-competitive effects and this balancing has to be conducted exclusively under the framework set out in Article 101(3)).[11]

The 'Chapter II' Prohibition: Abusive Conduct

This mirrors for UK purposes Article 102 TFEU (formerly Article 82 and before that Article 86) of the EU Treaty (ie existing European competition

---

[5] Commission Regulation 330/2010/EU of 20 April 2010 on the application of Art 101(3) of the Treaty to categories of vertical agreements and concerted practices. See also Guidelines on Vertical Restraints (2010/C 130/01).

[6] Commission Regulation (EC) No 772/2004 of 27 April 2004 on the application of Art 81(3) of the Treaty to certain categories of technology transfer agreements (OJ L 123/11).

[7] Regulation 1/2003.

[8] Article 1(2) of the Modernisation Regulation.

[9] This includes services.

[10] Notice: Guidelines on the application of Article 81(3) of the Treaty (Official Journal C 101, 27.04.2004, 97–118).

[11] Guidelines para 11.

law). It forbids conduct on the part of one or more persons, partnerships or companies which amounts to an abuse of a dominant position in a market and which may affect trade within any part of the UK. What is prohibited is not dominance in a market as such but an *abuse* of a dominant market position. The 'Chapter II' Prohibition does not however define 'abuse'. Nevertheless a non-exhaustive list in the Act[12] indicates that the likely problem areas may include:

(a) pricing (whether excessive, discriminatory or predatory); and
(b) discriminatory discounting, refusals to deal and tying.

Key to whether conduct may be abusive is whether or not a business has a *dominant position* in the relevant market—only abuses of a dominant position are caught by the 'Chapter II' Prohibition. In practice how the relevant market is defined will be crucial to both an analysis under the Chapter I and (in particular) the Chapter II Prohibitions, eg is it all software, all personal computer software, or all personal computer operating system software (rather than, say, application software or graphical user interfaces). Both the OFT and the European Commission have issued guidance in this area.[13]

The DGFT will generally consider that a business with a relevant market share below 40 per cent will not be dominant, unless there is other evidence to the contrary.

Unlike the 'Chapter I' Prohibition, there are only very limited exclusions to the 'Chapter II' Prohibition eg there are no block exemptions. Also 'Conduct of Minor Significance' where the undertaking in question has a turnover not exceeding £50 million will potentially be exempt from fines.[14]

5.2.2 Restraint of Trade Doctrine

This common law doctrine which prevents restrictions on competition which are against public policy still applies. This is notwithstanding the introduction of the Chapter I Prohibition in March 2000. In particular, unfair or unduly restrictive contracts between publishers and authors, for example where a publisher locks up an author's or artist's work for a long time with no obligation to publish or exploit, can fall foul of this doctrine. So the relevant restrictions may be held unenforceable as a matter of public policy. This was the case, for example, in *Macaulay v Schroeder Music Publishing Co Ltd*.[15] This doctrine could also be used to challenge unduly restrictive digital copyright contracts, for example.

---

[12] s 18(2).
[13] OFT Guideline 403: Market Definition (March 1999); Commission Notice on the definition of the relevant market for the purposes of competition law, OJ C372, 9.12.1997, 5.
[14] s 40 Competition Act.
[15] [1974] 1 WLR 1308 (HL).

5.3   EU LAW

Agreements, decisions, concerted practices and abuses of a dominant position which may affect trade between member states of the European Union may additionally be subject to EU competition law. EU competition law applies automatically in the UK and runs in parallel with UK competition law. Indeed, the Chapter I and Chapter II Prohibitions are modelled on earlier EU law so UK competition law is in effect the same as EU competition law. As noted earlier, Article 101 TFEU (formerly Article 81 of the EC Treaty) is equivalent to the Chapter I Prohibition and regulates agreements, decisions and concerted practices. As in the case of the Chapter I Prohibition, it is possible for an agreement to be exempted from Article 101 either individually or through a block exemption, as discussed above. Also agreements of 'minor importance' where the parties and their affiliates have very low market shares of 10–15 per cent or less, depending on the type of agreement and whether the parties are competitors, effectively fall outside the ambit of EU competition law provided they do not fix prices, share markets or contain certain other very serious restrictions on competition.[16]

Article 102 TFEU (formerly Article 82 of the EC Treaty) is equivalent to the Chapter II Prohibition and regulates abuses of a dominant position.

5.4   PENALTIES FOR BREACHING COMPETITION LAW

The OFT in the UK can impose fines on businesses which infringe the 'Chapter I' and 'Chapter II' prohibitions of up to a maximum of 10 percent of their worldwide group turnover.[17] It can also give directions to the persons or companies concerned to change or terminate the agreements or conduct in question, or request interim measures during an investigation. These directions are enforceable by court order on the application of the DGFT (Director General of Fair Trading). Interim measures directions will be published on the register maintained by the DGFT at the OFT and on a website on the Internet. There may also be publication in an appropriate trade journal.

The Commission which enforces EU competition law has similar powers to the OFT—here fines can be up to 10 per cent of worldwide group turnover.

[16] Commission Notice on agreements of minor importance which do not appreciably restrict competition under Art 81(1) of the Treaty establishing the European Community (*de minimis*) (2001/C368/07).

[17] Calculated in accordance with The Competition Act 1998 (Determination of Turnover for Penalties) Order 2000 (SI 2000/309) (as amended by The Competition Act 1998 (Determination of Turnover for Penalties) (Amendment) Order 2004 (SI 2004/1259)).

Persons that are adversely affected by the conduct of a dominant company (such as aggrieved competitors) or an anti-competitive agreement (such as customers forced to sign them) may also be able to seek redress in the UK courts by way of a claim for damages or an injunction.

Finally, the anti-competitive provisions in an agreement may be held to be void and therefore unenforceable by the courts.

In addition, very serious breaches of competition law (eg participating in cartels to fix prices) can amount to criminal offences.[18]

5.5   IMPLICATIONS FOR DIGITAL COPYRIGHT BUSINESSES

Businesses built on digital copyright have been driving forces in the world economy. They raise particularly interesting competition law issues. Some examples are discussed below.

5.5.1   E-commerce Generally

The key to success in e-commerce is often the first to market principle—online businesses want to enter the market first and rapidly build market share. This could mean they quickly become dominant in their markets and hence need to tread carefully as far as the 'Chapter II' Prohibition is concerned.

For example, in *Network Multimedia Television Ltd v Jobserve Ltd*,[19] Jobserve had built up an extremely successful online IT recruitment business ('job board') displaying advertising from many recruitment agencies. Jobserve had a significant market share. When Jobserve refused to allow certain agencies which were using another similar online 'job board' access to Jobserve's website, Jobserve found themselves accused of abusing a dominant position.

5.5.2   Software and Other Digital Copyright Licences

There is no specific EU block exemption for digital copyright licences as such. However, software copyright licensing agreements are now covered by the Technology Transfer Block Exemption (TTBER).[20] The Commission has

---

[18] In the UK under the Enterprise Act 2002.

[19] [2001] All ER (D) 57 (Apr).

[20] Commission Regulation (EC) No 772/2004 of 27 April 2004 on the application of Art 81(3) of the Treaty to certain categories of technology transfer agreements (OJ L 123/11) ('TTBER'). This came into force on 1 May 2004 and replaced the earlier Commission Regulation on the application of Art 81(3) of the Treaty to certain categories of technology transfer agreements, 240/96/EC. There was a transitional period for agreements in force on 30 April 2004 which do

also helpfully stated that it views the licensing of copyright for the purpose of the reproduction and distribution of a protected work (ie for resale) as similar to technology licensing (and therefore the Commission will apply the TTBER by analogy).[21] However, this will not be the case for the licensing of rights in performances and other rights related to copyright.[22]

As noted earlier, if an agreement falls within the application of the Block Exemption then Article 101(1) TFEU simply does not to apply.[23] The TTBER only applies below certain market share thresholds on the affected relevant technology and product market: a 20 per cent combined market share threshold if the parties are competing undertakings, and a 30 per cent combined market share if they are not competitors. Depending on whether or not the parties are competitors, when drafting the licence, certain hardcore restrictions on competition must be avoided in order for the TTBER to apply.

Whether or not the TTBER applies (for example, we may be talking about a database right and copyright licence for content where the TTBER does not apply, or the market share thresholds may be exceeded), to help avoid infringing competition law it is prudent to still draft such agreements as if the TTBER applied to them, especially if they grant *exclusive* rights to the licensee. In any event, the following provisions should always be avoided:

(a)   price fixing or resale price maintenance;
(b)   the licensee is obliged to assign the IPR in any improvements it may make to the software *back* to the licensor except in very limited circumstances;
(c)   non-compete obligations or territorial restrictions between the parties except in limited circumstances;[24]

---

not satisfy the new Regulation but were exempted by the old Regulation: this lasted from 1 May 2004 to 31 March 2006. The Regulation needs to be read in connection with Guidelines setting forth the European Commission's approach to interpreting and applying the Regulation, and intellectual property licensing generally, including licensing arrangements outside the scope of the Regulation (Commission Notice, Guidelines on the application of Art 81 of the EC Treaty to technology transfer agreements, OJ 2004 C101/02) ('Guidelines'). For a useful summary see: Steven De Schrijver and Mel Marquis, 'Technology Licensing in the EU after the Big Bang: The New Technology Transfer Block Exemption Regulation and Guidelines' (2004) *BLR* 161.

[21] Guideline 51.

[22] Guideline 52 (here the Commission sees value being created not by the reproduction and sale of copies of a product but by *each individual performance* of the work, eg by performance, showing, renting, and in such a context resale restrictions may give rise to less competition concerns; see also Case 26/81, *Coditel (II)* [1982] ECR 3381).

[23] Art 2, TTBER.

[24] Note for example the decision of the CJEU that territorial restrictions in broadcasting licence agreements against the supply of decoding devices outside the contract territory (here Greece) constitute absolute territorial restrictions by their object and therefore infringe Article 101 TFEU; free movement of services rules were also relevant to allow the importation of Greek decoder cards into the UK (*FA Premier League v QC Leisure* and *Karen Murphy v Media Protection Services Limited* 2011 EUECJ C-403/08). The territorial restrictions in the licence

(d)   restrictions on the quantities of product produced except in limited circumstances;

(e)   tying the digital copyright licence to the purchase of hardware or other tie-ins, for example; and

(f)   the licensee cannot challenge the validity of the licensor's copyright (generally).

Other provisions may also infringe competition law depending on the circumstances—this work is no substitute for reading the Technology Transfer Block Exemption (TTBER) and its Guidelines where there are concerns that the licence in question may restrict competition law.

5.5.3   Digital Copyright Distribution Agreements

Potentially anti-competitive software distribution agreements and other so-called 'vertical agreements' which involve the distribution of software or digital content and the grant of intellectual property rights may be open to challenge under the 'Chapter I' Prohibition or Article 101 TFEU. They should therefore be drafted to fall within the relevant block exemption if applicable[25] or where possible, especially if they grant exclusivity. In particular under EU law (the Vertical Agreements Exemption[26] and related Guidelines[27] and generally) the following provisions should be avoided (without taking specialist legal advice):

(a)   Price fixing or resale price maintenance (this is always a serious breach of competition law);

(b)   Restrictions on who the distributor can sell to within the EU;[28]

---

agreements were subsequently declared void by the High Court (*FA Premier League v QC Leisure* (3 February 2012 [2012] EWHC 108 (Ch)).

[25] This is primarily the Vertical Agreements Block Exemption Regulation (VABER) (Commission Regulation on the application of Art 101(3) of the Treaty to categories of vertical agreements and concerted practices, 330/2010/EU). The TTBER only applies to agreements which relate to the *production* of contract products (this must be the primary object). A pure sales licence or distribution arrangement does not fall within the TTBER; instead the VABER should be applied. However, where a software distributor is given a master licence and allowed to copy (ie *to produce*) the software for sale to end-users and to grant sub-licences then the TTBER ought to apply to the master licence arrangement, at least by analogy, and it ought to apply to the sub-licences (see Guideline 42). When dealing with a distribution agreement the licensing aspects should be scrutinised under the TTBER and the distribution and sales/marketing aspects under the VABER (see Guidelines 61–4).

[26] Commission Regulation on the application of Art 101(3) of the Treaty to categories of vertical agreements and concerted practices, 330/2010/EU.

[27] Commission Notice—Guidelines on Vertical Restraints, 2010/C 130/01. The Guidelines specifically discuss the Internet (paras 52–3).

[28] Article 4 (there are limited exceptions—see Guidelines on Vertical Restraints, paras 51–64.

(c)   Non-compete obligations lasting more than five years or which are indefinite in duration or which (except in limited circumstances) extend beyond the life of the contract.

5.5.4   Unfair Prices or Predatory Pricing

The imposition of obviously unfair prices, or the imposition of unfair trading conditions or discriminatory pricing in relation to software or other digital products may fall foul of the 'Chapter II' Prohibition or Article 102 TFEU. For example, industry-wide concerns about the high level of prices demanded by suppliers for millennium software upgrades led the OFT to launch an investigation in 1999 into incidences of unreasonable supplier behaviour. Also, in *Micro Leader Business v European Commission*[29] it was left open by the Court of First Instance of the European Communities (CFI) whether allegedly excessive pricing in France by a dominant software house (Microsoft) coupled with an attempt by Microsoft to prevent parallel importation of software into the EU from Canada to allegedly bolster prices in the EU could amount to an abuse of a dominant position.

Predatory pricing is where a dominant market player lowers its prices in the short term to uneconomic levels in an attempt to make it unprofitable for others to enter its market, thereby discouraging competition. This can also amount to an abuse of a dominant position.

It should also be noted cross-subsidising activities can in certain cases be an abuse of dominant position (eg using funds from a market where the trader is dominant to allow predatory pricing by that trader in a new market as opposed to that trader simply entering a new market).[30]

5.5.5   Maintenance

Competition law is relevant to the issue of maintenance: to what extent can a supplier insist that his customer obtains maintenance (eg spare parts, software upgrades, technical information) or other support services from that supplier? One effect of this practice is to restrict the establishment of third party service providers and therefore to reduce the choice available to customers. This could be held to be anti-competitive. This issue was before the English courts in *Synstar Computer Services (UK) Limited v ICL (Sorbus) Ltd*[31] but the judge stayed the proceedings as the matter was being considered

---

[29] Case T-198/98 [2000] CTLR N–113.
[30] *Getmapping v Ordnance Survey* [2003] ICR 1.
[31] High Court (Lightman J), 30 March 2001; unreported.

by the OFT and was likely to come before the Competition Commission in the UK.[32]

5.5.6   End-user Sales

It is in this area that 'tying' has the most appreciable impact. By way of example, take the Microsoft anti-trust action in the USA. If this had been brought in the UK or Europe, it would have been in respect of an abuse of the 'Chapter II' Prohibition or Article 102 TFEU. Here one concern was whether the provision of a product such as a free web browser with Microsoft's other software packages ('bundling') tended to drive other web browser suppliers out of the market—this is sometimes termed 'predatory innovation'. There were also similar concerns that Microsoft had been bundling its Media Player software into the Windows operating system and in 2009, Microsoft gave legally binding undertakings to the European Commission to deal with concerns that the company had tied its Internet Explorer to its near universally-used Windows system (see below).

Another example might be where a dominant software supplier designs and bundles its software to end-users in such a way that competitors either have difficulty making their products interoperable with the software, eg because they lack the relevant interface information, or their access to other markets is constrained because end-users are now locked into the dominant supplier's technology in these and related markets.

Indeed, concerns about Microsoft's alleged anti-competitive conduct in Europe resulted in a Commission decision against Microsoft on 24 March 2004.[33] In its decision, the Commission concluded, after a five-year investigation, that Microsoft Corporation infringed then Article 82 by (i) leveraging its near monopoly in the market for PC operating systems (OS) onto the markets for work group server operating systems (this stemmed from an alleged refusal by Microsoft to supply interface information to Sun Microsystems—information which Sun needed to allow them to create workgroup server operating systems that would interoperate with Microsoft's Windows desktop and server operating systems) and (ii) by tying its streaming media player to the Windows OS. Because the illegal behaviour was still ongoing, the Commission ordered Microsoft to disclose to competitors, within 120 days, the interfaces required for their products to be able to 'talk' with the

---

[32] The Director General of Fair Trading concluded that the defendants (ICL) were *not* in a dominant position in the relevant market so there could be no abuse of a dominant position (Decision ICL/SYNSTAR 20 July 2001 Case no CA98/6/2001).

[33] See Korah, *An Introductory Guide to EC Competition Law and Practice* (Oxford, Hart Publishing, 8th edn, 2004) section 5.7, and MacQueen, Waelde and Laurie, *Contemporary Intellectual Property Law and Policy* (Oxford, Oxford University Press 2008) 857–60, for a more detailed consideration of the Microsoft case.

ubiquitous Windows OS.[34] Microsoft was also required, within 90 days, to offer a version of its Windows OS without Windows Media Player to PC manufacturers (or when selling directly to end-users). In addition, Microsoft was fined €497 million for abusing its market power in the EU, the largest fine ever on a single firm.[35]

Microsoft appealed the decision to the Court of First Instance of the European Court of Justice (CFI).[36] The CFI gave judgement on 17 September 2007[37] and effectively upheld the Commission's decision. Microsoft said it would not appeal the CFI's judgement and said it would cooperate with the Commission and agree to changes to its licensing policies in order to comply with the Commission's decision.[38] The European Commission also imposed two penalty payments on Microsoft for failure to comply with the 2004 Decision: (i) €280.5 million on 12 July 2006 (for the period up to 20 June 2006) for failure to supply complete and accurate interoperability information, and (ii) €899 million on 27 February 2008 (for the period 21 June 2006 to 21 October 2007) for charging unreasonable prices for access to interface documentation for work group servers.[39]

Also in March 2013, Microsoft was fined €561 million over breach of undertakings given in 2009 to ensure website browser choice. Microsoft had agreed to display a screen offering users a choice over which website browser to use but the Commission found that the company had failed to display the browser choice screen from May 2011 to July 2012.[40]

5.5.7   Refusal to License Digital Copyright to Competitors

Article 102 TFEU (as well as the Chapter II Prohibition) prohibits undertakings in a dominant position in a given market from abusing this situation to the detriment of third parties. In its Thirtieth Report on competition policy in 2000, the European Commission expressed the view that undertakings which are free from competitive constraint commit a particularly dangerous abuse when they block or delay—through unfair practices—the entry of competitors into the market.

---

[34] The Commission followed *Magill* (see below and fn 41) in making this order.

[35] See Korah, above, and Commission press release IP/04/382.

[36] As of August 2008.

[37] *Microsoft v Commission (Competition)* [2007] EUECJ T-201/04 (17 September 2007).

[38] Microsoft press release, 22 October 2007; European Commission Press Release, 22 October 2007.

[39] European Commission press releases, 12 July 2006 (IP/06/979) and 27 February 2008 (IP/08/318). Microsoft appealed the decision but lost although it did receive a modest discount (see *The Guardian*, 27 June 2012). The fine was reduced from €899m to €860m; see Case T-167/08 (27 June 2012).

[40] European Commission press release, 6 March 2013 (IP/13/196).

It is a point of much debate whether IPR owners with valuable copyrights, database rights, patents or other IPR can be forced to license their IPR to competitors on the basis a refusal to license is an abuse of dominant position. The position following the landmark Magill[41] case of the 1990s (which concerned copyright in TV listings) is that competition law will only intervene in special circumstances where competition in a secondary market is affected or the introduction of a new product on this market is prevented. In the Magill case those providing TV listing information were obliged to make this available to those providing a new weekly TV guide, a new secondary market. It can also be argued that where an IPR is essential in enabling others to compete, then the IPR should be made available to competitors regardless (this is the so-called essential facilities doctrine[42]). If followed by the courts and competition authorities this latter approach could severely impact the value of IPR—after all, to be valuable IPR needs to provide exclusivity to its owners and licensees.

In July 2001, to general surprise, the Commission announced that it had granted interim measures ordering a US company IMS Health (IMS) to licence its 1860 marketing brick structure to its current competitors.[43] This was on the basis that by refusing to licence its competitors, IMS was abusing its dominant position. Also, the pharmaceutical industry itself had contributed to devising the 1860 structure.

Background

Pharmaceutical sales data and regional data are of great value to pharmaceutical companies. IMS is active in supplying information on sales and prescriptions of pharmaceutical products in Germany. Indeed. IMS is the world's number one supplier in this market with a worldwide turnover of US$1.4 billion in 1999. It has a dominant position in Germany.

IMS had developed a regional sales data method in Germany called the 1860 brick structure. IMS was the only provider of regional data in Germany until 1999, when two new competitors entered the market. The competitors initially attempted to distribute their regional sales information in a different structure but discussions with potential customers revealed that data analysed in this manner would not be marketable, as it did not correspond to the

---

[41] Cases C-241&242/91P *RTE and ITP v Commission* [1995] ECR I-743.

[42] *Port of Rodby* OJ 1994 L55/52. See also: *Bronner* [1998] ECR-I-7791 (Case C-7/97) (access to the only nationwide home-delivery scheme to rival daily newspaper: for there to be an abuse of a dominant position access to the service had to be *indispensable* in order for the rival to carry on their business—ie, there was no actual or potential substitute for the home delivery scheme).

[43] 'Commission imposes interim measures on IMS HEALTH in Germany', Commission press release IP/01/941, 3 July 2001.

territorial division already in place. So the competitors made use of the 1860 brick structure.

In 2000, IMS successfully obtained a German court order preventing the competitors from using the 1860 brick structure or similar structure, alleging copyright infringement. IMS then refused requests for a licence to use the structure from its competitors. Following a complaint by one of the competitors, the Commission investigated the matter and concluded that there did not seem to be a real and practical possibility of new entrants into the market employing another structure which would not infringe IMS' copyright. The Commission considered that refusal of access to the structure was likely to eliminate all competition in the relevant market and was not objectively justified. Hence IMS should be required to allow access and use of its data structure.

Implications

It is unclear how much of a sea change in competition policy *IMS* represents. As noted below, the ECJ has provided a narrow ruling on the subject. The facts here are very unusual—it seems that the case depended on whether the brick structure devised by IMS was in fact indispensable to the presentation of regional sales data or whether a different, non-infringing structure was possible. The Commission were at pains to stress it was a rare step and that the market concerned was very peculiar. IMS appealed the decision and in November 2001, the President of the Court of First Instance provisionally overturned the Commission's decision. The matter was referred to the European Court of Justice (ECJ) for a preliminary ruling on three questions on the interpretation of Article 82 (on a reference from the Landgericht Frankfurt am Main).[44] The Advocate General gave his opinion on 2 October 2003 and the court gave judgment on 29 April 2004.

The ECJ ruled that the refusal by an undertaking which holds a dominant position and owns a copyright of a brick structure *indispensable* to the presentation of regional sales data on pharmaceutical products in a Member State to grant a licence to use that structure to another undertaking which also wishes to provide such data within that Member State constitutes an abuse of a dominant position under Article 82 where the following conditions are fulfilled:

(a)   The undertaking which requested the licence intends to offer, on the market for the supply of the data in question, *new products or services not offered by the copyright owner* and for which there is a potential consumer demand;

(b)   The refusal is not justified by objective considerations; and

---

[44] *IMS Health GmbH & Co OHG v NDC Health GmbH & Co KG*, Case C-418/01.

(c)   The refusal is such as to reserve to the copyright owner the market for the supply of data on sales of pharmaceutical products in the Member State concerned by eliminating all competition on that market.

IMS is a narrow ruling. It does not open the floodgates by forcing copyright or database right owners to license their rights to all comers. It is consistent with earlier case law. The intangible asset/copyright work in question (here, the brick structure) had to be an essential input for operating in a secondary market (in this case the supply of data using the brick structure). This is crucial. The person seeking a licence must also be intending to offer new products or services not offered by the copyright owner and not merely duplicate those already provided by the owner.[45]

It should also be noted that the *IMS* case was referred to by the Court of First Instance of the European Court of Justice (CFI) in the *Microsoft* case discussed earlier in this chapter. The CFI applied *IMS* and earlier case law, and concluded that only in exceptional circumstances may a refusal to licence by an undertaking with a dominant position amount to an abuse of a dominant position. From the case law the CFI held that the occurrence of each of the following three circumstances amounted to exceptional circumstances:[46]

(a)   In the first place, the refusal relates to a product or service indispensable to the exercise of a particular activity on a neighbouring market;

(b)   In the second place, the refusal is of such a kind as to exclude any effective competition on that neighbouring market;

(c)   In the third place, the refusal prevents the appearance of a new product for which there is potential consumer demand.

According to the CFI, once it is established that such circumstances are present, the refusal by the holder of a dominant position to grant a licence may infringe Article 82 of the EC Treaty unless the refusal is 'objectively justified'. The CFI found these circumstances to apply, there was no objective justification for Microsoft's refusal and so Microsoft's behaviour was an abuse of a dominant position. In particular, Microsoft's argument that its technology was secret, protected by intellectual property rights and of great value and contained important innovations, so if Microsoft had to disclose this it would eliminate Microsoft's future incentives to invest in more intellectual property, was rejected by the CFI.[47]

So, whilst it remains the case that a digital copyright owner can only be forced to licence its copyright in very limited circumstances, what if the

---

[45] See in particular the Opinion of Advocate General Tizzano at 62, 66, 80, and his conclusion.

[46] *Microsoft v Commission (Competition)* [2007] EUECJ T-201/04 (17 September 2007) paras 331–6.

[47] Paras 688–711.

owner is dominant in its market and is already licensing third parties to use its copyright? In these circumstances if a new third party approached the owner and requested a licence and was refused, or an existing customer was refused a new licence, then this *refusal to supply* by the owner could still be an abuse of a dominant position unless objectively justified. This is on the basis of long established EU case law.[48]

Standards

Also, competitors who need to use a dominant industry standard owned by others in order to interface eg their software or hardware with other products may still be able to use *Magill* to their advantage as well as relying on the Software Directive and Article 102 generally.[49]

Compulsory Licensing

The CDPA also provides for 'compulsory licensing' of copyright and database rights.[50]

5.5.8   Excessive Pricing

It can be an abuse of a dominant position to charge excessive and/or discriminatory prices, for example for the supply of data where the data supplier is the only source of this data. This may also be linked to a threat to refuse to continue to supply the data unless a licence is taken at the price asked for, the latter also being a potential abuse of a dominant position. However, these cases need to be very carefully and comprehensively argued (ie pleaded) before the court and economic analysis provided by way of background, if they are to succeed.[51]

5.5.9   Content Bundling

It could be an abuse of a dominant position for a content owner such as a satellite broadcaster to bundle its offering to cable companies for redistribution

---

[48] *ICI and Commercial Solvents v Commission* [1974] ECR 223.

[49] Note for example, the now closed formal EU antitrust proceedings against Qualcomm Incorporated, a US chipset manufacturer, concerning an alleged breach of EC treaty rules on abuse of a dominant market position (article 82). The Qualcomm case raised important issues about the pricing of technology after its adoption as part of an industry standard. The investigation was opened on 1 October 2007 (see memo/07/389) and closed on 24 November 2009 (memo/09/516).

[50] (s 144) and the Database Regulations 1997 (sch 2, para 15).

[51] *Attheraces Ltd & Anor v The British Horseracing Board Ltd & Anor* Rev 2 [2007] EWCA Civ 38 (2 February 2007), para 20 (*per* Mummery LJ). See also *Attheraces Ltd & Anor v The British Horseracing Board Ltd & Anor* [2005] EWHC 1553 (Ch) (15 July 2005), and *BHB Enterprises plc v Victor Chandler (International) Ltd* [2005] EWHC 1074 (Ch) (27 May 2005).

in such a way that cable companies are forced to buy more programmes than they realistically might require.

5.5.10   Exhaustion of Rights in Digital Copyright Products

A major function of EU competition law is to enable the free movement of goods and services within the EU.[52] As copyright is a national right, could a copyright owner in the UK prevent the importation of CDs of his works placed on the market by a licensee of his in Germany? Could a database owner who has granted a licence to a user in the UK prevent that user from allowing a person in Germany *also* to have electronic access to the database as well? The key principle is that once copyright *goods* e.g. CDs, books or (subject to the discussion below as regards software) other copies which embody the copyright work in a *tangible article* have been put on the market with the consent of the copyright owner *within the EU* (as opposed to outside it), the owner cannot prevent their further circulation within the EU. In other words, the owner's rights are *exhausted* in respect of these goods—this is the *exhaustion of rights* doctrine. The principle applies to goods put on the market in the EU (which includes for this purpose the EEA). However, where goods are put on the market outside the EEA then the issue is one of consent: only if the rights holder has clearly consented to the export of the goods from outside the EEA into the EEA then will there be international exhaustion.[53] For example, Sony had no problem in preventing the import into the UK of PlayStation consoles offered for sale in the UK and the EEA via a website in Hong Kong where these products were only intended for sale in Japan. This was on the grounds that this clearly infringed Sony's intellectual property rights in the EEA.[54] In another case the operations of a Hong Kong Internet retail music business which shipped CDs into the UK market at the request of UK consumers had no tenable defence to a UK copyright infringement claim.[55]

It has been a matter of some debate as to how exhaustion of rights applies to copyright other than in the context of the distribution of *goods* eg CDs, books, records, software on CD and video tapes. For example, where a

---

[52] Arts 34–36 of the TFEU.

[53] 'Consent' must be unequivocal so will very rarely, if ever, be implied from the facts and certainly not from the silence of the rights owner (see *Zino Davidoff (Approximation of Laws)* [2001] EUECJ C-416/99 (20 November 2001) para 53.). Note that a different position applies in the USA—see the recent (2013) US Supreme Court decision in *John Wiley & Sons, Inc v Kirtsaeng*, No 11–697; 54 F 3d 210 (2d Cir 2011).

[54] *KK Sony Computer Entertainment & Anor v Pacific Game Technology (Holding) Ltd* [2006] EWHC 2509 (Pat) (18 October 2006).

[55] *Independiente Ltd & Ors v Music Trading On-Line (HK) Ltd (t/a CD-WOW) & Ors* [2007] EWHC 533 (Ch) (20 March 2007).

copyright product is delivered as a *performance* or otherwise transmitted (eg the cable transmission of a film), then there is no exhaustion of rights (see *Coditel Sa v Cine Vog Films SA*[56]). The owner can prevent any subsequent retransmission of the work within the EU.

In any event the Software Directive clarifies that the *first sale*[57] in the Community of copies of software exhaust the distribution right within the Community for those copies *with the exception of the right to control further rental of the software*.[58] Reference to 'Community-wide' exhaustion is also made in the Rental and Lending Right Directive.[59] Also, the Information Society Directive further clarifies that the exhaustion of rights doctrine only applies to the tangible original or tangible copies of a work where the first sale is by the right holder or with his *consent in the Community*.[60] This is also the position under the Copyright, Designs and Patents Act 1988.[61] So putting a CD on sale in the USA would not exhaust the owner's rights in Europe. For example, in *Micro Leader Business v European Commission*,[62] the lawful sale of Microsoft software in Canada did not exhaust Microsoft's rights to prevent import of the software from Canada into France.

The Information Society Directive also clarifies that where a work is communicated to the public over the Internet (eg images, text, music, film or video is included on a website), or where the works in question are by their very nature services (eg access to/use of a database or the rental or lending of works), then there is no exhaustion of rights.[63] So if I lawfully download an MP3 recording from a website and burn it onto CD then the right holder(s) can prevent any further sale or distribution of *that* CD, even if copies of the same CD were put on the market elsewhere in Europe by the right holder(s). At least this appears to be the case as regards content other than software. However, exhaustion of rights in software is now subject to a recent CJEU decision that permitted exhaustion of rights to apply in the case of downloaded software on the basis that in certain circumstances acquiring software through a digital download was the same (for exhaustion of rights purposes) as acquiring a copy on tangible media. This is an important case.

---

[56] C-262/81 [1983] 1 CMLR 49 (ECJ).

[57] What is meant by the first sale in the context of software is crucial—could it include a digital download? The CJEU recently said it could (*UsedSoft GmbH v Oracle International Corp*, Case C-128/11, 3 July 2012); this is discussed below.

[58] Art 4(c).

[59] Directive 92/100/EEC on rental right and lending right and on certain rights related to copyright in the field of intellectual property, Art 9(2) [now repealed and replaced by codified and amended version 2006/115/EC].

[60] Art 4(2).

[61] s 18.

[62] Case T-198/98, [2000] CTLR N–113.

[63] Art 3(3); Recital 29.

UsedSoft GmbH v Oracle International Corp, Case C-128/11, 3 July 2012

This case concerned Oracle's rights as software owner to control the resale of used 'databank' (client-server) software in Germany. In effect, software licences for Oracle's software were resold by original purchasers and buyers of the used licences then acquired a copy of the software direct from Oracle by a digital download from Oracle's website. Given Oracle's licence agreements are expressed to be 'non-transferable', the only way a buyer could be lawfully permitted to use the software is first, if exhaustion of rights applied to permit them acquiring the digital download in the first place, and second, on the basis they now have a lawfully acquired copy of the program, can they run it (including where necessary reproducing it—bearing in mind the reproduction right is not subject to exhaustion of rights—only the distribution right is).

The CJEU's decision is based on its interpretation of both the Information Society Directive and the Software Directive. Whilst the Information Society Directive appears to rule out digital downloads benefiting from exhaustion of rights (see in particular the discussion above including the fact that a digital download was a communication to the public and so not covered by exhaustion of rights), the Software Directive allowed this—given its interpretation and purpose—and so in effect trumped the Information Society Directive. Key were the provisions of Article 4(2) of the Software Directive which expressly dealt with exhaustion of rights in software and the CJEU's view that it was the intention of the EU legislature to assimilate both tangible and intangible copies of computer programs under Article 4(2). The CJEU also noted that from an economic point of view the sale of a computer program on CD-ROM and the sale of a program by downloading from the Internet are similar and that the online transmission method is the functional equivalent of the supply of a material medium. So the question was whether there was a 'sale' here. The CJEU took the view that as the software was licensed for an unlimited period and in return for a fee corresponding to the economic value of the copy of the work, then in light of the above discussion there was a first sale of the software exhausting the owner's rights in it. Given that these rights were exhausted, the buyer of a used licence was entitled to first download the software and having lawfully acquired it, then run the software for its intended purpose as permitted by Article 5(1) of the Software Directive.

It can be argued that this decision appears limited to software where the software is licensed for an unlimited time and an upfront fee—so if the licence is limited in time or and/or recurring fees are payable for its use then it appears the CJEU decision is not applicable. Also the CJEU made clear the original acquirer had to delete/render unusable the 'copy' they had resold—once they had resold the licence they no longer had the right to use the software. This gives some comfort to software proprietors who will want to carefully review their software licences in light of the CJEU decision. Of course, it is possible the CJEU could in future revisit this area or the legislature seek to further clarify exhaustion of rights in digital products.

5.5.11   E-books

The sale and distribution of e-books in the USA, UK and EU has been under scrutiny, including allegations of price fixing and other anti-competitive practices under Article 101 TFEU. In the UK in February 2011, the OFT opened an investigation focusing on whether the agreements between five major publishers and book retailers governing terms of sale (including pricing) were compatible with competition law. In particular, publishers had adopted an 'agency model' to seek to lawfully allow them to set resale prices on the basis their eBook retailers were their agents (not resellers/distributors) and under EU competition law true agency agreements are not subject to Article 101 TFEU.

The European Commission also investigated. The Commission was concerned not just about the agency issue but also whether there was collusion between publishers in that they all adopted the agency model in January 2010 with a most favoured nations clause (MFN) in each agreement that provided that if any retailer sold an eBook at a price that was lower than on Apple's iBookstore, the publishers were required to match the lower price on Apple's iBookstore. The Commission settled its investigation in December 2012 following commitments from Apple and the publishers to cease participation in the activities of concern. In particular, the publishers agreed to terminate all existing agency agreements that include retail price restrictions and a retail price MFN. The publishers further committed not to enter into new agreements that include price MFN clauses for five years. They also committed to a two-year 'cooling-off period', during which retailers will be free to offer retail price discounts for e-books up to an amount equal to the commission the retailer receives from the publisher over a one-year period. Apple committed to terminate its agency agreements with these four publishers as well as with Penguin. Apple further committed not to enter into or enforce any retail price MFN clauses they may have in any new or existing agency agreements for a period of five years.[64]

---

[64] Antitrust: Commission accepts legally binding commitments from Simon & Schuster, Harper Collins, Hachette, Holtzbrinck and Apple for sale of e-books; Commission press release Brussels, 13 December 2012. As of 13 December 2012, discussions with Penguin Books were continuing so not part of the settlement. Note that there is a separate US case where the US Department of Justice is taking action against Apple.

5.5.12 Collecting Societies

On 16 July 2008, the European Commission adopted an antitrust decision prohibiting European collecting societies from restricting competition by limiting their ability to offer their services to authors and commercial users outside their domestic territory. The prohibited practices consisted of clauses in the reciprocal representation agreements concluded by members of CISAC (the 'International Confederation of Societies of Authors and Composers') as well as other concerted practices between those collecting societies. The practices were held to infringe Article 81 of the EC Treaty. These were:

— The **membership clause**, currently applied by 23 collecting societies, that prevents an author from choosing or moving to another collecting society.

— **Territorial restrictions** that prevent a collecting society from offering licences to commercial users outside their domestic territory. These territorial restrictions include an **exclusivity clause**, currently contained in the contracts of 17 EEA collecting societies, by which a collecting society authorises another collecting society to administer its repertoire on a given territory on an exclusive basis and a **concerted practice** among all collecting societies resulting in a strict segmentation of the market on a national basis. The effect for a commercial user (such as the complainant companies RTL and Music Choice (a UK online music provider)) that wants to offer a pan-European media service is that it cannot receive a licence which covers several Member States from one society, but has to negotiate with each individual national collecting society.

The Commission decision required the collecting societies to end these infringements by modifying their agreements and practices, but did not impose fines. The removal of these restrictions will allow authors to choose which collecting society manages their copyright (eg, on the basis of quality of service, efficiency of collection and level of management fees deducted) rather than being limited to their national society. It will also make it easier for users to obtain licences for broadcasting music over the Internet, by cable and by satellite in several countries from a single collection society of their choice.[65]

---

[65] Commission press release, IP/08/1165 Brussels (16 July 2008). Note that the Commission is seeking to regulate this area further especially in the context of the multi-territorial licensing of musical works online—see Proposal for a Directive on collective management of copyright and related rights and multi-territorial licensing of rights in musical works for online use in the internal market (Brussels, 11.7.2012 Com(2012) 372 final 2012/0180 (COD)).

5.6   CONCLUDING COMMENTS

Digital copyright owners who are licensing or distributing content or digital copyright 'goods' such as software, CDs, eBooks, etc or providing online services need to bear in mind competition law when structuring and drafting their licences and distribution arrangements and commercial practices. Where they hold a dominant position in their markets they must take particular care to treat customers and potential customers fairly and not discriminate between them without good objective justification. They must also take other steps to avoid any allegation that their market conduct is otherwise 'abusive'.

Users of digital copyright may find competition law a useful weapon when faced with a refusal to licence by a dominant supplier, an inability to enter certain markets or where they are forced to enter into a highly restrictive agreement.

At the time of writing this area is fast-moving. As noted in this chapter, historically Microsoft has received much scrutiny from the EU competition law authorities. Now newer players such as Google are also under the spotlight.[66]

SUMMARY

(a)   Competition law applies to the exploitation of copyright/database right and the distribution of copyright products and databases.

(b)   UK and/or EU competition law can be relevant depending upon whether trade between EU countries may be affected.

(c)   Competition law regulates both anti-competitive agreements (licences, distribution agreements, etc) and abuses of a dominant position (refusals to supply or licence, unfair pricing, etc).

(d)   The first sale in the EU of tangible copies of a work (eg CD, DVD) will 'exhaust the right' to restrict any further circulation of the copy of the work within the EU.

(e)   Exhaustion of rights does not apply to tangible copies of works originating outside the EU, to the on-line exploitation of works or performances (subject to the special position of software), to making databases available, or to the rental of works.

(f)   Both owners and users of digital copyright works can use competition law to their competitive advantage.

---

[66] See for example: 'Antitrust: Commission Probes Allegations of Antitrust Violations by Google' (European Commission press release, 30 November 2010 (IP/10/1624)).

6

Software Copyright

6.1 CODE AND COPYRIGHT: THE BASICS[1]

Computer programs or software, as they are generally known, are in one sense simply instructions to operate a machine in machine-readable electronic form (binary code (010101 etc)) or in a higher level programming language. Software may be distributed:

(a) embodied on a physical carrier such as a disk or CD, in which case it is probably 'goods' under UK Sale of Goods law[2] (and will be so in the context of EU exhaustion of rights principles—see chapter five); or

(b) electronically (eg web downloads), in which case it is not 'goods' but probably services.

Software is typically written in a high level language such as FORTRAN, which a programmer will understand—this is source code. This will need to be compiled (ie translated) into machine-readable code (object code) for distribution on CD, disk or electronically to users.

Software may be protected by a variety of contractual and intellectual property rights (IP) in the United Kingdom, principally:

(a) **Copyright:** computer programs (object code) and their preparatory design materials (source code, etc) are defined as literary works under Section 3, Copyright, Designs and Patents Act 1988 (CDPA)). User manuals and software licences in printed or electronic form will also be protected by copyright and possibly database right in certain cases. This reflects the provisions of the Software Directive which are key in this regard.

---

[1] See generally: Bainbridge, *Legal Protection of Computer Software* (London, Tottel, 5th edn, 2008); Laddie, Prescott and Vitoria, *The Modern Law of Copyright and Designs*, ch 36, 'Computers and Copyright'; Lambert, 'Copyleft, Copyright and Software IPRs: Is Contract Still King?' [2001] *EIPR* 165; Lessig, *Code and Other Laws of Cyberspace* (New York, Basic Books, 1999); Stokes, 'United Kingdom Software Copyright: Cantor Fitzgerald v Tradition' [1999] *CTLR* 142.

[2] *St Albans v International Computers Ltd* [1997] FSR 251 (CA) 265–6.

(b) **Rights in confidential information:** the high level code generally used to write software (source code) is typically kept confidential—only the object code, the machine readable instructions in binary format (01010 etc), and related user manuals and licences, are distributed to users.

(c) **Patents:** software which has a 'technical effect,' for example it enhances PC memory capacity or operates or controls a technical process, and is otherwise novel and inventive can be patented.[3]

(d) **Designs/topography right:** for semi-conductor products.[4] As noted in chapter one, these rights are outside the scope of this book.

(e) **Registered designs/trademarks:** following recent case law and revisions to the Registered Designs Act 1949, to take account of EC legislation, it appears that computer icons, software fonts and on-screen displays are now eligible for registered design protection on the basis they are 'graphic symbols'.[5] Trademark protection may also be available.

(f) **Contract/software licensing:** because software needs to be copied in order to run and be used it is distinct from other literary works such as a book (which need not be copied in order to be read). Software owners will typically prescribe by way of a copyright licence (a contract) what rights users have to copy/reproduce, transfer and modify the software and for what purposes. It is desirable to clarify, where desirable, what use rights a user has, as from a licensor's perspective a licence 'to use' software will potentially be given a broad interpretation.[6] Licensors do not have complete freedom of contract here; in addition to con-sumer protection legislation (if relevant), licensors must have regard to Competition Law (see chapter five) and European law (the Software Directive—see below). Software licensing is given further consideration in chapter seven.

Because of the expense and perceived difficulties in securing patent pro-tection, by far the most common methods of software IP protection in the UK are copyright and confidential information. IP rights in software are not necessarily mutually exclusive, although full public disclosure of the software invention in the patent application (which is published) is required in order to obtain a patent.

---

[3] For a discussion and application of the principles relating to software patents see *Symbian Ltd v Comptroller General of Patents* [2008] EWCA Civ 1066 (8 October 2008), where a program that enabled a computer to run faster and more reliably was held to be patentable.

[4] Council Directive (87/54/EEC) of 16 December 1986 on the Legal Protection of Topographies of Semiconductor Products; Part III (Design Right), CDPA; Design Right (Semiconductor Topographies) Regulations 1989, SI 1989/1100.

[5] Council Directive 98/71 on the Legal Protection of Designs; *Apple Computer Inc v Design Registry* (ChD, Patents Court; Jacob J 24/10/01).

[6] *Cantor Gaming Ltd v Gameaccount Global Ltd* [2007] All ER (D) 2 (August).

Internationally, following the TRIPS Agreement, software generally is, and will be, protected by copyright (as a literary work, whether in object or source code), patents and rights in confidential information.[7]

In 1991, the European Community agreed the Software Directive[8] and this is now the basis for the copyright protection of software in the UK and elsewhere in the EU. The Software Directive was implemented into UK law by the Copyright (Computer Programs) Regulations 1992[9] (Regulations) and the CDPA was amended accordingly. The Directive clarifies the copyright protection to be given to software and provides for mandatory exceptions to copyright, including where de-compilation of a program is required in order to be able to determine the relevant interface information (such as the application programming interface: API). This will generally be needed to allow one program to inter-operate with another; for example, an application program (such as a word processing package) with a computer operating system.

6.2   THE SOFTWARE DIRECTIVE

Neither the Directive nor the CDPA define what is meant by 'computer program'. The recitals to the Directive state that:

> The term 'computer program' shall include programs in any form, including those which are incorporated into hardware. [It] also includes preparatory design work leading up to the development of a computer program provided that the nature of the preparatory work is such that a computer program can result from it at a later stage.

Are websites and in particular, the HTML code used to write them, 'computer programs'? This question is considered in section 7.7 of chapter seven. Note also that the CJEU has, reflecting the Directive, stated that 'computer program' includes the source code and object code with preparatory design work also included within the term 'computer program' under the Software Directive, 'provided that the nature of the preparatory work is such that a computer program can result from it at a later stage.'[10] The logic of the CJEU here is that a computer program must be capable of being reproduced to perform its task. So Graphical User Interfaces (GUIs), whilst not computer programs under the Software Directive (as they do not enable the

---

[7] ss 1 (Copyright and Related Rights), 5 (Patents) and 7 (Protection of Undisclosed Information), TRIPS.

[8] Council Directive (91/250/EEC) of 14 May 1991 on the Legal Protection of Computer Programs (note: repealed in 2009 and replaced by codified text: Directive 2009/24/EC; this edition maintains references to 1991 text (as amended)).

[9] SI 1992/3233.

[10] *Bezpecnostni softwarova asociace—Svaz softwarove ochrany v Ministerstvo kultury* ('BSA') Case C-393/09 at para 36. See also *SAS Institute* Case C-406/10 at para 37.

reproduction or creation of the computer program but are simply a means to make use of the features of the program), can also be protected by copyright where they are the author's 'own intellectual creation'[11] ie original. However, the CJEU also noted that a GUI will not be original if its expression as a copyright work is dictated by its technical function.[12] Note also that in light of the CJEU decision in *SAS Institute*, 'keywords, syntax, commands and combinations of commands, options, defaults and iterations [consisting] of words, figures or mathematical concepts in isolation' are unlikely to be protected.[13]

The main provisions of the Directive are as follows:

(a) **Copyright protection:**[14] Computer programs including their preparatory materials are protected by copyright as literary works within the meaning of the Berne Convention provided they are *original* in the sense of being the author's own intellectual creation. This test of originality is very similar to that for databases and is different from the traditional UK test of 'sweat of the brow' (see chapter two). The Regulations, however, do not require this test. Nevertheless, UK courts are obliged to interpret 'original' consistently with the Directive in respect of computer programs and are doing so.[15] Copyright also only extends to the expression in any form of a computer program: the ideas and principles which underlie any element of a program including those which underlie its interfaces are not protected by copyright; this is a restatement of the idea/expression dichotomy noted in chapters one and two.[16]

(b) **Restricted acts:**[17] Software copyright will be infringed by:
   (i) permanent or temporary copying of the program by any means including where this is required to load, store, run or display the program;
   (ii) any translation, adaptation, arrangement or other alteration of a program and copying the results thereof. So the compilation or de-compilation of a program would infringe copyright, as would any other translation between programming languages;
   (iii) any form of distribution to the public including rental of the original computer program or copies. But this is subject to the exhaustion of rights doctrine other than in the case of rental (see chapter five, section 5.5.10). In addition Member States must provide

[11] Paras 40–50.
[12] Paras 48–50.
[13] Case C-406/10 paras 66–9.
[14] Art 1.
[15] See eg *SAS Institute* [2013] EWHC 69 (Ch) discussed below.
[16] See also section 6.3 below.
[17] Art 4.

appropriate remedies dealing with secondary infringement and technical protection measures;

(iv) putting into circulation a copy of software knowing or having reason to believe it is an infringing copy;

(v) possessing a copy of a program for commercial purposes knowing or having reason to believe it is an infringing copy;

(vi) putting into circulation or possessing for commercial purposes any means the sole intended purpose of which is to facilitate the unauthorised removal or circumvention of any technical device which may have been applied to protect a computer program. So, for example, circulating a technique or algorithm designed to crack an encryption code applied to software or a device designed to unlock a 'dongle' used to protect software are not permitted. Section 296 CDPA already deals with this (See chapter seven, section 7.9.3).

(c) **Exceptions to the restricted acts:**[18]

(i) *Right to use program for intended purpose:*[19] A lawful acquirer of a computer program may use the program for its intended purpose, including error correction without infringing copyright unless agreed otherwise. This highlights the importance of contractual licence terms to clarify and restrict what users are entitled to do.

(ii) *Right to make a back-up copy:*[20] Where it is necessary in order for lawful use a person may make a back-up copy of a program regardless of any contract/licence to the contrary.[21] This right cannot be overridden by contract.

(iii) *Right to observe, study and test the program:*[22] No authorisation from the right holder is required for a person having the right to use a copy of the program to observe, study or test the functioning of the program in order to determine the ideas and principles which underlie it. But always provided he does so whilst performing any acts of loading, displaying, running, transmitting or storing the program which he is entitled to do. This right cannot be overridden by contract. This right was recently discussed and applied in *SAS Institute*[23]—see below.

---

[18] Arts 5 and 6.

[19] Implemented by s 50C CDPA.

[20] Implemented by ss 50A and 296A CDPA.

[21] Where software is supplied on CDs (or DVDs) which are robust and cannot be erased (and where replacement copies are available from the supplier), there is no necessity to make a back-up copy and so this exception cannot be relied on (see *Kabushiki Kaisha Sony Computer Entertainment Inc v Ball* [2004] EW HC1738 (Ch) para 30).

[22] Implemented by s 29(4A), s 50BA and s 296A CDPA.

[23] [2013] EWHC 69 (Ch).

(iv)   *Decompilation right:*[24] The authorisation of the right holder is not required where reproduction and translation of the code ('Acts') is *indispensable* to obtain the information necessary to achieve the interoperability of an independently created computer programs with other programs ('Information'). This right to decompile cannot be overridden by contract and is available provided that:

—   the Acts are performed by a licensee of the code or on their behalf;

—   the Information has not previously been readily available to the licensee or their agents; and

—   the Acts are confined to the parts of the original program which are necessary to achieve interoperability.

Also the Information may not be:

—   used for goals other than to achieve the interoperability of the independently created program;

—   given to others except where necessary for the interoperability of the independently created computer program; or

—   used for the development, production or marketing of a computer program substantially similar in its expression, or for any other act which infringes copyright.

6.3   WHAT DOES SOFTWARE COPYRIGHT PROTECT?

The scope of protection for computer programs is a matter of continuing debate in UK copyright law. The principles to be applied are those applying to the infringement of literary works. So literal copying of code which amounts to a substantial part of the program copied will infringe copyright.

But what if a program is copied not by simply copying its code but by writing a new program using the ideas behind the original program without literally copying the original code? Non-literal aspects of the program might include its 'look and feel', its structure, sequence and organisation and its input and output routines. If one were to apply the idea/expression dichotomy as baldly stated in the Software Directive, one might rule out a finding of infringement. This is clearly not correct, not least in light of the importance UK copyright law gives to protecting the skill and labour of authors, whether programmers or journalists. Also, Lord Hoffmann's analysis of the idea/expression dichotomy in *Designers Guild v Russell Williams*[25] (an artistic

---

[24]   Implemented by ss 29(4), 50B and 296A CDPA.
[25]   [2000] 1 WLR 2416, 2422D–2423E.

copyright/fabric design case) categorises the circumstances in which 'ideas' as such would not be protected:

(a) the ideas have no connection with the literary, dramatic, musical or artistic nature of the work;

(b) the ideas are not original or so commonplace as not to perform a substantial part of the work eg they are common programming techniques in the case of software—the Software Directive itself recognises this.[26]

In any event there is a slowly evolving body of case law in the UK in which the issues surrounding the non-literal copying of software have been considered. The most recent and important cases are *Cantor Fitzgerald v Tradition*,[27] *Navitaire Inc v Easyjet Airline Co. & Anor*,[28] *Nova Productions v Mazooma Games*,[29] and *SAS Institute Inc v World Programming Ltd.*[30] These are worth a detailed analysis to illustrate the relevant copyright principles. Before doing this it is, however, necessary to consider the two main UK cases on software copyright before *Cantor Fitzgerald, John Richardson Computers Ltd v Flanders*[31] and *Ibcos Computers Ltd v Barclays Mercantile Highland Finance Ltd.*[32]

6.3.1 *John Richardson Computers Ltd v Flanders*

This was the first full trial of the alleged infringement of copyright in a computer program to be held in the UK. It concerned allegations of literal and semi-literal copying of the plaintiff's program. Flanders had worked for the plaintiff in developing the plaintiff's program and had later developed his own. The programs were designed for pharmacists (they labelled prescriptions) and had a number of user features and routines in common.

The plaintiff's and defendant's programs were written in different programming languages. Hence there could be no literal similarities between the programs. The judge (Ferris J) focused on similarities at the user interface level and found that there was copying. Ferris J applied an American case, *Computer Associates v Altai (1992)*.[33] This case set out the three-step 'abstraction-filtration-comparison' test to determine the substantial similarity of the non-literal elements of computer programs. The aim is to

---

[26] Recital 14.
[27] [2000] RPC 95.
[28] [2004] EWHC 1725 (Ch) (30 July 2004).
[29] *Nova Productions Ltd v Mazooma Games Ltd & Ors* [2007] EWCA Civ 219 (14 March 2007).
[30] [2013] EWHC 69 (Ch).
[31] [1993] FSR 497.
[32] [1994] FSR 275.
[33] 3 CCH Computer Cases 46, 50.

determine what the 'kernel' of creative expression protecting the program in question is; this is then compared with the structure of an allegedly infringing program. The objective behind the test is to ensure that (1) programmers receive appropriate copyright protection for innovative utilitarian works containing expressions; and (2) non-protectable technical expressions remain in the public domain for others to use freely as building blocks for their own work. As Ferris J put it:

> ... at the stage at which the substantiality of any copying falls to be expressed in an English case the question which has to be answered, in relation to the originality of the plaintiff's program and the separation of an idea from its expression, is essentially the same question as the United States court was addressing in *Computer Associates*. In my judgment it would be right to adopt a similar approach in England.

The use by Ferris J of a modified version of the test for non-literal infringement set out in *Computer Associates* received much comment and some criticism at the time. However, the different approach taken by Jacob J in *Ibcos Computers* was generally welcomed as representing a common-sense application of traditional United Kingdom copyright principles to software infringement.

6.3.2   *Ibcos Computers Ltd v Barclays Mercantile Highland Finance Ltd*

The facts in this case were simpler than in the Richardson case. The defendant computer programmer (Mr Poole) had helped create an accounts payroll package for agricultural dealers (ADP) which was owned by his former company. Upon leaving his former company, in his spare time he developed a program (Unicorn) also for agricultural dealers, which was intended to be a more user-friendly program than ADP and which he commenced marketing. His former employers then sued him and the companies with which he was associated in marketing Unicorn on the grounds of copyright infringement, breach of restrictive covenant (not relevant here) and breach of confidence.

Rejecting the approach taken by Ferris J in *Richardson* and in particular the application of the *Computer Associates* test, Jacob J found that on the facts there was an overwhelming inference of literal copying of code (including disk to disk copying). Non-literal copying was also apparent. On the issue of applying *Computer Associates* and whether a substantial part of the plaintiff's work had been copied, Jacob J stated:[34]

> For myself I do not find the route of going via United States case law particularly helpful. As I have said, United Kingdom copyright cannot prevent the copying of

---

[34] Ibid 302.

a mere general idea but can protect the copying of a detailed 'idea'. It is a question of degree where a good guide is the notion of over-borrowing of the skill, labour and judgment which went into the copyright work. Going via the complication of the concept of a 'core of protectable expression' [as in *Computer Associates*] merely complicates the matter so far as our law is concerned. It is likely to lead to [the] over citation of United States authority based on a statute different from ours. In the end the matter must be left to the value judgment of the court. Having expressed this reservation however, I thoroughly agree with what Ferris J went on to say [in *Richardson*]: 'Consideration is not restricted to the text of the code ...'. That must be right: most literary copyright works involve both literal matter (the exact words of a novel or computer program) and varying levels of abstraction (plot, more or less detailed of a novel, general structure of a computer program).

Mr Poole's access to and use of the source code of ADP was also found to be in breach of confidence.

Following *Ibcos*, a further judgment involving non-literal copying of software was eagerly awaited, to see whether *Richardson* or *Ibcos* would be followed. The decisions of the High Court (Chancery Division) in *Cantor Fitzgerald* and *Navitaire* are therefore of considerable interest.

6.3.3 *Cantor Fitzgerald v Tradition*

Facts

The plaintiffs (CFI) and the first and second defendants (Tradition) carried on business as inter-dealer brokers (IDBs) in bonds in London. An IDB facilitates trading between persons wishing to buy or sell bonds. The case concerned an action for infringement of copyright in certain computer programs which form part of a bond-broking system, and for breach of confidence in relation to those programs. The software primarily in question causes the particulars of bids for and offers of bonds to be displayed on dealing screens and enables brokers to input details and so effect deals—this is a so-called 'front office' system. The action also concerned an allegation of infringement in respect of the related 'back office' (records and accounting) system. However, the majority of the case centres on the front office system.

The third defendant, Mr Howard, left CFI (effectively being dismissed) and thereafter set up an IDB business for the first and second defendants (Tradition). Mr Howard also recruited the fourth defendant, Mr Harland, from CFI, where he was head of systems, together with several programmers who had worked with Mr Howard in developing CFI's IDB system. These persons took up employment with Tradition on 27 January 1992. By 15 April 1992 they had written a front office IDB system for Tradition which worked on similar computers and used the same programming language as the CFI system.

CFI then started proceedings on the basis that it was impossible to have written the Tradition system in the time available without access to the source code of the CFI system. Tradition initially denied that their programmers had access to CFI's source code and said that they had written the system from scratch in the very limited time available. However, following discovery, Tradition learnt that the programmers did have access to the CFI source code and there had been some copying. In the light of this, Tradition then admitted that copying had taken place and sought an indemnity from Mr Howard. Tradition's principal expert, Dr McKenzie, also discovered that, based upon an analysis of lines of code in each system, the copied code definitely amounted to 2 per cent of the Tradition system. The percentage rose to 3.3 per cent if questionable code was included.

At trial Tradition admitted that the source code for the whole of CFI's front and back office systems had been loaded on to a computer at Tradition and hence copied. This counted as an infringement. Tradition also further admitted copying those parts of the code which their programmers had admitted copying. Tradition made no admissions in respect of any other code, including that identified as questionable by Dr McKenzie.

CFI asserted that much of the questionable code had been copied. They also identified a small amount of other code which had been copied, but which had been removed from the Tradition system before it 'went live'—that is, run for the first time as a working system, and relied on this as well. In the end CFI restricted its claim to copying of a substantial part of each of 35 modules (out of 48 modules chosen from the 363 modules making up the Tradition system). They also made two claims for breach of confidence (not considered here).

Judgment

It was clear law that copyright protects computer programs in the same way as literary works. In analysing whether there was copyright infringement, Pumfrey J cited *Ibcos* and Jacob J, who said that a claim in copyright was to be tested as follows:

(a)   What are the work or works in which the plaintiff claims copyright?
(b)   Is each such work 'original'?
(c)   Was there copying from that work?
(d)   If there was copying, has a substantial part of that work been reproduced?

Pumfrey J considered that as a general principle this was right. In this case, however, he felt that it was of considerable importance to deal with the inter-relationship of the originality of the work (the prerequisite for copyright) and the substantiality of the part of the work copied (the prerequisite for infringement). There was a real risk of making an error when adapting well-known principles developed in the context of literary works and applying them uncritically to literary works whose only purpose is to make a machine operate in a specific manner. Indeed, following the Australian case of *Autodesk v Dyason*,[35] it could be argued that *any* part of a program is substantial, since without it the program would either not work at all or not work as desired.

In fact, the judge considered this approach as a whole simplistic. The correct approach to substantiality relies on the fact that it is the function of copyright to protect the relevant skill and labour extended by the author in making the work.[36] It therefore follows that a copyist infringes if he appropriates a part of the work on which a substantial part of the author's skill and labour was expended. In the context of computer programs, substantiality is to be judged in the light of the skill and labour in design and coding which went into the piece of code alleged to be copied. It is not determined by whether the system would work without the code, or by the amount of use the system makes of the code.

Furthermore, in the context of a computer program there did not need to be literal copying of the code. Following literary copyright cases it was well established that a substantial part of the author's skill and labour may reside in the plot of a novel or play and copyright could be infringed by taking the plot without taking any part of its particular manner of expression. The closest analogy to a computer program lies in its algorithms, structure or 'architecture'.

Applying this and other relevant law, the judge found that in respect of the disputed allegations of copyright infringement, Tradition's programmer had definitely appropriated a substantial part of the skill and labour which went into the CFI modules and so infringed copyright.

6.3.4 *Navitaire Inc v Easyjet Airline Co. & Anor*[37]

Facts

Navitaire claimed that easyJet had infringed the copyright in Navitaire's computer-based 'ticketless' reservation system 'OpenRes'. OpenRes was used by easyJet until it introduced its own replacement system, 'eRes'. Easyjet specifically wanted eRes to be substantially indistinguishable from OpenRes in its user interface. (ie the appearance the running software presents to the user who may be an agent in a call centre or a private individual seeking to make a booking by use of the World Wide Web). Easyjet did not have access to the source code for OpenRes. It was also not in dispute that none of the underlying software in eRes in any way resembles that of OpenRes, save that it acts upon identical or very similar inputs and produces very similar results:

---

[35] [1992] RPC 575.
[36] *Catnic Components v Hill & Smith* [1982] RPC 182 at 223.
[37] [2004] EWHC 1725 (Ch) (30 July 2004). See also press release by the defendant's solicitors Herbert Smith, 4 August 2004.

the claimant Navitaire argued that the copyright in OpenRes was infringed by what was called 'non-textual copying'.

The non-textual copying had three aspects. The first was the adoption of the 'look and feel' of the running OpenRes software. The second, not always clearly distinguished from the first during the trial, was a detailed copying of many of the individual commands entered by the user to achieve particular results. The third was the copying of certain of the results, in the form of screen displays and of 'reports' displayed on the screen in response to prescribed instructions. In other words, as used by easyJet the systems are very similar in use. Internally, the judge noted it was correct to say that they are completely different, subject to a point on the names used to identify certain data in the databases in eRes. Given that near identity in appearance and function could not have been achieved without a close analysis of the OpenRes system in action, Navitaire argued that there was 'non-textual' reproduction of either the whole of the OpenRes software considered as a single copyright work or alternatively of the various copyrights subsisting in 'modules' going to make up the system. In essence Navitaire maintained that the screens, command codes and the 'business logic' of their OpenRes system had been infringed by easyJet's eRes system.[38]

The Judge (Mr Justice Pumfrey again) noted that:

> There is here an issue of general importance. To emulate the action of a piece of software by the writing of other software that has no internal similarity to the first but is deliberately designed to 'look' the same and achieve the same results is far from uncommon. If Navitaire are right in their most far-reaching submission, much of such work may amount to the infringement of copyright in the original computer program, even if the alleged infringer had no access to the source code for it and did not investigate or decompile the executable program.[39]

There was also an allegation that Easyjet had infringed Navitaire's copyright in respect of the OpenRes databases in two respects: (a) that in transferring or 'migrating' the data contained in their OpenRes databases, which contained a record of every passenger and every flight on an easyJet aeroplane, to the new system, easyJet made interim copies of the existing OpenRes databases that they were not entitled to make; and (b) that easyJet and BulletProof (the second defendant) used their knowledge of the OpenRes databases to design the eRes databases in such a way that the copyright or copyrights alleged to subsist in certain 'schemas' which define aspects of the structure of the OpenRes database had been reproduced in the structure of the eRes database.[40]

---

[38] See paras 1–3.
[39] Ibid para 5.
[40] Ibid para 7.

Judgment

The judge summarised the main copyright issues as follows:

> Navitaire contend that copyright subsists in the command set as a copyright work distinct from the source code. This claim has a number of aspects: (i) the collection of commands as a whole is entitled to copyright as a 'compilation'; (ii) each of the commands is a copyright work in its own right; (iii) alternatively, each of the 'complex' commands is a work in its own right. As to the displays, Navitaire contend that (i) in respect of the so-called VT100 screen displays, the 'template' (fixed data and layout of variable data) is a separate copyright work for each display and (ii) certain GUI (graphical user interface) screens on the separate Schedule Maintenance module are copyright works as they stand and have been copied. Then it is said (and this is a quite distinct allegation) that the similarity exhibited by eRes to OpenRes in the eye of the user is such that there has been 'non-textual copying' of the whole of the source code. This is said to be strictly analogous to taking the plot of a book: an author who takes the plot of another work and copies nothing else will still infringe copyright if a substantial part of the earlier author's work is represented by that plot, and the same goes for computer programs [see *John Richardson Computers v Flanders* [1993] FSR 497 (Ferris J)].[41]

The judge held as follows:

The Commands

These were not protected by copyright. The individual command words and letters used did not qualify for protection as literary works—they do not have the necessary qualities as literary works.[42] The 'complex' commands[43] were not protected as the judge viewed them as a sort of ad hoc programming language not protected by the Software Directive.[44] The compilation of commands was not protected as it was either a computer language (and therefore not protected at all by virtue of the Software Directive) or there was no 'compilation' at all in the copyright sense.[45]

The judge also made the following important observation:

> Copyright protection for computer software is a given, but I do not feel that the courts should be astute to extend that protection into a region where only the functional effects of a program are in issue. There is a respectable case for saying that copyright is not, in general, concerned with functional effects, and there is some advantage in a bright line rule protecting only the claimant's embodiment of the function in software and not some superset of that software. The case is not truly analogous with the plot of a novel, because the plot is part of the work itself.

---

[41] Ibid para 73.
[42] Para 79: *Exxon Corp v Exxon Insurance Consultants International Ltd* [1982] RPC 69 followed.
[43] These are command words that have a syntax.
[44] See Recital 14; see also paras 81–9.
[45] Paras 90–94.

The user interface is not part of the work itself. One could permute all the letters and other codes in the command names, and it would still work in the same way, and all that would be lost is a modest mnemonic advantage. To approach the problem in this way may at least be consistent with the distinction between idea and expression that finds its way into the Software Directive, but, of course, it draws the line between idea and expression in a particular place which some would say lies too far on the side of expression. I think, however, that such is the independence of the particular form of the actual codes used from the overall functioning of the software that it is legitimate to separate them in this way, and not to afford them separate protection *when the underlying software is not even arguably copied* [emphasis added].[46]

The Screens

The screens were part of the user interface. Certain screens (those which were graphical in nature and were classed as 'artistic works') were copyright works and protected by copyright.[47] Others (the so-called VT100 screens showing only printable characters) were not protected as they were ideas which underlie the interfaces of the software and not protected by virtue of the Software Directive.[48]

Business Logic and Non-textual Copying

The judge noted that the case advanced by Navitaire was based on the fact that the functions of OpenRes and eRes are identical to the user so far as the aspects of the system of interest to easyJet are concerned. The case had its origin in the suggestion that what was called the 'business logic' of OpenRes had been appropriated.[49] However, it was clear that:

easyJet and BulletProof had no access to the source code of OpenRes, and it is not in dispute that in languages used, actual code and architecture (subject to [a] claim in respect of the database) the systems are quite different. There is no suggestion that the eRes code represents a translation or adaptation of the OpenRes code. The term 'non-textual copying' might be replaced by the more accurate 'copying without access to the thing copied, directly or indirectly'.[50]

The judge did not find any infringement of Navitaire's copyright. The skill and labour Navitaire were seeking to protect were not 'relevant' skill and labour:[51]

Navitaire's computer program invites input in a manner excluded from copyright protection, outputs its results in a form excluded from copyright protection and creates a record of a reservation in the name of a particular passenger on a particular flight. What is left when the interface aspects of the case are disregarded is the business function of carrying out the transaction and creating the record, because none of the code

---

[46] Para 94.
[47] Paras 97–9.
[48] Art 1(2).
[49] Para 107.
[50] *Per* Pumfrey J at para 113.
[51] See Lord Hoffmann in *Designers Guild* [2000] 1 WLR 2416 at para 119.

was read or copied by the defendants. It is right that those responsible for devising OpenRes envisaged this as the end result for their program: but that is not relevant skill and labour. In my judgment, this claim for non-textual copying should fail.

I do not come to this conclusion with any regret. If it is the policy of the Software Directive to exclude both computer languages and the underlying ideas of the interfaces from protection, then it should not be possible to circumvent these exclusions by seeking to identify some overall function or functions that it is the sole purpose of the interface to invoke and relying on those instead. As a matter of policy also, it seems to me that to permit the 'business logic' of a program to attract protection through the literary copyright afforded to the program itself is an unjustifiable extension of copyright protection into a field where I am far from satisfied that it is appropriate.[52]

Other Allegations of Copyright Infringement

There were additional allegations of copyright infringement including: (a) unauthorised alterations to Navitaire's 'TakeFlight' source code (the only piece of Navitaire's source code which easyJet had access to: there was no agreement permitting this use and the judge found copyright infringement);[53] and (b) (as noted above) allegations of copyright infringement in respect of the OpenRes databases on the basis that Easyjet had migrated certain data to eRes and also copied the structure of the OpenRes database. Except in limited respects concerning the process of migrating the data to the eRes system and the supply of certain database extracts to the second defendant BulletProof, these claims failed.[54]

It is worth noting that the judge accepted that section 50D of the CDPA ('Acts permitted in relation to databases') enabled the use of 'screen shots' to assist in data migration;[55] those involved in data migration would do well to read the judgment in *Navitaire* for pointers as to what is likely to be permissible. In light of *Navitaire*, database users would also be advised to ensure that any software and/or database licences they have allow them to migrate their data to a new platform or database, to avoid any risk of infringement.

6.3.5 *Nova Productions v Mazooma Games; Nova Productions v Bell Fruit Games*[56]

Facts

Nova Productions (claimant) owned a computer game based on pool and called 'Pocket Money'. The claimant brought copyright infringement

---

[52] Paras 129–30.
[53] Paras 132–49.
[54] Para 286.
[55] Para 280.
[56] *Nova Productions Ltd v Mazooma Games Ltd & Ors* [2007] EWCA Civ 219 (14 March 2007) (Court of Appeal); *Nova Productions Ltd v Mazooma Games Ltd & Ors Rev 1* [2006] EWHC 24 (Ch) (20 January 2006) (High Court).

proceedings against both Mazooma Games (the developers of a coin-operated video game called 'Jackpot Pool') and Bell Fruit (the developers of a coin-operated video game called 'Trick Shot'). The claimant lost the case in the High Court and also lost the case on appeal. The main thrust of the claimant's argument was that the defendants' games infringed their copyright, in particular copyright in:

(a)   artistic works (the bitmap graphics and the frames generated and displayed to the user of Pocket Money)
(b)   literary works (Nova's designer's design notes and the software program he wrote to implement the Pocket Money game)

This case is interesting as this is another example where there was no copying of code—the defendants did not have access to or copied the code itself. What was alleged was that the defendants had copied a number of features of Pocket Money. In particular, both defendants had used the claimant's game as inspiration for aspects of their game and this was supported by the facts. Indeed, there were some similarities between the games but the visual appearance and rules of the games were all very different.

Judgement

Nova Productions lost their claim both in the High Court and on appeal. The claim that certain artistic works had been copied failed as either there was no copying at all (as the frames themselves were not copied) or even if there was, it was not substantial. As far as the claim based on literary copyright was concerned, this was also rejected both in the High Court and on appeal. The Court of Appeal dismissed the literary copyright claim on two grounds. First, on the basis of the idea–expression dichotomy discussed earlier in this book—what inspired some aspects of the defendants' game was just too general to amount to a substantial part of the claimant's game—as the trial judge noted, 'they are ideas which have little to do with the skill and effort expended by the program and do not constitute the form of the expression of the literary works relied upon.'[57] Second, the Court applied the principles applied by Mr Justice Pumfrey in *Navitaire*.

Indeed, the Court of Appeal thought the facts were stronger in *Navitaire* than in the present two cases, yet in *Navitaire* the claimants still lost. Importantly, the Court of Appeal made clear (as envisaged by the Software Directive) that ideas are not protected by software copyright law and what is protected by way of preparatory design work is that work *as a literary work—* the expression of the design which is to go into the ultimate program, not the ideas themselves contained in the program. The Court further stated that

---

[57] *Nova Productions Ltd v Mazooma Games Ltd & Ors* [2007] EWCA Civ 219 (14 March 2007) (Court of Appeal) para 44.

a written work consisting of a specification of the functions of an intended computer program will of course attract protection as a literary work but the functions themselves do not. Indeed, the Court of Appeal said that the judge in *Navitaire* was quite right to say that merely making a program which will emulate another but which in no was involves copying the program code or any of the program's graphics is legitimate.[58]

6.3.6 *SAS Institute Inc v World Programming Ltd*[59]

Facts

SAS Institute Inc (SAS Institute), was a developer of analytical software known as SAS (referred to in the case as 'the SAS System'). The SAS System is an integrated set of programs which enables users to carry out a wide range of data processing and analysis tasks, and in particular, statistical analysis. The core component of the SAS System is 'Base SAS', which enables users to write and run application programs (also known as 'scripts') to manipulate data. Such applications are written in a language known as the 'SAS Language.' The functionality of Base SAS may be extended by the use of additional components ('the SAS Components'). The SAS System had been developed over a period of 35 years.

Over the years SAS Institute's customers have written thousands of application programs in the SAS Language. Prior to the events giving rise to this case, SAS Institute's customers had no alternative to continuing to license use of the necessary components in the SAS System in order to be able to run their existing SAS Language application programs, as well as to create new ones. So a customer who wanted to change over to another supplier's software would be faced with rewriting its existing application programs in a different language.

World Programming Ltd (WPL) saw that there was market demand for alternative software able to execute application programs written in the SAS Language. So WPL created a product called World Programming System or WPS to do this. In developing WPS, WPL attempted to emulate much of the functionality of the SAS Components as closely as possible in the sense that, subject to only a few minor exceptions, the same inputs would produce the same outputs. This was to ensure that WPL's customers' application programs executed in the same manner when run on WPS as on the SAS Components. In doing so WPL had *no* access to the source code of the SAS Components, did not copy any of the text of the source code of the SAS Components or copy any of the structural design of the source code of the SAS Components. Nevertheless, SAS Institute contended that WPL had committed a series of

---

[58] Paras 50–52.
[59] [2013] EWHC 69 (Ch).

infringements of copyright and acted in breach of contract in creating WPS and its accompanying documentation, and SAS Institute instituted proceedings against WPL in the High Court in September 2009.

SAS Institute's principal claims were as follows:

(a)   A claim that WPL copied the manuals for the SAS System published by SAS Institute ('the SAS Manuals') when creating WPS and thereby infringed the copyright in the SAS Manuals.

(b)   A claim that, by copying the SAS Manuals when creating WPS, WPL indirectly copied the programs comprising the SAS Components and thereby infringed the copyright in the SAS Components.

(c)   A claim that WPL used a version of the SAS System known as the Learning Edition in contravention of the terms of its licences, and thereby both acted in breach of the relevant contracts and infringed the copyright in the Learning Edition.

(d)   A claim that WPL infringed the copyright in the SAS Manuals in creating its own documentation, namely a manual ('the WPS Manual') and some 'quick reference' guides ('the WPS Guides').

Judgement

The case was originally heard in June 2010 and Arnold J gave judgment on 23 July 2010.[60] As regards the claims made, Arnold J was able to conclude in respect of the fourth claim that WPL had infringed the copyrights in the SAS Manuals when creating the WPS Manual, but not when creating the WPS Guides. However, to decide the other claims the judge considered it was necessary to refer certain questions on the interpretation of the Software Directive and the Information Society Directive to the CJEU for a preliminary ruling. The CJEU gave judgment on 2 May 2012.[61] Arnold J then applied the CJEU judgment, giving judgment on 25 January 2013.[62] As regards the four claims he found:

(i)   This claim was dismissed, referring to the reasons Arnold J gave in his first judgment.[63] The SAS Manuals were ordinary literary works so not governed by the Software Directive. However they are detailed descriptions of the functionality of the SAS System. Here the judge followed Pumfrey J in *Navitaire* (in light of the CJEU judgment which supported this reasoning)[64] that it is not an infringement of copyright in a computer program to replicate its functions without copying its source code or

---

[60]   [2010] EWHC 1829 (Ch).
[61]   Case C-406/10, 2 May 2012.
[62]   [2013] EWHC 69 (Ch).
[63]   [2010] EWHC 1829 (Ch) at [251]–[261].
[64]   Case C-406/10 (2 May 2012) para 46.

design. So 'by parity of reasoning' it is not an infringement of copyright in a manual describing those functions to use the manual as a specification of the functions that are to be replicated and, to that extent, to reproduce the manual in the source code of the new program. It is a question of the kind of skill, judgement and labour involved. Copyright in a literary work, be it a computer program or a manual, does not protect skill, judgement, and labour in creating ideas, procedures, methods of operation or mathematical formulae. So it follows it is not an infringement to reproduce these things either from a computer program or a manual.[65]

(ii) This claim was dismissed. In his judgment the CJEU had endorsed Pumfrey J's interpretation of Article 1(2) of the Software Directive: copyright in a computer program does not protect either the programming language in which it is written or its interfaces (specifically, its data file formats) or its functionality from being copied.[66] Although it was not necessary to decide the point, Arnold J also opined on whether a programming language as such could ever be protected by copyright—this was because it could be debated whether it was a 'work' at all—a putative copyright work has to be a literary or artistic work within the meaning of Article 2(1) of the Berne Convention[67]—this definition is expansive and open-ended but not unlimited eg it does not include sound recordings or broadcasts.[68] Arnold J commented:

> Based on the evidence which was adduced at trial, and my general understanding of the position, my provisional view is that a programming language such as the SAS Language is not capable of being a work. A dictionary and a grammar are works which describe a language. Such works record, and thereby fix, the elements of the language they describe: the meanings of its words and its syntax. It does not follow that the language is a work. Rather, the language is the material from which works (including dictionaries and grammars) may be created. The evolutionary or organic aspect of language can be left on one side for the moment, since it is clear that it is possible to create a language from scratch. Even when a language is created from scratch, however, what it amounts to is a system of rules for the generation and recognition of meaningful statements. Programming languages such as the SAS Language are no different in this respect.[69]

In addition he also followed Pumfrey J in *Navitaire* in holding that the functionality of a program is not protected by copyright.[70] In particular

---

[65] [255].
[66] At [16].
[67] CJEU Case C-5/08, *Infopaq International A/S v Danske Dagblade Forening* [2009] ECR I-6569 at [32]–[37].
[68] *SAS Institute* [2013] EWHC 69 (Ch) at [27].
[69] At [33].
[70] [2010] at [249].

the CJEU had held that neither the functionality, nor the programming language, nor the data file formats of a computer program constitute a form of expression of that program and so they are not protected by the copyright in the program.[71] The test for infringement following the CJEU in *Infopaq*[72] being, 'there will only be reproduction of a substantial part of a literary work ... where what has been reproduced represents the expression of the intellectual creation of the author of that literary work.'[73] Because neither the functionality nor the programming language nor the data file formats of a computer program constitute a form of expression of that program they are not protected by the copyright in the program, and, accordingly, in applying the *Infopaq* test, those elements must be disregarded. There can only be a reproduction of a substantial part of the computer program if the defendant has reproduced something that represents the expression of the intellectual creation of the author of the program.[74]

(iii) This claim was dismissed: WPL's use of the Learning Edition was within Article 5(3) of the Software Directive (ie WPL were allowed to observe, study and test to program to determine the ideas and principles underlying it) and to the extent that such use was contrary to the licence terms they are null and void by virtue of Article 9(1)[75] of the Software Directive, with the result that none of WPL's acts complained of was a breach of contract or an infringement of copyright.

(iv) The same as in his earlier judgment.

Discussion

The *SAS Institute* case has clarified a number of areas in software copyright by virtue of the reference to the CJEU. In particular it affirms the approach of Pumfrey J in *Navitaire*.

It is also relevant in passing to note the recent US case *Oracle America Inc v Google Inc*.[76] Here the judge held that Oracle could not claim copyright protection for its Java APIs (ie interfaces) which Google had used in its Android

---

[71] The CJEU interpreting Article 1(2) of the Software Directive (which states that: 'protection in accordance with this Directive shall apply to the expression in any form of a computer program. Ideas and principles which underlie any element of a computer program, including those which underlie its interfaces, are not protected by copyright under this Directive)—Case C-406/10, para 46 and ruling 1.

[72] Case C-5/5/08 *Infopaq International* [2009] ECR I-6569.

[73] [2010] at [244].

[74] [2013] at [46].

[75] This edition uses the original Software Directive references which Arnold J uses; the 2009 codified version (Directive 2009/24/EC) which repealed the earlier Directive has different referencing. For the correlation between the two see: Annex II Correlation Table to the 2009 Directive.

[76] Case No. C 10-3561 (US District Court, Northern District of California) (judgment—May 2012).

operating system. The judge's reasoning reflects principles inherent in the Software Directive and the *SAS Institute* decision:

> So long as the specific code used to implement a method is different, anyone is free under the Copyright Act to write his or her own code to carry out exactly the same function or specification of any methods used in the Java API. It does not matter that the declaration or method header lines are identical. Under the rules of Java, they must be identical to declare a method specifying the same functionality—even when the implementation is different. When there is only one way to express an idea or function, then everyone is free to do so and no one can monopolize that expression. And, while the Android method and class names could have been different from the names of their counterparts in Java and still have worked, copyright protection never extends to names or short phrases as a matter of law.[77]

This case is currently on appeal.

6.3.7 Software copyright following *Cantor Fitzgerald, Navitaire, Nova Productions* and *SAS Institute*

Cantor Fitzgerald indicated that in the UK, software copyright can be infringed by non-literal copying. It followed the approach of Jacob J in *Ibcos Computers* and traditional United Kingdom copyright principles (rather than United States authorities). If a substantial part of the programmer's skill, labour and judgement has gone into them, the algorithms or sequences behind a computer program (as well as its architecture) are potentially protected by copyright, although the recent CJEU decision in *SAS Institute* must now be borne in mind, as must the test for copyright infringement in light of the CJEU decision in *Infopaq,* in answering the question.

   Cantor Fitzgerald also provides some helpful pointers as to the relation between copyright and breach of confidence when ex-employees misuse their former employer's source code. The possibility of this being in breach of confidence was recognised by Jacob J in *Ibcos Computers*, but the extent to which software and its preparatory materials are protected by the law of confidence is given fuller consideration in *Cantor Fitzgerald.*

   The later case of *Navitaire* does not rule out a finding of non-literal copying but where the infringer has *not* had access to the source code of the original program, the case suggests that a finding of copyright infringement will be difficult, if not impossible. In light of *Navitaire* the chances of a successful software copyright 'look and feel' case appear limited unless there is a clear misappropriation of a copyright work (eg GUIs) or underlying source code.

---

[77] http://jurist.org/paperchase/2012/06/federal-judge-rules-in-favor-of-google-in-java-case.php (accessed 23 June 2013).

The approach taken by the High Court in *Navitaire* has now been followed by the Court of Appeal in *Nova Productions* and by the High Court in *SAS Institute*.

So based on current case law, the English courts will not protect the functionality of a piece of software through the law of copyright unless program code has actually been copied or the program's graphics have been copied. This approach has been reinforced by the decision of the CJEU in *BSA*.[78] Nor will the look and feel of a computer game be protected, for similar reasons. The Court of Appeal in *Nova Productions* did not want to see copyright law being used to stifle the creation of works that are very different, as in the different games in *Nova Productions,* nor was it right that the courts should give protection to ideas at such a high level of abstraction as those in *Nova Productions*.[79] If this were to happen, copyright would become an instrument of oppression rather than the incentive for creation which it is intended to be.[80] This point was also made by the Advocate General and the CJEU in *SAS Institute*: 'to accept that the functionality of a computer program can be protected by copyright would amount to making it possible to monopolise ideas, to the detriment of technological progress and industrial development.'[81]

Having said this, it is not inconceivable that depending on the facts a future court might find that there has been copyright infringement where the architecture or structure or 'design' of a computer program has been copied. This is by analogy to literary copyright cases such as *Baigent v The Random House Group Ltd*[82] (which involved an allegation of copyright by *The Da Vinci Code*), which have left the door open for a successful infringement claim on the basis that whilst copyright law does not protect the themes and ideas in a novel, it can potentially protect how those facts, themes and ideas are put together (the architecture or structure of the novel).[83] Also, in *SAS Institute* Arnold J referred to the 'design' of a program as well as its code as potentially benefitting from protection.[84]

---

[78] Case C-393/09.

[79] See the discussion about the level of abstraction in sections 6.3.1 and 6.3.2 above.

[80] *Nova Productions Ltd v Mazooma Games Ltd & Ors* [2007] EWCA Civ 219 (14 March 2007) (Court of Appeal), paras 54–5.

[81] Case C-406/10 at para 40.

[82] [2006] FSR 44; [2008] EMLR.7 (CA).

[83] [2006] FSR 44, paras 176, 227.

[84] [2010] EWHC 1829 (Ch) at [251]–[261].

6.4   THE CHALLENGE OF THE OPEN SOURCE MOVEMENT TO SOFTWARE COPYRIGHT

Traditionally software licensors have sought to control the bug fixing/error correction (maintenance) and further development of their software by users by:

(a)   granting limited software licences restricting such acts;

(b)   not allowing users or third party maintainers or contractors access to source code which would facilitate such acts;

(c)   providing such services themselves (typically for a fee).

This policy is often justified by licensors on the basis that it preserves the integrity of their code. All lawful users will know that the code has been or will be maintained or developed to a certain standard in a consistent manner on the basis of properly documented upgrades and new releases. This ultimately benefits users as rogue developments and updates can be avoided. It also enables the licensor to more easily maintain the software.

In contrast the open source, 'copyleft' [as opposed to 'copyright'] and free software movements in varying degrees support a different licensing and development model. By making source code available on license terms to encourage collaboration between users, users can develop and maintain the software on a collaborative basis: developments are shared within the wider developer community. Users can fix their own problems. Also by sharing code between developers, technical progress is promoted.

The open source movement is often equated with a desire to abolish or at least relinquish copyright protection for software and the concomitant 'privatisation' of knowledge. Whilst some would take this position, typical open source licences such as the General Public Licence (discussed in chapter nine) in fact rely upon copyright as a means of ensuring users comply with the licence and hence the principles underlying open source software.

In any event, the benefits of 'open source' licensing need to be weighed against the possible disadvantages. Suppliers have been reluctant in the past to effectively give their source code, their 'crown jewels' away for free. The issues are also somewhat different depending on whether you are a supplier or a user. In each case, the relevant open source licence needs to be carefully scrutinised to ensure it meets your requirements. It must never be taken on trust that because the code is 'open' it can be freely used without any restrictions or obligations.

6.4.1   Some Issues

Supplier Perspective

(a)   By exploiting 'open source' software in conjunction with the supplier's own proprietary software, there is a risk that the proprietary software must also be made public as a condition of exploiting the 'free'/'open' source software. The licensing and exploitation rights in respect of the open source software *and* the consistency of these with the supplier's own software licensing strategy must be carefully analysed.

(b)   It is unlikely there will be any performance or intellectual property rights warranties in respect of the open source software. Therefore use and exploitation is at the supplier's risk.

User Perspective

(a)   Does the user have the ability to maintain the open source software if there is no adequate third party support?

(b)   Again, it is unlikely there will be any performance or intellectual property rights warranties in respect of the open source software. Therefore, use and exploitation is at the User's risk.

Section 9.5.4 of chapter nine looks at these issues in more detail.

SUMMARY

(a)   Software in both source code and object code form is protected by copyright as a literary work.

(b)   There is a debate as to how 'original' software has to be to benefit from protection given that the key European legislation (the Software Directive) speaks of software needing to be the author's own intellectual creation, a higher test than has traditionally been applied in the UK.

(c)   The Software Directive has restricted how licensors can use software copyright and software licences to prevent the creation of back-up copies, the testing/observation/study of how software works and access to interface information where required to create an interoperable program. UK cases are now exploring the scope of this right.[85]

(d)   Software copyright can potentially protect a program from both literal and non-literal copying (ie where the code is not copied), but this protection is likely to be very limited in the case of non-literal copying. In particular, the CJEU has recently clarified that under the Software Directive the functionality of a computer program, its programming language and the format of its data files are not protected by copyright.[86]

(e)   The open source movement seeks to use software copyright to promote new co-operative licensing models rather than abolishing the very notion of copyright. However, suppliers and users must take care when exploiting or using open source software to ensure that the model and licence terms used are appropriate for their business.

---

[85]   *SAS Institute v World Programming* [2013] EWHC 69 (Ch) 25 January 2013.
[86]   *SAS Institute* Case C-406/10.

7

Digital Copyright and E-Commerce

This chapter looks at the relationship between digital copyright and electronic commerce/e-business, as broadly defined. Here there is a rapidly developing international case law and an equally fast-moving legislative agenda. In the EU, for example, the adoption of the Information Society Directive in 2001 is the foundation for digital copyright protection for years to come.[1] This chapter needs to be read alongside chapter eight, which focuses on current copyright and database right issues relating to Web 2.0 and beyond, in particular user-generated content. As Web 2.0 develops further, more and more businesses will operate in this space, so the issues raised in chapter eight will become increasingly important.

The areas covered in this chapter are:

(a) re-use of analogue content in the digital environment
(b) licensing and linking—how best to exploit your digital copyright assets
(c) the protection of digital images
(d) how search engines can be lawfully used
(e) Napster, Grokster, MP3 and online copyright infringement
(f) the liability of service providers
(g) the protection of standards and web content
(h) steaming media and piracy
(i) protecting copyrights electronically—technical protection measures and fair use.

---

[1] The best general introduction to the area is Macqueen, 'Copyright and the Internet' (chs 5 and 6) and Waelde, 'Search Engines and Copyright' (ch 7) in Edwards and Waelde (eds), '*Law and the Internet*, (Oxford, Hart Publishing, 3rd edn, 2009). See also: Calleja, 'Copyright and E-commerce: Getting the Balance Right' *Electronic Business Law*, May 2001, 6, and Dickie, *Internet and Electronic Commerce Law in the European Union* (Oxford, Hart Publishing,1999) for background to EU developments.

7.1   CONTENT REUSE[2]

The ability to exploit existing media content (books, magazines, newspapers, films, sound recordings and so on) in digital form, whether in online, CD-ROM, DVD, MP3, e-book or other format, is crucial to the success of the digital economy. Multimedia publishers have been aware of the need to acquire electronic/digital rights for new content for a number of years. Other publishers have more recently recognised the potential value in digitising their extensive archives and are only now making them available to the public in various electronic formats. The streaming of films and other content via websites and apps has also become common, especially as Internet users continue to migrate to higher bandwidths and there is a wide take-up of mobile devices that can access the content.

Of course, such rights issues are not new. In the USA, for example, the courts have had to deal with issues such as: do 'motion picture rights' include the right to broadcast a film on television? Is home video distribution of films permitted where the contract in question is silent on this express point or simply refers to 'motion picture' rights?

Unless the publisher or distributor is in the happy position of owning the relevant copyright for the work in question, they will need to be sure they have a licence to use the work sufficient for their purposes. In this case there will be either:

(a)   **an existing licence agreement:** this will need to be read carefully to determine:
  (i)   the scope of the rights granted; and
  (ii)   was the licensor able to license the rights in the first place; or
(b)   **no written agreement:** the work may simply have been commissioned, for example. In this case the author will retain the copyright in the work unless:
  (i)   equity intervenes and transfers the copyright to the commissioner— this is only likely to happen where it is absolutely clear that the work was created for the commissioner alone and the author clearly intended to relinquish all rights, current and future, in the work;[3] or
  (ii)   the author is an employee of the commissioner and it was created during the course of that person's employment.

Otherwise, the court will imply a copyright licence where reasonable and equitable and only to the extent necessary to give business efficacy to the

---

[2] See generally, Radcliffe, 'New Media Convergence: Acquiring Rights to Existing Works for the Internet under U.S. Law' [2001] *EIPR* 172. For background on the publishing industry and publishing agreements see Jones, *Publishing Law* (London, Routledge, 1996).
[3] *Ray v Classic FM* [1998] FSR 622.

contract.[4] In certain cases the amount of money paid for the work can also be relevant in determining whether there is an equitable assignment or the scope of any implied licence.[5]

In either case the scope of any express or implied licence will be limited to what was in the joint contemplation of the parties at the date of the licence. Under English law it will not extend to enable the licensee to take advantage of new, unexpected uses of the work unless this is absolutely clear from the circumstances or the express terms of the contract, although ultimately it depends on the facts. For example, in a relatively recent case an implied licence from the 1970s to reproduce recordings as vinyl records and cassettes was held to also cover CDs and DVDs.[6]

7.1.1 Specific Issues for Audio-visual Content

Audio-visual works such as films and animation pose particular challenges. Such works tend to have complex rights histories. Also, there are several technologies available for watching content and the technology here may be relevant to what rights are required. The two main methods are:

(a) **Downloading** a digitally compressed file for viewing later: this is only really feasible where the user has broadband or high capacity and speed mobile Internet access. Here a copy of the work is made on the user's hard drive, memory card or other storage media for storage and replay purposes.

(b) **Video streaming.** Here the film or other work (eg webcast) is viewed in real time. No permanent copy is made on the user's hard drive. Streaming is discussed in more detail later in this chapter in section 7.8.

It is becoming more common to deal with 'Internet rights' in film contracts and related 'Video on Demand' rights may also be expressly carved out. However, Internet film distributors will nevertheless need to ensure they have all the rights they need on the basis of the above analysis including the use via tablets and mobile devices. For example, they might be able to take advantage of a licence of rights in 'future media' from the producer in question. Other commercial issues such as territory of distribution, term of agreement and period of Internet release, royalty/revenue sharing arrangements, etc will also need to be fully documented.

[4] *BP Refinery (Westernport) Pty Ltd v The President, Councillors and Ratepayers of the Shire of Hastings* (1978) 52 *ALJR* 20, 26 (PC).
[5] *Ray v Classic FM* [1998] FSR 622.
[6] *Ray v Classic FM* [1998] FSR 622, 643; *Meikle v Maufe* [1941] 3 All ER 144; *Barrett v Universal-Island Records Ltd* [2006] EWHC 1009 (Ch) para 360.

7.1.2   Some Examples from the Case Law

Freelance Journalists and Photographers[7]

Take the case of a freelance journalist commissioned in the early 1980s to write a newspaper column. No written contract was executed. The newspaper wants to reuse the journalist's work in an online news database accessible via the Internet. Under English law the analysis above suggests that the newspaper needs the express consent of the journalist to do this. For example, in a recent case involving a freelance newspaper photographer who retained copyright in his photographs it was held that an exploitation of the photographer's rights not contemplated at the time of the relevant licence (in this case the inclusion of his photographs in a back numbers website) was not within the scope of the licence.[8] In the USA it appears that any such reuse would infringe the journalist's copyright.[9] Various European countries have also had to decide on the position here including:

(a)   **The Netherlands:** In *De Volkskrant*[10] the reuse of newspaper articles on CD-ROM and on a website was held to go beyond any implied licence the newspaper had to reuse the articles in question.

(b)   **Germany:** Germany has an author-friendly copyright law. It is not possible for an author to grant rights to exploit their works in respect of uses unknown at the time the contract is made—any such attempt will be null and void under German law.[11] There have been a number of cases where photographers and others have successfully prevented Internet or CD-ROM reuse of their works.

(c)   **France:** The French courts have treated online publication as fundamentally different from print publication in a number of decisions favouring journalists over publishers, for example *Le Figaro*[12] and *Le Progres*[13] (which concerned reuse on the Internet and Minitel—a French online information service).

Electronic Books

A large number of publishers are now actively marketing 'e-books' ie books that can be viewed on PCs, PDAs, dedicated readers, and via apps on mobile

---

[7] For a review of the position internationally see: D'Agostino, 'Should Freelancers Be Allowed to Keep their Copyrights in the Digital Era?', WP 10/03, *OIPRC Electronic Journal of Intellectual Property Rights.*

[8] *Grisbrook v MGN Limited* [2009] EWHC 2520 (Ch).

[9] *New York Times Co Inc et al v Tasini et al* (Case no: 00-201, Supreme Court, 25 June 2001); section 201(c) (US) Copyright Act 1976.

[10] *Rechtbank Amsterdam* (District Court) 24 September 1997.

[11] Art 31(4), German Copyright Act.

[12] Tribunal de grande instance Paris, 14 April 1999.

[13] Tribunal de grande instance Lyon, 21 July 1999; Cour d'appel de Lyon, 9 December 1999.

devices. These books are supplied by the publisher in electronic form and require separate reader software (eg Microsoft Reader, Adobe Acrobat Reader or the use of hardware and related software that can read proprietary formats such as the Amazon Kindle's AZW format or Sony's BBeB format) in order to be read on screen, often these days using electronic paper (eg the Amazon Kindle, various devices from Kobo, the Barnes and Noble 'Nook' and Sony Reader all use this display technology) or on mobile devices via reading apps. What are the rights issues here?

Take a publisher who has been granted the exclusive right by the author to publish a book 'in book form', a not uncommon term in publishing agreements. The author then licenses another publisher to exploit the 'electronic rights' in his book. Can the first publisher prevent this? The English courts would probably take a similar view to the US court in *Random House v Rosetta Books*[14] where the term 'book' in publishing contracts was held not to automatically include electronic books. In this case, Rosetta Books began selling electronic versions of books (e-books) by Kurt Vonnegut, Robert Parker and William Styron with the authors' consent (via their agents). Random House claimed it had the right to prevent this on the basis it had the exclusive right from the author to 'print, publish and sell the work in book form'. Random House sought a preliminary injunction to prevent Rosetta Books' activities but this was denied. Random House appealed but the US Court of Appeals for the Second Circuit rejected their appeal and held that the District Court was entitled to deny the injunction.[15]

Moral Rights
Moral rights might also be a problem. Take the 1997 French case *Queneau*, in which the heir of the poet Raymond Queneau objected to the inclusion of Queneau's poems on a website on the grounds the structure of the poems was distorted by the website and so infringed the moral right of integrity.

7.1.3 Lessons to be Learnt

These examples illustrate the need always to seek clear grants of rights to the extent required. Many publishers will want to go down the route of acquiring broad rights but this may not always be possible. There has been a backlash from journalists and their unions over attempts to acquire all rights.

In any event, it should be noted that 'electronic rights' has no special meaning: every effort should be made to clarify what is meant by this term if it is used particularly if multimedia or other interactive use is considered. Also care should be taken to define what is meant by an 'e-book' as well as some

---

[14] US District Court, Southern District of New York, 01 Civ. 1728; Stein J, 11 July 2001.
[15] 8 March 2002.

e-books are simply text files that can be read using a reading device; others may be 'enhanced', containing graphics, animation and other audio-visual content.

Publishers will also want to seek waivers of moral rights where available.

7.2   LICENSING AND LINKING

Digital copyright owners ('licensors') will frequently exploit their rights by granting 'licences' of some or all of their rights to others. A licence is simply permission to do that which would otherwise be unlawful: it does not confer any proprietary rights on the licensee, the person who is granted the licence.[16] In other words, a copyright licence simply prevents the licensee from infringing the licensor's copyright.

Although many licences will be contractual in nature, there is no need for a licence to be in the form of a binding contract—a licence need not be contractual, although many are. An explicit or tacit consent to reproduce a work can amount in law to a licence, whether or not the person giving the consent meant to contract.[17]

Under English law the three key components to establish a binding contract are:

(a)   offer eg an offer to supply software on certain terms
(b)   acceptance of the offer by conduct or by assent (eg clicking an 'I agree' icon)
(c)   consideration (typically money but it could be non-monetary)

A benefit of contractual licences as opposed to 'bare' licences/permissions is that where a licensee breaches the licence he will be both in breach of copyright and contract. A contractual licence will impose obligations on the licensee and these are likely to go beyond terms simply setting out what use the licensee can make of the licensor's copyright. Also, a bare licence is potentially revocable at will (or depending on the circumstances, on reasonable notice) whereas a contractual licence can only be revoked in accordance with the contract terms.

A licence can be made orally or in writing. However, exclusive licences, where the licensee has the right to exploit the copyright to the exclusion of all other persons including the licensor, should always be in writing and signed by or on behalf of the owner of the right. This is to ensure the licensee has all the benefits of being an exclusive licensee, including the right to sue infringers and recover damages.[18]

---

[16]   *Thomas v Sorrell* (1673) Vaugh 330, Ex Ch.
[17]   *Barrett v Universal-Island Records Ltd* [2006] EWHC 1009 (Ch) (para 362).
[18]   ss 92 and 101 CDPA.

Licences can also be express or implied from the circumstances. This issue is considered in greater detail in sections 7.2.1 and 7.4.3 below.

As discussed in chapter one, copyright licences, whether express or implied are central to the lawful operation of the Internet. In this section, two areas are looked at in detail: how digital copyright works can be licensed, with particular reference to the Internet, and to what extent copyright can control 'linking', ie the use of hypertext links.

7.2.1   Licensing Digital Copyright Works

Digital copyright/database right is typically licensed in one of the following ways:

Express Written Contractual Licence

In return for a payment to the licensor or some other promise by the licensee (ie consideration), the licensee is granted the right to exploit the work in question subject to clear restrictions. The document will be in writing on paper and be executed by both parties. Because of this, there is generally no issue about its enforceability unless certain provisions are invalid eg, they contravene the Software Directive, etc. Many licensors and collecting societies (see chapter nine) will only deal on this basis.

Nevertheless, it is often bureaucratic and cumbersome, if not impossible, to require all licensees to enter into such written contracts. Other licensing models have therefore been developed:

Shrink Wrap Licences

These are commonly used for 'off the shelf' software and some information products/databases on CD-ROM. The licensee will typically buy the product from a shop. When he gets home he will find the box or packaging for the CD-ROM will contain a seal; by breaking the seal he will be deemed to have accepted the enclosed licence terms. There has been a debate in both the UK and the USA about the enforceability of these licences. The argument against is that the binding contract governing the sale and use of the software is made when the user makes the purchase in the shop. At that point he will probably be unaware of the precise terms and conditions in the box. So they will not bind him.

However in *Beta Computers (Europe) Ltd v Adobe Systems (Europe) Ltd*[19] (a Scottish case) Lord Penrose held that if the user opens the 'shrink wrap' packaging this would constitute acceptance of the contract terms. Although there are conflicting US authorities, *ProCD v Zeidenberg*[20] came down strongly in favour of the enforceability of these sorts of licences.

---

[19] [1996] FSR 367.
[20] 86 F 3d 1447 (7th Cir, 1996).

In any event, in an English case the judge, in considering whether a shrink-wrap licence applied, said that, 'it is common ground that such deemed agreement is effective in law as agreement.'[21] So this seems to settle the matter, at least until shrink wrap licences are ever revisited by the courts.

Click Wrap Licences

These licences present an on-screen message to the user. This explains that unless the user clicks on an icon signifying agreement to be bound by the terms of an on-screen licence (which can be viewed before the icon is clicked and which can also generally be printed out for further reference), the product will not be available for use.

Whether these licences are enforceable depends on the circumstances:

(a) **Packaged product:** here the product is sold off the shelf. The user only sees the on-screen message after he has purchased the product. In this case the situation is surely analogous to a shrink wrap licence.

(b) **Online product:** here the product is made available for downloading from a website and before the download can take place, the click wrap procedure must take place. In this case there appears little doubt the English courts would find a valid contract provided there was offer, acceptance and consideration. US courts have also found such contracts binding.

Browse Wrap (and Web Wrap) Licences

Here the user may be made aware of the existence of the licence before he downloads software or some other digital product eg via a hypertext link but there is no procedure where he gives his unambiguous assent to the licence terms eg by clicking on an icon as in a click wrap licence. Web wrap licences are similar by way of a notice attempting to make entry into and further use of the website conditional on posted terms and conditions.[22]

In a US case, *Specht and Others v Netscape Communications Corp and America Online Inc*,[23] which involved the free download of Netscape's SmartDownload software, the court was of the view that knowing consent or assent was required in order for there to be a binding contract. In this case it was not enough that there was a download icon associated with a statement beneath it (viewed by scrolling down the page) that stated 'Please review and agree to the terms of the Netscape SmartDownload software licence

---

[21] *Per* His Honour Judge Richard Havery QC in *Microsoft Corporation v Ling & Ors* [2006] EWHC 1619 (Ch) (3 July 2006) para 10.

[22] See the discussion in Riefa and Hornle, 'The Changing Face of Electronic Consumer Contracts in the Twenty-first Century: Fit for Purpose?' in Edwards and Waelde (eds), *Law and the Internet*.

[23] Case 00 Civ 4871 (AKH), US District Court, Southern District of New York, 3 July 2001; Hellerstein J; reported in *Electronic Business Law* (September 2001) 15.

agreement before downloading and using the software.' There was also a hypertext link to the licence agreement. The judge required a clear assent to the licence terms, as in a click wrap licence.

It is probable that the UK courts would take a similar approach.[24] However, all may not be lost as far as licensors are concerned—they still may have certain rights in the context of a bare licence; see below.

Bare or Implied Licences

Much Internet content is made available without any attempt to impose a contractual licence on the user. Most websites simply contain a copyright notice or use statement setting out what rights the user has to download and use the content. It is submitted that although such terms may not be a binding contract, they are nevertheless indicative of the terms of the permission granted by the copyright owner to use the rights in question. If use outside these terms would infringe copyright or database right, then there is no reason why the licensor should not be entitled to commence infringement proceedings against the user for this misuse.

Also, as noted above, it is possible the court may in any event imply a licence and this may be of limited scope.[25] In the USA, there has been consideration of this area in a number of cases, including *Blake A. Field v Google, Inc.*[26] This case involved Google's cache feature, which allows users to access snapshots of web pages automatically copied and stored by Google using 'Googlebots'. The court held that what Google was doing was 'fair use' under US copyright law; this area is discussed in greater detail in section 7.4 below. But the court also said that Google had an additional defence—by putting up content on his website Mr Field had granted Google an implied licence. This was because Mr Field was aware of how Google's caching worked and in particular that if he did not want his content cached it was very easy to prevent this by using a 'no-archive' meta tag on his site (this tag (ie machine-readable instructions on the website) would in effect tell search engines not to archive or cache the site). But he chose not to do this, and so it was reasonable for Google to assume that he consented to what they were doing. The judge noted that, 'consent to use the copyright work need not be manifested verbally and may be inferred based on silence where the copyright holder knows of the use and encourages it.'[27] This seems to be a sensible approach, although as discussed in chapter eight in the context of the Google News litigation, not all courts have taken this view and there is no express

---

[24] See the discussion in Riefa and Hornle, above, 110–11.
[25] *Trumpet Software Pty Ltd v OzMail Pty Ltd* (1996) 34 IPR 481, FC; [1996] 18 (12) *EIPR* 69 (Australia).
[26] US District Court, District of Nevada, Case 2:04-cv-00413-RCJ-GWF, Robert C Jones, J (12 January 2006).
[27] *Ibid* p 10.

UK authority on this point, although the UK courts have had no problem in finding an implied copyright licence where the facts justify this, even without it being a contractual licence.[28]

Of course, where valuable content is made available online, the licensor is well advised to consider the use of a click wrap licence and not just rely on browse/web wrap or a bare or implied licence. Nevertheless for practical reasons, this may not be possible in all cases.

A Statutory Regime for Digital Licences

The UK and the European Commission appear unwilling at present to produce a model code or law dealing with the supply and licensing of digital products akin to the US UCITA (Uniform Computer Information Transaction Act of July 1999). So digital licences will be governed by:

(a)   general copyright and contract law principles
(b)   where relevant, consumer protection legislation and legislation aimed at online sales (Unfair Contract Terms Act 1977, Distance Selling Regulations,[29] Unfair Terms in Consumer Contracts Regulations,[30] Electronic Commerce Regulations, other consumer law, etc)
(c)   e-commerce law such as the Electronic Signatures Directive[31] dealing among other things with the validity of such contracts

7.2.2   Linking

Web pages can easily be linked. The classic link is highlighted in blue on a web page: by clicking on the link the browser is taken to the URL of the linked website. This is achieved by including the relevant HTML code in the original site. For example, a link to the Vatican website would read as follows in HTML script:

<A HREF='http://www.vatican.va/'>The Vatican website</A>

It can be argued that anyone setting up a website impliedly licenses others to link to that site, as this is a fundamental technical and commercial feature of the Internet. But it is also suggested that the terms of any implied licence will be overridden by any express licence terms, linking policies, or website terms and conditions on the basis of section 7.2.1 above. Certainly all websites should at the very least include a linking policy and commercial sites will want to ensure a full linking agreement is entered into to protect their

---

[28] *Barrett v Universal-Island Records Ltd* [2006] EWHC 1009 (Ch) (para 362).
[29] Consumer Protection (Distance Selling) Regulations 2000, SI 2000/2334.
[30] Unfair Terms in Consumer Contracts Regulations SI 1999/2083 and Unfair Terms in Consumer Contracts (Amendment) Regulations SI 2001/1186.
[31] Directive 99/93/EC of 13 December 1999 on a community framework for electronic signatures.

IPR (see chapter nine for a precedent). Website operators should give careful thought as to the extent they need contractually binding website conditions, in light of the discussion in section 7.2.1 above. It would also be sensible to take technical measures to prevent deep linking.

Deep Linking

It is important to distinguish between a simple link, such as that to the Vatican above where the user is taken to the Vatican home page and leaves his home site, and a deep link. In a deep link the linked home page is bypassed and the user goes straight to the linked pages, bypassing any copyright notices, terms and conditions and (which may be significantly prejudicial) advertising on the home page.

An example occurred in the US case *Ticketmaster Corp et al v Tickets.com Inc.*[32] The defendant's website contained a deep link to the plaintiff's site, bypassing the plaintiff's homepage. In this case the judge did not consider that the defendant's actions amounted to copyright infringement because the defendant merely took factual information and this was not protected by copyright. Also the judge considered that no copying was involved in hyperlinking.

Framing

It is also possible for other websites to be 'framed' so that they appear on the home site surrounded by material from the home site—this may well cause confusion and lead users to assume the third party material to be part of the home site.

An example of framing is the US case *Washington Post v The Total News*[33] where *Total News* framed third-party news from the *Washington Post* and other papers' websites in conjunction with *Total News'* own advertising material. The plaintiffs claimed trade mark infringement, copyright infringement, deception, unfair competition and various others claims. Unfortunately the case settled without any decision although *Total News* was allowed to maintain links to the news websites without framing.

Linking and Digital Copyright: A UK Legal Analysis

Linking may amount to passing off or trade mark infringement, especially if framing is used, as was reportedly alleged in an action commenced by Haymarket against Burmah Castrol.[34] However, succeeding on the basis of copyright or database right infringement is less certain.

---

[32] US District Court, Central District of California, 27 March 2000; Hupp J; reported in *Electronic Business Law* (June 2000) 13.
[33] No 97 Civ 1190 (PKL) (SDNY 1997).
[34] *Electronic Business Law* (March 2001) 1.

Take the 1996 Scottish case *Shetland Times v Wills*.[35] Here the defendants who operated a news service called *Shetland Times* deep-linked to news items on the plaintiff's site by reproducing headlines from the plaintiff's site on their site. These headlines were hyper-linked to the original stories on the plaintiff's site. The plaintiffs succeeded in gaining an interim interdict (interlocutory injunction). This was on the basis that the plaintiffs had a prima facie case of copyright infringement against the defendants. This was under two heads:

(a) The headlines on the plaintiff's website were cable programmes under section 7 of the CDPA. The defendants were also operating a cable programme service and so the inclusion of the headlines on the defendant's site was an infringement of copyright under section 20 CDPA.

(b) The headlines were themselves original 'literary works' and the defendants were copying them (storing the works by electronic means), so infringing copyright under section 17 CDPA.

It must be stressed that *Shetland Times* was only an interim, interlocutory decision; the case settled before full trial, so it is not persuasive authority. In particular there was very little technical discussion put to the judge; it can certainly be argued that the interactive nature of the Internet should rule out cable programme protection. In any event, the 2003 Regulations have now done away with a separate protection for cable programmes; these now fall within the definition of 'broadcasts' in Section 6 of the CDPA. To succeed under the current law *Shetland Times* would have had to argue successfully that the linking amounted to infringement by 'communication to the public' (section 20 CDPA).

The judge also noted there was a question mark over whether headlines of eight or so words designed to impart information are original literary works. Indeed, the House of Lords held in *Exxon Corporation v Exxon Insurance*[36] that a literary work must be 'intended to afford either information and instruction or pleasure in the form of literary enjoyment.' Query whether news headlines satisfy this test although recent UK case law (*Meltwater*) indicates they can on the basis of the recent CJEU *Infopaq* case noted in section 2.6.2. These issues have come up again more recently in the Google News litigation discussed in chapter eight.

In any event, although there are arguments that hyperlinks can infringe copyright by amounting to a 'communication to the public', strong arguments have been raised against such a finding by the European Copyright Society (ECS) on the basis, among other things, that a hyperlink is simply

---

[35] [1997] FSR 604.
[36] [1982] Ch 119.

a location tool and hyperlinks do not transmit a work, a hyperlink is not a 'work' and nor is it a communication to a 'new public'. In other words, the original web page linked to has already made the work in question available to the public and by reference to CJEU case law, there must be communication to a 'new public' (ie wider than that originally contemplated by the original communication to the public[37]).[38] These arguments will be considered by the CJEU in the *Svensson* reference which deals with copyright liability in hyperlinking and which the ECS addresses in its opinion. In any event, as the ECS note in their opinion their argument that hyperlinking in general is not an activity covered by the communication to the public right in Article 3 of the Information Society Directive does not mean that in no circumstances will there be liability and they cite potential areas of liability under national law as follows:

— accessory liability (particularly where there is the knowing facilitation of the making of infringing copies) (see the discussion below in section 7.5 below)
— unfair competition (in UK law passing off)
— infringement of moral rights
— circumvention of technological measures[39]

Database Right and Linking

As noted in chapter three, there have been continental European cases where deep linking has been held to amount to database right infringement. In *StepStone v Ofir*[40] Ofir (an online job agency and direct competitor of StepStone) deep-linked to StepStone's job advertisements and allowed its users to access the advertisements via the links. Its users were the ones extracting the data. Nevertheless, this was held to infringe StepStone's right to control the distribution of its database by making parts of the database available on a repeated and systematic basis to the detriment of StepStone, albeit that what was taken was not in itself a substantial part of the database. However, in the French case *Cadremploi v Keljob*,[41] a different conclusion was reached on appeal. Keljob had extracted information from Cadremploi's site using a search engine for the benefit of its users. The information extracted was presented in a form which identified it as originating from another site

---

[37] See CJEU Joined Cases C-403/08 and C-429/08 *Football Association Premier League and Others* [2011] ECR.
[38] See European Copyright Society, Opinion on the reference to the CJEU in Case 466/12 *Svensson*.
[39] Ibid, para 7.
[40] Case no Az 28 0 692/00, Landgericht Koln, 28 February 2001; reported in *Electronic Business Law* (June 2001) 13.
[41] Cour d'appel de Paris, 14th Chambre, s B, 25 May 2001, reported in *Electronic Business Law* (August 2001).

and containing a link to Cadremploi's website. The court was of the view that the data extracted by Keljob was not a substantial part of Cadremploi's database nor was Keljob engaging in anything other than normal use of the database—its search engine was simply exploring sites open to the public.

In the German case *Roche Lexikon Medizin*[42] the publishers of an online medical encyclopaedia were able to prevent a medical information and news portal from linking to their encyclopaedia. What was prevented was not simple linking: here the defendants had framed the plaintiff's content. The court had no trouble finding a clear case of copyright and database right infringement and that there was no implied licence to link by framing. Also, the private use exception in German copyright law did not apply to databases whose elements are searchable by electronic means.

Other continental cases have also considered database right infringement in the context of framing and/or linking. In the German case *Der Poet*[43] a database of lyrical texts and poems maintained on a website by the claimant was held to be a protected database and the activities of the defendant in linking and framing the claimant's content along with the defendant's advertisements were held to infringe the *sui generis* database right: the court was of the view that whilst a mere link might be the subject of an implied licence, framing was not. In *Danish Newspaper Publishers' Association v Newsbooster*[44] the text collections of headlines and articles which made up certain news websites of the claimant's members were found to be protected databases. The defendant (a search service and electronic newsletter provider) was prohibited from reproducing and publishing the newspaper headlines and deep-linking. However, in the *Paperboy* decision[45] Germany's highest court held that deep-linking to online newspaper articles was permitted. This did not constitute copyright infringement, database right infringement or unfair competition.[46]

---

[42] Case no AZ 3U 247/00, Oberlandesgericht Hamburg, 22 February 2001, reported in *Electronic Business Law* (November 2001).

[43] Case no AZ 28 O 141,01 Landgericht Koln, 2 May 2001, reported in *Electronic Business Law* (February 2002) 13.

[44] Bailiffs Court, Copenhagen, Denmark, 5 July 2002, reported in *Electronic Business Law* (October 2002).

[45] Federal Court of Germany, Case No I ZR 259/00, 17 July 2003, reported in *Electronic Business Law*, November 2003.

[46] The database right argument appeared to fail as the court held that as the claimant had made the database available on its website, the addition of hypertext links was not something the owner could control. The copyright argument failed as among other things, creating a hypertext link could not itself amount to an infringing act of copying by the defendant and furthermore as the claimant had made the works available, it could not prevent subsequent linking—deep linking merely facilitates access. NB As Julia Hornle notes in her comment on the case, the court did point out it might have decided the case differently had the claimant used technical measures to prevent deep linking (see *Electronic Business Law* (November 2003) 13, and see also Thudt,

As discussed in section 3.3 of chapter three, under UK law it is possible that hyper-linking to another's website might amount to the reutilisation of data, assuming the website in question is a database for database right purposes. 'Reutilisation' is defined to mean making the contents of a database available to the public by any means.[47] However, query whether a 'substantial' part of the database is reutilised or, if it is insubstantial, whether the linking conflicts with the normal exploitation of the database or unreasonably prejudices the legitimate interests of the maker of the database.[48] Although not binding on UK courts, *StepStone v Ofir* and *Roche Lexikon Medizin* would appear to support this interpretation, *Cadremploi v Keljob* does not.

In any event, where the in-line linking in question itself involves the substantial *reproduction* of information held in another's database (eg the copying of newspaper article headlines and/or other information taken from another site into the links where this copying is substantial) then there is a greater risk that this will be held to be database right infringement.[49]

Meta Tags

Internet search engines work among other things by picking up tags included in the HTML source code at the top of a web page. For example, a website might contain meta tags as follows:

<meta name='keywords' content='st isidore, london, church, church of england'>

<meta name='description' content='The website of St Isidore of Seville, London. The site contains details of services and events.'>

This would indicate to a search engine that it was a church website with some additional information.

Unscrupulous website operators may use third party names, trade marks or slogans in their meta tags in an effort to divert business to their site. A classic example is the use of 'playboy', as in the US case *Playboy Enterprises Inc v AsiaFocus Inc*.[50] In this case by using 'playboy' as a meta tag, among other things, the defendants were found liable for trade mark dilution. In the UK it was reported that Road Tech Computer Systems successfully sued a rival Mandata after Road Tech's trade marks were used as meta tags on Mandata's site.[51]

'Recent Developments in E-commerce Law in Germany', *Electronic Business Law* (August 2004) 10.

[47] Regulation 12, Copyright and Rights in Databases Regulations 1997. See also discussion in section 3.3 above and CJEU case *Football Dataco* (Case C-173/11).

[48] See the ECJ in *William Hill*, ch 3, section 3.3.2.

[49] Beunen, *Protection for Databases* (Nijmegen, Wolf Legal Publishers 2007) 177.

[50] ED Va Civil Action No 97-734-A 4/28/98.

[51] *Road Tech Computer Systems v Mandata (Management and Data Services Ltd)*, 25 May 2000 (unreported).

Whilst the use of meta tags might amount to trade mark infringement or passing off, it is less likely to amount to copyright infringement. Copyright (as a literary work) will not protect mere words or slogans.[52] So it is hard to see how meta tags can infringe copyright. It should be noted that there has now been trade mark related litigation relating to keyword advertising and Google's AdWords service but this is outside the scope of this book.[53]

Linking and Service Provider Liability

The US Digital Millennium Copyright Act (DMCA) effectively limits the liability for those operating or providing hyperlinks, online directories and search engines, as well as other service providers (broadly defined), where users are referred to or linked to a site that contains infringing material using such so-called 'information location tools'.[54] This is on the basis the provider does not have the requisite level of knowledge that the material is infringing, does not receive a direct financial benefit (where it is able to control the infringing activity), and upon notice takes down or blocks access to the material.

As noted in chapter two, the Electronic Commerce Directive does not currently limit liability in respect of the use of information location tools. In any event, it can be debated whether providing a link to infringing material is currently copyright infringement even if you know the material is infringing. This area is discussed in more detail in section 7.5 below.

7.3   DIGITAL IMAGE PROTECTION

7.3.1   Copyright in Digital Images

The Internet is a highly visual medium. Still digital images in a compressed format (gif, jpeg, etc) are features of nearly all websites. As discussed in chapter two, these images may benefit from copyright protection in the following ways:

(a)   **A computer-generated work:** a digital image generated by a computer in circumstances where there is no human author of the work.[55] If the work is 'original' then it will benefit from protection. It ought to be

---

[52] See *Exxon Corporation v Exxon Insurance Consultants International Ltd* [1982] ch 119, noted in ch 2 and above.

[53] For a discussion of this area see Bednarz and Waelde, 'Search Engines, Keyword Advertising and Trade Marks: Fair Innovation or Free Riding?' in Edwards and Waelde (eds), *Law and the Internet*.

[54] s 512 (d).

[55] s 178 CDPA.

'original' if the creation by a human author of a similar work would satisfy the threshold for originality.

(b) **A digital photograph:** a photograph is defined under the CDPA as a recording of light or other radiation on any medium from which an image is produced or from which an image may by any means be produced.[56] An 'original' digital photograph will therefore benefit from copyright protection in its own right. Most photographs will be original. However there is some doubt about photographs that are simply attempts to slavishly copy existing artistic works. There are many websites using art gallery, museum or similar images. Museums and galleries also generate income from licensing picture rights. So this issue is of some significance.

In *Interlego v Tyco*[57] Lord Oliver commented that 'skill, labour and judgment merely in the process of copying cannot confer originality.' This was followed by a US judge in *Bridgeman v Corel*[58] which concerned the reproduction by Corel on CD-ROM of photographs of Old Master paintings. Bridgeman claimed copyright in these photographs. The judge held they were not sufficiently original to warrant copyright protection in the USA, applying English copyright law. However, when the matter was before the English courts recently in *Antiquesportfolio. com v Fitch*[59] the High Court had no problem in granting copyright to photographs of antiques albeit the items photographed were 3D objects rather than 2D paintings.

(c) **Digital scanning of artistic works:** artistic works in copyright are digitally scanned into image file format. Here the copyright subsists in the artistic work of which the digital image is a copy. There is no separate copyright in the digitally scanned image. This is because although such an image is technically a photograph, the image is not sufficiently *original* to qualify for copyright protection. Following *Interlego v Tyco* noted above it is a mere slavish, mechanical copy of an existing artistic work. For example, in *The Reject Shop v Manners*[60] a photocopy as such was not protected by copyright.

(d) **A computer-assisted or aided work:** a scanned artistic work or other digital image is electronically enhanced or manipulated by a human author. If sufficient independent skill or labour is involved, the work ought to benefit from copyright protection, regardless of the protection of the underlying work.

---

[56] s 4(2) CDPA.
[57] [1987] FSR 409.
[58] 25 F Supp 2d 421 (1998).
[59] [2001] FSR 345.
[60] [1995] FSR 870.

7.3.2   Infringing Image Rights

As discussed in chapters one and two, the mere act of viewing a digital image from a website potentially infringes copyright (subject to the outcome of the CJEU reference in the *Meltwater* case, where the Supreme Court took the view that those browsing such an image potentially benefit from the temporary copying exception under Article 5(1) of the Information Society Directive—see section 1.5.1). Likewise, uploading a digital image to a website (where the Article 5(1) exception will not apply). Anyone creating a website must ensure they either own or have the rights to copy and publish the image on the Internet. Alternatively it is possible the use may amount to fair dealing or otherwise benefit from an exception under Part I, Chapter III of the CDPA (see section 2.4 of chapter two).

In *Antiquesportfolio.com v Fitch*[61] the failure by a web design agency to properly clear digital image rights to photographs of antiques taken from *Millers Antiques Encyclopaedia* used on a client's (Antiquesportfolio) website was considered to be copyright infringement.

The use of digital image search engines might also infringe copyright; this is considered below.

7.3.3   Protecting Digital Images

There are various techniques for preventing and/or minimising the risk of copying, making copying easier to detect, and assisting in proving infringement. These include:

(a)   **Technical measures:**
    (i)   only uploading low resolution image files to websites (this reduces their economic value if copied)
    (ii)   embedding a 'digital watermark' in the image—this is code which is impossible or very difficult to detect and/or remove and which will identify the source of the copied image. This will aid in proving copyright infringement.
    (iii)   only making the image publicly available in encrypted form
    (iv)   use of technology which restricts access to high-resolution images (eg Zoomify software)
    (v)   using digital technology such as web crawlers and image search engines to scour the web for infringing images
(b)   **Contractual/legal steps:**
    (i)   ensure you can prove copyright title to the original image eg by carefully making records of its creation, or perhaps even registering

---

[61] [2001] FSR 345.

the work in jurisdictions such as the USA where this is possible, or alternatively making use of various commercial or voluntary copyright registration schemes operating in jurisdictions where there is no state-legislated copyright registration system (see eg, www.acid.uk.com)

(ii) ensure a copyright notice is placed alongside the image or even tagged to it

(iii) ensure any person accessing or using the images is bound by appropriate copyright licence terms

7.4   LAWFUL USE OF SEARCH ENGINES

7.4.1   Background

The Internet can be viewed as a huge library of interconnecting databases. But although the library is constructed using a common language (HTML), there is no electronic card index or some other type of library catalogue. Users must therefore rely on a host of search engine providers to track down what they are looking for.

Search engines consist of large databases put together and searched in a number of ways. Search engines can obtain their data by soliciting information from website operators, their ISPs or their domain name registrars. Alternatively automated search devices (web crawlers, spiders, robots (including 'Googlebots')[62] and the like) can be used to automatically trawl the web for appropriate data. This data will need to be stored and indexed.

As databases, search engines potentially benefit from database right and possibly copyright protection. Those operating search engines need to protect their data from automated extraction by web crawler or similar technologies. This can be done through both technical and legal steps, such as monitoring hits and having clear, binding conditions of use and access, as well as informational steps, eg by using meta tags to instruct web crawlers and the like not to copy the site, as discussed above.

However, of greater debate and importance is whether those operating search engines could themselves be accused of copyright or database right infringement. This is not far-fetched. Extracting data from a website for such purposes could potentially infringe any database rights in the website (see chapter three). It could also infringe copyright if what is taken amounts to the whole or a substantial part of a copyright work; this is very likely to be the case where images are copied into thumbnail form for indexing and

---

[62] www.googleguide.com/google_works.html.

subsequent searching. Of course, what is being done might amount to fair use or fair dealing, or a licence to copy for these purposes might be implied. But this is far from certain in all cases.

7.4.2   The US Experience

There are a number of US cases which shed light on this issue. In particular, there have been cases where websites containing valuable databases have been trawled by competitors. One of the best-known examples is *eBay Inc v Bidder's Edge, Inc.*[63] eBay operates an extremely successful online auction site. Bidder's Edge operated an auction aggregation site. Instead of buyers accessing hundreds of online auction sites themselves, Bidder's Edge essentially automated the process by using a software robot to extract information from relevant websites. The resulting database was then made available for searching.

Bidder's Edge sought a licence from eBay for its activities but the parties could not agree on the scope of the licence: eBay was only prepared to allow 'real time' as opposed to automated searches. Negotiations broke down and eBay sued Bidder's Edge for, among other things, trespass, copyright infringement, unfair competition, and computer fraud and abuse. [Note: US law does not have the equivalent of database right.] eBay successfully obtained an injunction on the basis there had been 'trespass to chattels'—a concept not so far recognised by English law in the context of the Internet.

Another similar case also involved the use of a web spider by Verio to extract domain name registrant information for marketing purposes from Register.com Inc, a domain name registrar. This was also in breach of Register.com Inc's terms of use. Here Verio was also held to have committed trespass.[64]

Both these cases were decided on grounds other than copyright infringement. However in December 1999, in *Leslie A. Kelly v Arriba Soft Corp,*[65] a US District Court held that the use by an Internet, 'search engine' of others' copyright images was prima facie copyright infringement but was justified under the US 'fair use' doctrine. The case is the subject of two Appeals Court Decisions.[66]

---

[63] United States District Court, ND California, 24 May 2000; reported in *Electronic Business Law* (February 2001) 14.

[64] US District Court for the Southern District of New York, reported in *Electronic Business Law* (February 2001) 4.

[65] United States District Court, Central District of Southern California, Southern Division, Case No SA CV 99–560, Gary L Taylor J, 15 December 1999.

[66] 6 February 2002; 7 July 2003. See below.

7.4.3 *Kelly v Arriba Soft (USA)*[67]

Facts

Arriba (now known as ditto.com (Ditto)) operates a 'visual search engine' on the Internet. Unlike other Internet search engines it retrieves images instead of text, and produces a list of reduced 'thumbnail' pictures related to the search query. These can be clicked on to view the images and the originating website.

The search engine operates by maintaining an indexed database of approximately two million thumbnail images. These thumbnails are obtained by the operation of Ditto's 'crawler', a computer program that travels the web in search of images to be converted into thumbnails and added to the index. Ditto's employees then screen and rank the images and eliminate any which are inappropriate.

The plaintiff was a photographer specialising in photographs of the California gold rush country and also in photographs related to the works of Laura Ingalls Wilder (of *Little House on the Prairie* fame). He publishes his photographs in books and on the Internet.

In January 1999, around 35 of the plaintiff's images were indexed by the Ditto crawler and put in the defendant's image database. As a result of this, these images were made available in thumbnail form to users of the defendant's visual search engine.

The plaintiff objected and Ditto removed the images from its database, although due to some technical difficulties, some reappeared on occasion. In the meantime, the plaintiff sued the defendant for copyright infringement and also violation of the US Digital Millennium Copyright Act (DMCA) by removing or altering the copyright management information associated with the plaintiff's images.

The hearing was one for summary judgment.

Decision (at First Instance)

The judge had no difficulty in finding a prima facie case of copyright infringement: the defendant did not dispute the validity of the plaintiff's copyright or his ownership. Nor did it dispute it had reproduced and displayed the plaintiff's images in thumbnail form without authorisation.

So the issue was whether the infringement was justified on the basis of 'fair use' under US copyright law. In determining whether the use made of a

---

[67] See Stokes, *Art and Copyright* (Oxford, Hart Publishing, 2001), and Stokes, 'Leslie A Kelly v Arriba Soft Corp: A View from the United Kingdom' [2000] *EIPR* 599, for further background.

work in any particular case is a fair use the factors to be considered by a US court include:

Purpose and Character of the Use

The court found the 'transformative' nature of the use of the plaintiff's images very significant. The judge considered the defendant's use of the images was very different from the use for which the images were originally created. The plaintiff's works are artistic works used for illustrative purposes. The defendant's visual search engine and related thumbnail images are for a functional not an artistic, aesthetic purpose: to catalogue and improve access to images on the Internet. The court found that the purpose and character of the defendant's use was on the whole significantly 'transformative' and therefore this factor weighed in favour of fair use.

Nature of the Copyright Work

The court found this factor weighed against fair use.

Amount and Substantiality of the Portion Used

The court found this factor weighed slightly against fair use.

Effect of the Use on the Potential Market or Value of the Copyrighted Work

No significant adverse effect was demonstrated so the court therefore found this factor weighed in favour of fair use.

Conclusion: fair use

The court therefore found two of the four factors weighed in favour of fair use, and two weighed against it.

Having weighed all of the fair use factors together, the court found that the defendant's conduct constituted fair use of the plaintiff's images. Decisive here was the first factor. The defendant never held the plaintiff's work out as its own, or even engaged in conduct specifically directed at the plaintiff's work. According to the judge:

> [the] plaintiff's images were swept up along with two million others available on the Internet, as part of [the] defendant's efforts to provide its users with a better way to find images on the Internet. [The] defendant's purposes were and are inherently transformative, even if its realization of those purposes was at times imperfect [eg the ability to display full images of the plaintiff's photographs without the other aspects of the originating website]. Where, as here, a new use and new technology are evolving, the broad transformative purpose of the use weighs more heavily than the inevitable flaws in its early stages of development.

Digital Millennium Copyright Act (DMCA)

The plaintiff raised an interesting argument that the defendant had violated section 1202(b) of this Act by displaying thumbnails of the plaintiff's images without displaying the corresponding copyright management information consisting of a standard copyright notice in the surrounding text. This section states that:

No person shall, without the authority of the copyright owner or the law:

(1) intentionally remove or alter any copyright management information;

...

(3) distribute ... copies of works ... knowing that copyright management information has been removed or altered without authority of the copyright owner or the law, knowing, or, with respect to civil remedies under section 1203, having reasonable grounds to know, that it will induce, enable, facilitate, or conceal an infringement of any right under [federal copyright law].

This argument was given short shrift by the judge and appears not to be the subject of the appeal. In particular, although the thumbnail images created by the defendant did not contain any of the plaintiff's website copyright notices, it was clear from the defendant's site that the images were subject to the originator's copyright and also the defendant clearly indicated on their site the address (with hyper-link) to the originating website where this information would be available.

Two Appeals Court Decisions

Kelly v Arriba Soft has been the subject of two Appeals Court decisions.[68] The first decision (filed on 6 February 2002) affirmed in part and reversed in part the order of the US District Court. Unlike the District Court, the Appeals Court focused in some detail on the linking and use made of the thumbnail images obtained by using Arriba's search engine. The creation of the thumbnail images and their use for search purposes was found to be fair use. However, where by clicking on the thumbnails they gave access to larger, full-size framed images (so that they were viewed, divorced from their original website—'in-line linking'), then it was held that the plaintiff photographer's public display rights were infringed and this was not justified by the fair use doctrine.

The second decision (re-filed on 7 July 2003) withdrew the Appeals Court's earlier ruling that in-line linking (see Glossary) violated a copyright owner's public display right, but retained the ruling that the creation of thumbnail images by search engines is fair use. The decision left open for a further hearing whether the display by Arriba of Kelly's full-sized images was fair use. This is important, as the display of the full-size images involved the use of linking (including in-line linking initially). However, this fascinating case now seems to have ended with a default judgement in Kelly's favour.[69] But the

---

[68] US Court of Appeals for the Ninth District, No 00-55521.
[69] US District Court, Central District of California, 18 March 2004.

issues raised in this case have continued to be considered by the US courts, in particular in the action by publisher Perfect 10 against Google.

Perfect 10 v Google

Perfect 10 is a US adult entertainment publisher. Images of its models have appeared on unauthorised websites. Google operates a well-known web search service which includes image searching and Google had indexed these images and made thumbnail images available through the normal operation of its search service. Perfect 10 complained to Google in May 2001 that Google's creation of thumbnail images and in-line linking to full-size images infringed Perfect 10's copyright and legal action against Google was commenced in November 2004.

In February 2006, the District Court ruled in favour of Google on several grounds (in particular that Google's use of frames and in-line links did not amount to the display (in a US copyright sense) by Google of the full-size images stored on and served by infringing third party websites—in other words, Google was not liable for direct copyright infringement by merely linking to these sites). But the court ruled against Google for its creation of thumbnails.[70] In particular, the District Court determined that Google's use of thumbnails as part of its image search function was likely to infringe Perfect 10's copyrights as Google's Image Search service copied Perfect 10's images as thumbnail images in its cache and displayed them to users. The District Court's holding distinguished *Kelly* (see above) (which held that creating and using thumbnails for search purposes was fair use) based on the fact that Perfect 10 also sells reduced-size images for download to mobile phones, and Google's thumbnails might affect the market for those reduced-size images. Also, Google's use of the thumbnails was held to be more commercial than Arriba's as, in the opinion of the judge, Google's AdSense program appeared to be available to the websites infringing Perfect 10's copyright and Google derived a benefit from this program.

Both sides appealed and on 16 May 2007, the Ninth Circuit Court of Appeals reversed the District Court's finding on fair use and held that Google benefited from a fair use defence in so far as Google were copying Pefect 10's images to create thumbnail images. The Appeals Court applied the fair use principles discussed in *Kelly* (see above) and came to the conclusion that Google were putting Pefect 10's thumbnail images ('along with millions of other thumbnail images') to a use fundamentally different from that intended by Perfect 10 which provided a significant benefit to the public and was a significant transformative use—this convinced the court that Google's use was fair use.

The Appeals Court also considered whether Google could be secondarily liable for its in-line linking to infringing full-size images under the doctrines

---

[70] *Perfect 10 v Google, Inc* (US District Court, Central District of California, CV 04-9484 AHM (SHx), February 2006 (A Howard Matz J)).

of contributory and vicarious infringement. The District Court considered that Perfect 10 was unlikely to succeed in proving Google could be held liable on these grounds. The Appeals Court took the view that further fact-finding by the District Court was necessary here in particular as to whether Google knew of infringing activities yet failed to take reasonable and feasible steps to refrain from providing access to infringing images (in other words, was there secondary liability). After this Google moved for summary judgment, asserting that it was protected from secondary liability by the relevant provisions of the DMCA. The Court's decision on this was appealed by Perfect 10. However, the case appears not to have progressed beyond this.[71]

A View from the UK

It is interesting to speculate what the outcome of the *Kelly* case might have been if the case had involved infringement in the UK of photographs by a living British photographer. The analysis that follows focuses on copyright and moral rights protection for the photographer; database rights aspects (of primary relevance to the person constructing a search engine database or a website hosting the images) are not therefore considered.

Would there be prima facie infringement of copyright?

On the facts clearly yes: copying of all or any substantial part of a copyright work is 'primary' infringement of copyright in the work[72] and copying includes for these purposes both 'storing the work in any medium by electronic means'[73] and also making copies 'which are transient or are incidental to some other use of the work'.[74] In the *Antiquesportfolio* case discussed above, the judge was clearly of the view that even small-scale reproduction by digital means of entire photographs on a website was copyright infringement. Also, the new 'communication to the public right' might be infringed by the linking carried out by Arriba Soft and (more probably) by the display of the images on Arriba's website.

Would there be a defence analogous to that of 'fair use'?

It would appear not. The fair dealing defences in English law are much more narrowly drawn than the US 'fair use' doctrine and only include fair dealing in the context of research and private study,[75] and for criticism, review and news reporting.[76] These do not appear particularly relevant here. The only such defence potentially relevant seems that of fair dealing for purposes of research or private study—it is submitted that what is being carried out here

---

[71] See status of case at www.eff.org/cases/perfect-10-v-google (accessed 11 June 2013).
[72] s 16 CDPA.
[73] s 17(2) CDPA.
[74] s 17(6) CDPA.
[75] s 29 CDPA—see section 2.4 of ch 2 above.
[76] s 30 CDPA.

is not 'research or private study' within their ordinary meanings; of course the defendant might argue that the whole purpose behind its activities is to permit research (ie web searching). Also, under the 2003 Regulations the research must be for a non-commercial purpose, but search engines are surely commercial in nature?

But even if accepted, this argument appears to probably fall foul of s 29(3) (b) CDPA ('copying by a person other than the researcher ... is not fair dealing if ... The person doing the copying knows or has reason to believe that it will result in copies of substantially the same material being provided to more than one person at substantially the same time and for substantially the same purpose.') Also the pre CDPA cases of *Stillitoe v McGraw-Hill Book Co*[77] and *University of London Press Ltd v University Tutorial Press Ltd*[78] held that facilitating private study or research *for others* did not fall within the similar exemptions in the earlier copyright Acts.

Nor is it very probable that an English court would be swayed by any argument that the public interest in this case would demand that the copying be permitted.[79]

Moral Rights Aspects

Under UK law, as discussed in chapter four, 'authors' such as photographers benefit from moral rights protection in addition to copyright. An English court in these circumstances would therefore also have to entertain any claim by the photographer that his 'moral rights' had been infringed, by, for example, if (having asserted this right) he was not identified in connection with the commercial publication of his works (which would include web publishing).[80] Of more interest in this case is whether the production of the thumbnail image could be said to infringe the photographer's moral right not to have his work subjected to derogatory treatment.[81] Treatment includes any alteration or adaptation of the work, and such treatment is derogatory 'if it amounts to distortion or mutilation of the work or is otherwise prejudicial to the honour or reputation of the author.'[82] It might therefore be argued that a thumbnail image is a clear distortion of the work, although this may be difficult to sustain in the light of the limited case law in this area noted in chapter four.

However, the defendant might in any event seek to raise the defence that moral rights do not apply as the database and search results produced by

[77] [1983] FSR 545.
[78] [1916] 2 Ch 601.
[79] *Hyde Park Residence v David Yelland* [2000] *ENTLR* N-77; [1999] RPC 655; [2000] 3 WLR 215.
[80] s 77 CDPA—see section 4.2.1 of ch 4.
[81] s 80 CDPA.
[82] s 80(2)(b) CDPA.

the search engine are 'a collective work of reference.'[83] This would, however, appear to stretch such a definition beyond its context in the CDPA of '... encyclopaedia, dictionary, yearbook or other collective work of reference.'

Implied Licence

As discussed in chapter one and section 7.2 above, it can be argued that both express and implied copyright licences are central to the effective functioning of the Internet. Could it therefore be argued under UK law that by making their images available on the Internet, photographers and other creators of images have granted implied licenses to enable the copying and cataloguing of their works where necessary to search the Internet?

There is a debate about the circumstances in which such a copyright licence will be implied. The classic approach, based on contract cases dealing with the implications of terms into contracts, is to be cautious about the existence and scope of any such licence. In any event as there is unlikely to be a contract between the photographer and search engine, and the photographer will probably have included an on-screen licence on his website restricting copying without his consent, it is perhaps difficult to see why such a licence would be implied from the circumstances.

Nevertheless, the operation of search engines might either fall within a public interest defence to copyright infringement or the more general legal doctrine of 'non-derogation from grant'.[84] This doctrine says that in certain circumstances a licensor of intellectual property cannot take away what he has purported to licence. The classic case is whether there is a right to repair a car or software, even if this means copying in order to develop spare parts or code—the so-called spare parts defence.[85] As noted in chapter two above, any general public interest defence must be doubted, given the Court of Appeal's rejection of a broad public interest defence in *Hyde Park Residence Ltd v Yelland*,[86] although the impact of human rights law on copyright is a developing area, as noted in section 2.4 of chapter two. The scope of the 'non-derogation from grant' principle is very narrow and is really based on public policy.[87] There is also authority that the spare parts defence does not in any event apply to software or databases protected by database right.[88] So without any further judicial clarification of the matter, the existence and scope of any implied licence in such circumstances remains unclear.

It should, however, be noted that there are cases from other jurisdictions that suggest an image copyright owner who displays his works on the Internet

---

[83] s 79(5) and s 81(4) of the CDPA.
[84] *British Leyland v Armstrong* [1986] AC 577.
[85] *Mars UK Ltd v Teknowledge Ltd* [2000] FSR 138.
[86] [1999] RPC 655.
[87] *Canon Kabushiki Kaisha v Green Cartridge Co (Hong Kong) Ltd* [1997] AC 728 (PC).
[88] *Mars UK Ltd v Teknowledge Ltd* [2000] FSR 138.

must take technical steps to prevent automated searching or they will be deemed to have consented to the operations of search engine operators;[89] other cases, however, have taken a different position.[90]

European Developments

The Electronic Commerce Directive contains no exceptions to copyright infringement that appear relevant in this case: the 'mere conduit', 'caching' and 'hosting' exceptions from liability do not appear to be relevant. Nor does the Information Society Directive provide any clear guidance on this area. So it is suggested an English court might well decide *Arriba* rather differently.[91]

Indeed in a German case (September 2003), the Hamburg regional court held that thumbnail images published by the German version of Google's news site infringed the photographer's copyright. No 'fair use' or other defences were available.[92] In October 2008, the same court took a similar decision where Google had indexed thumbnails of the images of an artist and a photographer.[93]

7.4.4 Practical Issues

It seems that the use of search engines can in certain circumstances amount to copyright infringement. Certainly the use of web crawlers or similar technologies to scour specific websites in order to extract information to be reproduced/re-presented for commercial gain could well infringe copyright or database right in the UK. In any event, those who want to attempt to protect their websites from such practices should ensure they have clear, binding website terms prohibiting this and take technical steps (eg using 'No archive' meta tags) to prevent this.

Those constructing search engines also need to ensure they do not infringe copyright. Simply collecting meta tag information from sites may be justified (eg by way of an implied license), as the very reason for including it is to alert searchers to the content of the site in question. However, more extensive copying from a site could well infringe. Readers are referred to the discussion in section 7.2 of this chapter regarding linking and framing for

---

[89] See decision of the German Federal Supreme Court, File Number I ZR 69/08 (29 April 2010) regarding Google.

[90] See discussion at 7.2 above. See also: *Blake A Field v Google Inc*, 412 F.Supp.2d 1106 (D Nev 2006).

[91] For a fuller discussion of the possible application of the Electronic Commerce Directive see: Stokes, *Art and Copyright* (Oxford, Hart Publishing, 2nd edn, 2012) 154–5.

[92] Regional Court, Hamburg, 5 September 2003; see the news item in *Electronic Business Law* (May 2004) 1. See also the Google News cases discussed in ch 8.

[93] Cases 308 O 42/06 and 308 O 248/07, Hamburg Regional Court (see report in *Bloomberg. com*, 13 October 2008).

a further consideration of these issues. In particular, search engines should avoid framing any indexed websites they make available for browsing.

7.5 NAPSTER, GROKSTER, MP3 AND BEYOND: A UK VIEW

It is clear law on both sides of the Atlantic that a person who directly copies a digitised work or communicates it to the public without the permission of the copyright owner will infringe copyright (primary infringement) or where a person knowingly distributes infringing copies there will also be infringement (secondary infringement). What is more difficult is whether a person not directly involved in the infringing activity can be held liable for the conduct of another. In particular, can manufacturing and/or distributing a device or operating an Internet based service that can facilitate copyright infringement by others *itself* amount to copyright infringement by the person providing the service or supplying the device in question?

This area has already been a fertile source of litigation in the context of home cassette taping and video recorders. In the USA there have been a number of Internet-related cases involving devices or services which facilitate copyright infringement and the key cases initially related to MP3 music files, of which *Napster* is probably the highest profile.[94] By way of background, MP3 (or MPEG 3) is a standard for storing music in digital, compressed form established in 1987 by the Motion Pictures Experts Group (MPEG). Digital music on CD can be converted to MP3 through a process called 'ripping'. Once in MP3 format, music can be efficiently transmitted and distributed as file attachments via the Internet. It can easily be converted back into audible form or burnt back on to CD, although there will be some loss of quality. MP3 files were the first to be 'ripped' and distributed online but in due course video files have also been treated in a similar way.

Commentators have inevitably sought to apply the US MP3 and similar cases to a European context. But as noted below, US and European/UK law are not necessarily the same in this area. So whilst the US cases provide food for thought it may be doubted whether the UK courts would in all cases come to the same result. In any event, since the last edition of this book the UK courts have now considered cases similar to *Napster*.

---

[94] *A&M Records Inc et al v Napster Inc* Case No 00-16401 (26 July 2000—District Court for Northern District of California; 12 February 2001—US Court of Appeals, Ninth Circuit). Later cases include *MGM v Grokster Ltd et al* (2 April 2003—District Court for Central District of California, Case Nos 01-08541-SVW, CV 01-09923-SVW; see case comment by Julia Hornle in *Electronic Business Law* (July 2003) 15, and subsequent cases discussed in this chapter).

Others have considered to what extent MP3 technology and cases such as *Napster* pose challenges to the distribution models and the economics of the music industry. This section simply focuses on the legal position of services such as *Napster* going forward. The intention is to shed light on the legal position in the UK of those operating peer-to-peer services such as *Napster* and others who may be held to facilitate digital copyright infringement. In this section UK law is stated as of 17 April 2013. US law is stated as it stood in 2005 when the US Supreme Court gave its decision in *Grokster*.

7.5.1   The UK Position: Legal Overview

Service providers and others who are not themselves *copying* material or communicating it to the public can still be liable for copyright infringement in the following circumstances:

(a)   *Authorising infringement*: under UK law a person can be liable for copyright infringement by *authorising* another person to do any act restricted by copyright.[95] The authorisation in question must come from someone having or purporting to have authority and the person authorising the infringement must have some degree of actual or apparent control over the person authorised: an act is not 'authorised' by a person who merely enables or possibly assists or even encourages another to do the act but does not purport to have any authority which he can grant to justify the doing of the act.[96] For example, in *CBS Songs Ltd v Amstrad plc*[97] the sale of hi-fi systems which were able to copy cassette tapes at high speed was not 'authorisation' even though the almost inevitable consequence was that purchasers would use the machine to make infringing music audio tapes. A more recent definition of 'authorise' is:

> that 'authorise' means the grant or purported grant of the right to do the act complained of. It does not extend to mere enablement, assistance or even encouragement. The grant or purported grant to do the relevant act may be express or implied from all the relevant circumstances. In a case which involves an allegation of authorisation by supply, these circumstances may include the nature of the relationship between the alleged authoriser and the primary infringer, whether the equipment or other material supplied constitutes the means used to infringe, whether it is inevitable it will be used to infringe, the degree of control which the supplier retains and whether he has taken any steps

---

[95] s 16(2) CDPA.
[96] *CBS Inc v Ames Records and Tapes Ltd* [1982] Ch 91; *Amstrad Consumer Electronics plc v British Phonographic Industry Ltd* [1986] FSR 159 (CA); *CBS Songs Ltd v Amstrad plc* [1988] 1013 (HL).
[97] [1988] 1013 (HL).

to prevent infringement. These are matters to be taken into account and may or may not be determinative depending upon all the other circumstances.[98]

(b) ***Secondary infringement***: a person can also be liable for (secondary) copyright infringement of a work by among other things:
   (i) Possessing, importing or dealing in copies of a work knowing or having reason to believe they are infringing.[99]
   (ii) Making, importing, possessing in the course of business or selling or hiring an article 'specifically designed or adapted for making copies of that work knowing or having reason to believe that it is to be used to make infringing copies.'[100]
   (iii) Transmitting the work by means of a telecommunications system (otherwise than by communication to the public) knowing or having reason to believe that infringing copies of the work will be made by means of the reception of the transmission in the UK or elsewhere.[101]

(c) ***Circumventing technological measures and removing or altering ERMI***: the CDPA also prevents persons from circumventing (knowing or having reasonable grounds to know they are doing this) or making or dealing in devices or services designed to circumvent copy-protection or other 'effective technological measures' designed to protect copyright works and which achieve the intended protection.[102] There are also criminal offences for dealing in unauthorised decoders etc. In addition, there is protection against a person knowingly and without authority removing or altering electronic rights management information (ERMI) or dealing in copies where the ERMI has been altered or removed.[103] This area has been expanded by the Information Society Directive and is considered in greater detail in section 7.9 below.

(d) ***Vicarious liability***: it is also possible for a person to be vicariously liable for copyright infringement by virtue of the acts of his servants or agents done with his authority.[104]

(e) ***Joint tortfeasor***: there is also the possibility of liability for copyright infringement on the basis of being a joint tortfeasor (infringement of copyright is a 'tort' and a tortfeasor is someone who carries out the tort)—a common law concept. There must be a concerted/common design to infringe on behalf of the parties involved. The principle being that to

---

[98] *Per* Kitchin J in *20C Fox v Newzbin* 2010, EWHC 608 (Ch) 90.
[99] ss 22 and 23 CDPA.
[100] s 24(1) CDPA.
[101] s 24(2) CDPA.
[102] Part VII, ss 296–299 CDPA.
[103] s 296ZG CDPA.
[104] *Performing Right Society Ltd v Mitchell and Booker, etc., Ltd* [1924] 1 KB 762; *Canadian Performing Right Society v Canadian National Exhibition Association* [1934] 4 DLR 154.

be liable the joint tortfeasor must have been so involved in the commission of the tort as to make himself liable for the tort. 'Unless he has made the infringing act his own, he has not himself committed the tort.'[105] So for example, in a recent Court of Appeal case involving database rights (but equally applicable to copyright) *Football Dataco Ltd v Stan James plc*[106] the bookmaker Stan James on its website provided a pop-up box providing live football scores ('Live Scores') unlawfully extracted and reused by the German company Sportradar from the 'Football Live' database created by Football Dataco which data Sportradar sold to Stan James. The court found that users (punters) of the website pop-up box infringed database right as they extracted a substantial part of Football Live when they used the pop-up facility on the Stan James website—this was primary infringement. Stan James (and Sportradar) were also held to be joint tortfeasors with the UK punters using the website. Jacob LJ commented:

> The provider of such a website is causing each and every UK user who accesses his site to infringe. His very purpose in providing the website is to cause or procure acts which will amount in law to infringement by any UK user of it. *The case is not one of a mere facilitator, such as eBay or Amstrad where the choice to infringe ultimately lay with the consumer. Here Stan James is in reality* responsible *for the punter's infringement* [emphasis added].[107]

This decision is being much discussed, not least the implications of Jacob LJ's comment that 'the owner of any website anywhere in the world will be a joint tortfeasor with a UK user of that website if the inevitable consequence of access to that site by the user is infringement by that user.'[108] In contrast with previous case law involving eBay[109] or Amstrad,[110] where the service/product can be used to facilitate infringement (or not) and it is the user's choice whether to use the service/product to infringe, here Stan James by providing the website would inevitably cause or procure acts which amount in law to infringement by any UK user of it.[111]

7.5.2   US Law[112]

Liability here can arise either vicariously or, a more limited subset, by contributory infringement. These are broad concepts which can affix copyright

---

[105] *Per* Peter Gibson LJ in *Sabaf v Meneghetti* [2002] EWCA Civ 976.
[106] [2013] EWCA Civ 27.
[107] At para 97.
[108] At para 96.
[109] A case relating to trade mark infringement: *L'Oréal v eBay* [2009] EWHC 1094.
[110] *CBS Songs Ltd v Amstrad Consumer Electronics plc* [1988] 1 AC 1013.
[111] *Per* Jacob LJ at paras 96–8.
[112] See Halpern et al, *Fundamentals of United States Intellectual Property Law* (The Hague, Kluwer Law International, 1999).

liability in a wide range of circumstances; for example, simply posting addresses on a website directing users to other websites containing infringing materials can amount to contributory infringement if the person posting the addresses knows or has reason to know they point to sites containing infringing materials.[113] It is not necessary for hyper-links to be provided.

Vicarious Liability

In US copyright law vicarious liability is a broad concept: 'when the right and ability to supervise coalesce with an obvious and direct financial interest in the exploitation of copyrighted materials—*even in the absence of actual knowledge that the copyright monopoly is being impaired* [emphasis added] ...—the purpose of copyright law may be best effectuated by the imposition of liability upon the beneficiary of that exploitation.'[114]

Contributory Infringement

The doctrine of 'contributory infringement' is that 'one who, with knowledge of the infringing activity, induces, causes, or materially contributes to the infringing conduct of another, may be held liable as a 'contributory' infringer'.[115] Unlike vicarious liability, there must be actual or constructive knowledge for there to be contributory infringement: 'Benefit and control are the signposts of vicarious liability, [whereas] knowledge and participation [are] the touchstones of contributory infringement'.[116]

The US Supreme Court in *Sony Corp of America v Universal City Studios Inc*,[117] a case involving inter alia the use of VCRs for 'time shifting' purposes, gave guidance on this area. There would not be contributory infringement solely on the basis that the defendant sold equipment with constructive knowledge that customers might use the equipment to make unauthorised copies of copyright material; there needs to be a closer relationship between the infringer and the alleged contributory infringer and some ability to control the infringement. Furthermore, dealing in an article with a substantial non-infringing use would not be contributory infringement.

The Digital Millennium Copyright Act 1998 (DMCA) also contains anti-piracy provisions outlawing both direct and contributory conduct in relation to circumventing copyright protection systems or impairing copyright management information. These are discussed in more detail in section 7.9 below.

Because of the economic interests at stake in the distribution and copying of digitised music in MP3 format via the Internet, it is not surprising that

---

[113] *Intellectual Reserve Inc v Utah Lighthouse Ministry Inc* 75 F Supp 2d 1290 1999 US Dist LEXIS 19103; 53 USPQD2D (BNA) 1425; Copy L Rep (CCH) no 28,013.
[114] *Shapiro, Bernstein & Co v HL Green Co*, 316 F.2d 304, 307 (2d Cir 1963).
[115] *Gershwin Publishing v Columbia Artists Management* 443 F 2d 1159, 1162 (2d Cir 1971).
[116] *Demetriades v Kaufmann* 690 F Supp 289, 293 (SDNY 1988).
[117] 464 US 417, 104 S Ct 774 (1984).

there have been a number of US cases of which *Napster* is one of the latest and the best known. The cases tend to have common themes:

(a)   For vicarious or contributory infringement under US law there must be an act of direct copyright infringement. So the defendants have tended to plead a 'fair use' defence (following the similar principles discussed in *Kelly v Arriba Soft* in section 7.4.3 above). For example, in *RIAA v MP3.com*,[118] MP3.com's service 'MyMP3.com' allowed users to access online copies of music they had previously purchased by allowing users to replay remotely copies of their recordings held on the defendant's servers. MP3.com created these copies by itself copying thousands of CDs without the permission of the record companies concerned. MP3. com argued that their activities were permitted by the fair use defence (for example, by analogy to the use of VCRs to 'time shift' recordings) but this argument was rejected by the court, not least as MP3.com and not its users was the person actually making the infringing copies. Other defences have also been pleaded, eg that the Audio Home Recording Act 1992 applies; this permits the non-commercial use by consumers of digital audio recording devices for making digital musical recordings.

(b)   Defendants have also argued that there is no vicarious or contributory infringement on the basis:

(i)   they do not exercise *control* over their users,

(ii)   the device/service in question has substantial non-infringing uses (a classic example is a device used to 'burn' CDs), or

(iii)   they have no knowledge about what users are doing.

(c)   Also the provisions of the Digital Millennium Copyright Act (DMCA) which provide a defence to ISPs for innocent copyright infringement have been pleaded. As noted in chapter two, the DMCA provisions here are similar in scope to those dealing with service provider liability in the Electronic Commerce Directive.

7.5.3   Napster, Grokster and Beyond

Background to Napster

Napster made its proprietary MusicShare software freely available for Internet users to download. Users who obtained Napster's software could then share MP3 music files with other users of the Napster service. The Napster service enabled users to exchange MP3 files stored on their PC hard drives directly with other users without payment. In essence, Napster managed a file index-ing and directory service but did not itself copy/store MP3 files. Napster also

---

[118]   2000 US Dist. LEXIS 5761 (SDNY 2000).

provided software which allowed users to search for, request, download and play the MP3 files.

On 26 July 2000, the District Court granted a preliminary injunction to prevent Napster from among other things facilitating copyright infringement by others. On 12 February 2001, the Appeal Court upheld the original injunction but ordered the District Court to modify its scope.

Legal Issues

The plaintiff record companies in *Napster* claimed that users of Napster's service were engaged in the wholesale reproduction and distribution of copyrighted works (direct infringement). Users who upload file names to the search index for others to copy violated the plaintiff's distribution rights and users who download files containing copyrighted music violated the plaintiff's reproduction rights.

Napster raised various defences including that its users were engaged in fair use of the MP3 material. In particular, users might use the service to 'sample' recordings before deciding to purchase them. Alternatively, what their users were doing could be space shifting ie, as in MyMP3.com, a user downloads MP3 music files in order to listen to music he already owns on audio CD. The courts were not impressed by these arguments.

The courts seemed to have little difficulty finding Napster liable for vicarious or contributory copyright infringement in a peer-to-peer setting. As far as contributory infringement was concerned, the Appeal Court made clear Napster would be liable to the extent it had knowledge of specific infringing material available on its system and failed to purge such material from the system. As far as vicarious liability was concerned, it was clear Napster had the right and ability to supervise the infringing activity of its users and also had a direct financial interest in such activities. So Napster was obliged by the Appeal Court to police its system within the limits of what was technically practicable. Failure to so police would open up Napster to vicarious liability.

It should be noted that a different conclusion was initially reached in the more recent *Grokster* case.[119] In this case the defendants were distributing software enabling the use of *decentralised* file-sharing.[120] This was held by the

---

[119] *Metro-Goldwyn-Mayer v Grokster* US Court of Appeals for the Ninth Circuit, 19 August 2004 (Case No 03-55894); 259 F Supp 2d 1029 (CD Cal.2003) (District Court). The Appeals Court agreed with the District Court's analysis that what Grokster and the other defendants were doing (software distribution—distributing file-sharing software to users) did not give rise to contributory or vicarious copyright infringement. See also Vanessa Smith Holburn, 'Landmark File-sharing Ruling' *Electronic Business Law* (September 2004) 5.

[120] The technology used by all three defendants (Grokster, StreamCast (formerly MusicCity Networks) and Kazaa BV (formerly known as Consumer Empowerment) was 'Fast Track' originally developed by the founders of one of the defendants Kazaa BV). (Note: Kazaa BV did not defend this US action and had a default judgment made against them; Kazaa have also

District Court and Appeals Court not to amount to contributory or vicarious copyright infringement—unlike in *Napster* the defendants had no control over the file sharing and no ability to do so. What the defendants were doing was not significantly different from the sale of home video recorders or copy machines such as in the *Sony* case noted above.[121]

In *Grokster* the Appeals Court opined about the limits of copyright law and the need for legislative change (ie a new US copyright law from Congress) as opposed to judicial decision if cherished principles were to be revised by the courts on public policy grounds in order to better protect the plaintiffs:

> ...We live in a quicksilver technological environment with courts ill-suited to fix the flow of internet innovation ...The introduction of new technology is always disruptive to old markets, and particularly to those copyright owners whose works are sold through well-established distribution mechanisms. Yet, history has shown that time and market forces often provide equilibrium in balancing interests, whether the new technology be a player piano, a copier, a tape recorder, a video recorder, a personal computer, a karaoke machine, or an MP3 player. Thus, it is prudent for courts to exercise caution before restructuring liability theories for the purpose of addressing specific market abuses, despite their apparent present magnitude.[122]

However, on appeal to the US Supreme Court, the position taken by the Appeals Court was reversed.[123] Grokster were found liable. Following common law principles and criticising the Appeals Court's over reliance on *Sony*, the Supreme Court held that a person who distributes a device capable of both lawful and unlawful use with the object of promoting its use to infringe copyright, as shown by clear expression or other affirmative steps taken to foster infringement, going beyond mere distribution with knowledge of third-party action, is liable for the resulting acts of infringement by third parties using the device, regardless of the device's lawful uses.[124] This was found by the court to be the position as regards Grokster. Unlike the Appeals Court, the Supreme Court considered that existing liability theories did provide a remedy for MGM and it was appropriate to find Grokster liable:

> The tension between the competing values of supporting creativity through copyright protection and promoting technological innovation by limiting infringement liability is the subject of this case. Despite offsetting considerations, the argument for imposing indirect liability here is powerful, given the number of infringing downloads that occur daily using respondents' software. When a widely shared

been the subject of similar litigation in the Netherlands—see Alfred P Meijboom, 'The Dutch *Kazaa* Case: Does File Sharing Infringe upon Copyright or Unfortunate Litigation?' (2004) 25 *BLR* 183.)

[121] See fn 117.
[122] At 11746–11747.
[123] *MGM v Grokster*, 545 US (2005).
[124] Pages 10–24.

product is used to commit infringement, it may be impossible to enforce rights in the protected work effectively against all direct infringers, so that the only practical alternative is to go against the device's distributor for secondary liability on a theory of contributory or vicarious infringement.[125]

The application by the Supreme Court of common law principles to find Grokster liable has been a controversial decision.[126] Indeed, the Supreme Court in the view of some US commentators, appears to have created a new form of 'secondary liability' for copyright infringement—'inducement'—in addition to contributory infringement and vicarious liability.[127] Given that the Supreme Court justices produced two sets of concurring opinions with different reasons, this case is likely to continue to be scrutinised carefully.

7.5.4   The UK Experience

In the previous edition of this book the question was asked '[h]ow would a UK court treat the operation of an Internet-based service such as Napster that can facilitate copyright infringement by others?'. At that time (2008) such a case had yet to be decided by the English courts, and it was noted that:

> some believe that UK judges may find reasons not to follow the 1980s 'home taping' precedents such as *CBS Songs Ltd v Amstrad plc* noted above. For example, a plaintiff might argue that the defendant has the ability to prevent downloading, transmission and distribution of copyright material or has reason to believe it is hosting or transmitting infringing material. But this would appear more difficult to argue in the case of a decentralised P2P system such as KaZaa or Grokster noted above.[128] In any event if the earlier cases were followed then a defendant in such a case ought to be in an even better position to avoid liability by drawing users' attention to copyright laws in website terms and conditions and making it clear that reproduction of copyright works may require permission.[129]

Since 2008 there have now been a number of cases which indicate the UK courts are taking a robust view against those infringing copyright online. Of particular importance are *Twentieth Century Fox Film Corp v Newzbin Ltd*[130] (*'Newzbin'*) and *Dramatico Entertainment Ltd v British Sky Broadcasting*[131] (*'Pirate Bay'*).

---

[125] Pages 10–13.

[126] See eg Fred von Lohmann, 'Remedying Grokster', law.com, 25 July 2005.

[127] See above and also Lawrence Lessig, 'Make Way for Copyright Chaos', *New York Times*, 18 March 2007.

[128] See comment by Gavin Sutter in *Electronic Business Law* (June 2002) 14. He sees *CBS* as being applicable to the facts in *KaZaa*.

[129] Stokes, *Digital Copyright Law and Practice*, 3rd edn (Oxford, Hart Publishing, 2009) 153–4.

[130] [2010] EWHC 608 (Ch) (29 March 2010).

[131] [2012] EWHC 268 (Ch) (20 February 2012).

Newzbin

Newzbin Ltd ran a website called 'Newzbin' which provided a search and indexing facility for the users of 'Usenet'—a worldwide Internet discussion (messaging) system. Usenet allows content to be posted but large files (eg films) need to be split into multiple parts and in effect a large number of related messages posted. Anyone wanting to download a film from Usenet would have to identify the messages in question and in effect reassemble the film. The arguments the claimants (film studios) raised was that the Newzbin service operated to provide a facility for users to search easily for unlawful copies of films on Usenet and have ready access to them, including by categorising them and displaying their titles and allowing users to search for and obtain access to unlawful copies of their choice. The Newzbin service was only available to members and premium members were able to download content from files searched and found via Newzbin. Newzbin said their service was simply a search engine like Google directed to Usenet.

It was clear that in using Newzbin premium members were able to download unlawful copies of films and in doing so infringe copyright themselves. But how could Newzbin itself be liable? Obvious avenues to explore based on the above discussion was whether Newzbin was authorising copyright infringement by its members, was it a joint tortfeasor with its members, or was it unlawfully communicating the film studios' films to its members? If any of these were the case, then Newzbin would infringe copyright. In the alternative the claimants also said that the defendant is a service provider with actual knowledge of other persons using its service to infringe copyright and consequently the claimants sought an injunction under s.97A of the CDPA. The s.97A claim failed but the claimants were successful in all their arguments that Newzbin infringed copyright with the judge leaving the door open for an award of additional damages under s.97 CDPA for the flagrancy of the infringement.

Looking at each area of potential copyright infringement in turn:

(a) **Authorising infringement:** looking at all the facts (including the ready possibility of Newzbin being able to filter out infringing content, the nature of the service offered by Newzbin (which was clearly aimed at making copies of infringing films available and was under Newzbin's control) and the close relationship between Newzbin and its members), the judge took the view that a reasonable member would deduce from the defendant's activities that the defendant purported to possess the authority to grant any required permission to copy any film that the member may choose from the 'Movies' category on Newzbin and that the defendant has sanctioned, approved and countenanced the copying of the claimants' films.

(b) **Joint tortfeasor:** the judge had no difficulty in finding that the defendant had procured and engaged in a common design with its premium members to infringe the claimants' copyright.

(c) **Infringement by communication to the public:** in light of the CJEU case *Rafael Hotels*,[132] communication to the public was a broad concept and Newzbin's activities taken as a whole amounted to making the claimants' copyright films available to premium members and in that way communicated them to the public.

Pirate Bay

The Pirate Bay (TPB) is the world's largest 'BitTorrent' tracker. BitTorrent is a file-sharing protocol that in a reliable way enables large and fast file transfers by breaking files up into small chunks that can be provided by different members of a P2P network. TPB is also an 'open' tracker, where anyone can download content files. To be able to upload files, write comments and personal messages one must register at the site. Like Newzbin, TPB is a peer-to-peer (P2P) service where the service provider does not itself copy store and make available content but relies on its users to do so.

In TPB, users download and install the uTorrent software for free and once installed, the user's computer becomes part of a P2P network allowing the user to both download content files made available by other P2P users on the network and also to make content files available for downloading by others (ie for upload). The key part of the BitTorrent protocol is the creation and distribution of 'torrent files' associated with particular content files. The torrent files do not contain content but enable the identification (and hence uploading and downloading) of the relevant content files. TPB provides an organised directory of content which users can browse and from which they can select the content of their choice. Among the search options available are 'music' and 'audio'.

By use of the various search options it is easy to find, among other things, recordings by particular artists. It is also possible to select files that are popular with other users. Furthermore, users can select file types including 'music' and 'FLAC' (ie Free Lossless Audio Codec, an audio format similar to MP3). Having selected the content, the user downloads the relevant torrent file for that content from TPB. The BitTorrent software on the user's computer will then use the information in the torrent file to download the chunks of the content file from the 'swarm' (the community of Bittorrent users sharing a file at any time).[133]

---

[132] *SGAE v Rafael Hoteles SL* Case C-306/05 2006.

[133] For a discussion of the technical aspects see *Dramatico Entertainment Ltd & Ors v British Sky Broadcasting Ltd & Ors* [2012] EWHC 268 (Ch) (20 February 2012) paras 19–29.

It is fair to say that TPB is a very widely used website. In December 2011 its index listed over four million torrent files, of which it was estimated that over one million of these were music torrents and of these over 750,000 were commercially available (ie copyright-protected works). The site also generated substantial advertising revenue. Needless to say, the record industry were concerned about the mass copying and distribution of music facilitated by TPB but rather than seeking to bring a claim against TPB itself, they sought an injunction against the defendants (being the main UK ISPs) pursuant to section 97A CDPA (which implemented Article 8(3) of the Information Society Directive) requiring the defendants to take measures to block or at least impede access by their customers to TPB, see Section 8.3.4.

7.5.5   Where To Next?

The net seems to be closing in on services such as Napster, Grokster, Newzbin etc, which have been held to facilitate digital copyright piracy. Developments such as the Digital Millennium Copyright Act (DMCA) in the USA and the Information Society Directive have given rights' owners greater rights and remedies against both direct and contributory infringers of digital copyright works. Also, once a service operator or provider has knowledge that it is facilitating copyright infringement, then it would be well advised to remove it in order to benefit from the exemptions to ISP liability under the Electronic Commerce Directive and to avoid a damages claim and reduce the risk of injunctive relief against it.[134]

7.6   SERVICE PROVIDER LIABILITY

7.6.1   Background

The *Napster*, *Grokster* and other cases discussed in section 7.5 above raise a more general issue: should those who *innocently* host, store or facilitate the transmission of infringing copyright content over the Internet be liable for copyright infringement?

As discussed in chapter one, the Internet involves a large number of intermediaries involved in enabling the hosting and transmission of Internet content. In the early years of the Internet and Internet law, a number of US cases examined the liability of website or electronic bulletin board operators and Internet service providers where they were involved in hosting

---

[134] See Section 2.6.1 of ch 2.

infringing content.[135] These centred on the application of the US copyright law doctrines of contributory and vicarious liability for copyright infringement discussed in section 7.5 above. In particular it soon became apparent there were a number of issues including:

(a) Are service providers or operators under a duty to monitor the sites they host or control for infringing material or otherwise obliged to take steps to prevent infringement?

(b) What if they made clear in their terms of use that users posting or hosting material on their sites were responsible for infringing content, not the host or operator?

(c) Once such persons became aware they are hosting infringing content, are they then under a duty to remove it and, by doing so, cease to be liable?

(d) What if such persons are innocent throughout and have facilitated infringement with no knowledge, actual or constructive?

In due course courts in Europe have also had to consider similar issues.[136]

7.6.2 Clarifying the Position

Over the last few years, states have taken action to try to clarify when liability arises in such circumstances. An early example is the German Teleservices Act 1997. The first major international precedent was the US Digital Millennium Copyright Act (DMCA) 1998, which provides 'safe harbours' for those transmitting, caching, hosting or linking to, infringing materials. Then the matter was also dealt with in the EU Electronic Commerce Directive. Both pieces of legislation are discussed in detail in section 2.6 of chapter two.

As noted in chapter two, the effect of the Electronic Commerce Directive and the Information Society Directive is that those acting as caches, hosts or 'mere conduits' benefit from certain exemptions, eg if they take down material as soon as they become aware it is infringing. In all cases, a lack of knowledge on the part of the operator is very important in order to escape liability.

In any event, operators should consider the merits of establishing a notice and take down policy to deal with any requests to take down infringing material as discussed in chapter two, section 2.6.1. They also need to ensure their online terms and conditions with users permit this as well. ISPs are also

---

[135] For example: *Religious Technology Center v Netcom On-Line Communications Serv* 907 F Supp 1361 (ND Cal 1995); *Sega Enterprises Ltd v Maphia* US District Court for the District of Northern California, 16 December 1996.

[136] For example: *Church of Spiritual Technology v Dataweb BV* District Court of the Hague, 9 June 1999; *Cee Dee Empire v IFPI* Eastern Division, High Court, Denmark, 8 December 1998, [1998] *EIPR* N-203; *Belgacom Skynet v IFPI Belgium & Polygram Records*—as discussed in section 2.6.1 of ch 2. See also the CJEU Cases *Scarlet* Case C-70/10 and *SABAM* Case C-360/10/.

being encouraged to ensure their terms and conditions are consistent with the above approach and the voluntary use of 'notice and take down' schemes across industry is being promoted on the basis they are consistent with the Electronic Commerce Directive.

7.7   STANDARDS AND WEB CONTENT

The Internet and various e-commerce products rely upon standards. Examples include the various MPEG standards dealing with the compression of digital data for audio and audio-visual use and also the technology behind DVDs. Many standards involve the 'pooling' of IPR rights, typically patents, between rights holders. Careful consideration of competition law/anti-trust issues is required in order to establish such standards.

Technical standards frequently involve 'patent pools'. The pooling of copyright is less common. This in large part is a feature of what copyright does and does not protect. The ideas and techniques underlying much of the Internet and e-commerce will not benefit from copyright protection. They are more properly protected by patents. Copyright will, of course, protect software and this may include programs relating to interfaces. However, as discussed in chapter six, the Software Directive constrains the extent to which interface information/technology can be 'privatised' in any event, as can competition law.

Much web content is written in HTML or XML code. XML was developed by the World Wide Web Consortium (W3C), which among other things develops standards for the Internet. Although similar to HTML, XML effectively describes what, as well as how, information is presented. The CDPA does not define a 'program' but it can be argued that the HTML source code typically used to generate web pages *is* a program—it is instructions to a web browser akin to a classic computer program. Therefore, web page source code ought to benefit from copyright protection as a computer program.

What of the HTML or XML languages: could they be protected by copyright as computer programs in their own right? Both the Software Directive[137] and an Australian case, *Data Access Corp v Powerflex Services Pty Ltd*,[138] suggest not. It is one thing to protect a program written in a programming language, quite another thing to protect the language itself. See also the discussion in Section 6.2.

---

[137] Recital 14. This was also the position recently reached in the *Navitaire and SAS Institute* cases—see section 6.3 of ch 6.

[138] [1999] HCA 49 (30 September 1999) (High Court of Australia) on appeal from the Federal Court [1997] 490 FCA (4 June 1997).

7.8   STREAMING MEDIA AND DIGITAL COPYRIGHT

A popular technology for enabling consumers to access audio and video content over the Internet is a process known as 'streaming'. This typically makes use of a software program called a 'codec' (Coder/DECoder) and has the advantages of:

(a)   *compressing* the initial digital video/audio data using a 'coder' program, so allowing more efficient transmission over the Internet;

(b)   leaving no trace of the compressed file (or the decompressed (ie decoded data) played to the user by the 'decoder') on the user's computer, unless the content owner has permitted the user to actually download the file; and

(c)   potentially only allowing access to streamed media by users having the right decoder/player.

So to view a streamed film, for example, the user will have to return to the original website each time the user wants to watch it. There will be no copy stored on the user's hard drive.

Streaming is therefore to be contrasted with 'downloading'. In downloading, a complete copy of an audio or video file is delivered to and stored on the user's computer. Once a user has downloaded a file, he/she can access the file at will, and can also redistribute copies of that file to others.

To prevent the unauthorised copying, re-use and redistribution of their content and also to facilitate transmission over the Internet, many copyright owners do not make their content available for downloading. Instead they distribute the content using streaming technology in a manner that does not permit downloading.

Many Internet web pages that deliver streaming music or video have historically used the RealNetworks format (ie RealAudio or RealVideo or RealMedia). The user needs a RealPlayer in order to access and play this material. Now Internet users have access to high bandwidth connections (eg via cable, ADSL broadband or satellite), the use of streaming technology has become even more widespread.

Of course, those using streaming technologies need to have the relevant licences in place both to use the technology and from the audio/video content owners whose work they intend to 'stream'. For example, in the US case *Bonneville International Corp et al v Marybeth Peters, as Register of Copyrights et al*,[139] it was held that under US copyright law (as applied by the United States Copyright Office), the simultaneous streaming over the Internet of radio broadcasts of sound recordings required a licence from the owner

---

[139]   Civ No 01-0408 (ED Pa, 1 August 2001).

of the copyright in the sound recordings and the payment of appropriate royalties. Similarly in another US case, *The Rodgers and Hammerstein Organization et al v UMG Recordings Inc. and The Farm Club Online Inc.*,[140] various music publishers were successful in requiring the defendant record companies to acquire additional rights to allow Internet streaming of recordings of the publishers' songs.

7.8.1   Piracy and Streaming

Not surprisingly, pirates have tried to devise ways to circumvent streaming, for example in order to:

(a)   allow users to download and copy streaming media files
(b)   allow users to convert files from proprietary streamed formats such as 'RealMedia' to 'open' formats such as MP3, for example

7.8.2   Defences Against Piracy

The best defence against piracy is for content suppliers to bind users to contractually binding online terms expressly prohibiting the retransmission, copying, modification or redistribution of streaming media files. However, it may be difficult in many cases for content suppliers/owners to bind users or enforce any such licences. In these circumstances, rights owners will need to fall back on the protection digital copyright law gives against the unauthorised adaptation, modification, reproduction, distribution or otherwise of copyright works. In addition, as streaming technology can be viewed as a technical measure designed and used (at least in part) to prevent copyright infringement, any attempt to circumvent this technology may also give rise to liability under anti-circumvention legislation such as the US Digital Millennium Copyright Act 1998 and the Information Society Directive.

For example, in the US case *RealNetworks, Inc. v Streambox, Inc.*,[141] RealNetworks sued a maker of products that allow users to capture and record streaming media files, and to convert streaming files into other formats such as MP3. It was alleged by RealNetworks that Streambox were violating the provisions of the Digital Millennium Copyright Act 1998 (DMCA) by distributing and marketing the so-called Streambox VCR and a product called a Ripper: the VCR enables end-users to access and download copies of RealMedia files that are streamed over the Internet despite RealNetworks' technical measures in place to prevent this. The Ripper is a file conversion application that enables RealMedia formatted files to be converted into other

---

[140]   00 Civ.9322 (JSM) (SDNY, September 2001).
[141]   2000 US Dist. LEXIS 1889 (WD Wash, 2000).

formats such as MP3. Another product, the Streambox Ferret, was also alleged to be unlawfully designed to permit consumers to make unauthorised modifications to a software program to which RealNetworks held the copyright.

The court granted a preliminary injunction preventing sales of the so-called Streambox VCR (recorder) product and Streambox Ferret (search tool) product, but reversed a temporary restraining order and allowed sales of the Streambox Ripper (file converter) product.

7.8.3 Concluding Thoughts

Decisions such as *RealNetworks* certainly help to bolster the attractions of streaming as a mechanism for delivering digital content.

7.9 TECHNICAL PROTECTION MEASURES AND FAIR USE: THE END OF COPYRIGHT?

7.9.1 Background[142]

The ease of copying, reproducing, modifying and transmitting digital copyright works has made many rights owners look to technical measures to protect their copyrights. Technical measures can work in a number of ways, which are not necessarily exclusive, including:

(a) preventing material from being copied, eg RealNetworks' streaming media products discussed above or the Content Scramble System (CSS) encryption technology used to protect DVDs from copying, or through using meta tags to prevent the copying of a web page by a web crawler;

(b) only allowing authorised users access to the works in question, eg by encrypting/scrambling content as in CSS or in the case of the 'conditional access systems' used to protect digital satellite broadcasts;

(c) marking the material either in a digitally 'indelible' manner to identify its source, eg through using digital watermarks or adding redundant code to software;

(d) embedding copyright notices in or adjacent to the material in question; and

(e) secure distribution, DRM systems and SDMI (see Glossary for more details).

---

[142] See generally: Hansbridge, 'DRM: Can It Deliver?' [2001] *ENTLR* 138, and Thomas, 'DVD Encryption—DECSS' [2000] *ENTLR* 135.

But just as technology can be used to protect technology, hackers and others have shown themselves equally creative in circumventing technical measures. For example, hackers have devised the DeCSS decode scrambling system to circumvent the CSS system used to protect DVDs. Once an encryption code is cracked, all systems using the code are potentially vulnerable. So it is strongly argued by rights owners that the circumvention of technical measures should be made unlawful (ie giving rise to civil liability) or even illegal (ie a criminal offence). Although civil libertarians and others argue that such laws potentially restrict free speech and the 'fair use' of copyright material, such 'anti-circumvention' laws seem here to stay.

Anti-circumvention laws are not new. As noted below, even before the implementation of the Information Society Directive, the CDPA contained a number of provisions dealing with this area. Some also implement the European Conditional Access Directive.[143] But to be fully effective, there needs to be international harmonisation. The 1996 WIPO Copyright and Performances and Phonograms Treaties seek to do this by requiring adequate legal protection and effective legal remedies against:

(a)   the circumvention of technological measures used to protect copyright; and
(b)   persons removing or altering any electronic rights management information (ERMI), or distributing, broadcasting, etc works where the ERMI has been removed or altered with the requisite knowledge.

7.9.2   The Position in the USA

Background to the DMCA
The USA implemented the anti-circumvention protections in the 1996 WIPO Treaties through the Digital Millennium Copyright Act 1998 (DMCA). This predates the Information Society Directive. In light of its importance it is worth looking at the DMCA in some detail.

The DMCA prohibits:

(a)   *Circumventing technological measures which control access to copyright works*[144]
       This also includes facilitating the circumvention of technological measures that effectively control access to a copyright work by, for example, manufacturing, importing or providing products or services (a) primarily designed or produced for this purpose, (b) with only a limited commercially significant purpose other than to circumvent technological

---

[143] Directive 98/84/EC of 20 November 1998 on the legal protection of services based on, or consisting of, conditional access.
[144] s 1201(a)(1)(A).

measures, or (c) marketing them for use in circumventing technological measures;[145]

(b)   *Manufacturing, importing, offering to the public, providing or otherwise trafficking in any technology, product, service, device or component that:*

    (i)   is primarily designed or produced for the purpose of circumventing the protection afforded by technological measures that effectively protect the rights of a copyright owner. An example of this would be a device preventing a work from being copied.

    (ii)   has only a limited commercially significant purpose or use other than to circumvent technological measures protecting the rights of a copyright owner;

    (iii)   is marketed for use in circumventing technological measures protecting the rights of a copyright owner.[146]

(c)   *The impairment of copyright management information (CMI)*[147]

This includes dealing with false CMI and removing or altering CMI.

The Preservation of the Right to 'Fair Use' and Exceptions to the DMCA

It should be noted that the DMCA does not prohibit the act of circumventing a technological measure that prevents copying, as opposed to one controlling access. This was deliberate: the intention is to ensure the public has the continued ability to make fair use of copyrighted works. The DMCA also contains certain express but limited safeguards to preserve the right to have access to certain works for certain purposes such as education, research, news reporting and so on.[148] There are also other limited exceptions to the prohibitions in the Act. These include circumventing access control measures for encryption research and security testing. Reverse engineering is also permitted to a very limited extent—to achieve interoperability between computer programs.

Remedies

Liability under the Act is both civil[149] and, where the acts are wilful and for commercial advantage or private financial gain, criminal.[150]

The DMCA in Practice

This Act has been the subject of a number of decisions including the *Napster* and *Arriba* cases discussed above. For example, in *Universal City Studios Inc v*

---

[145] s 1201 (a)(2).
[146] s 1201 (b)(1).
[147] s 1202.
[148] s 1201(a)(1)(B),(C), (D), and (E).
[149] s 1203.
[150] s 1204.

Reimerdes,[151] the court (in granting a preliminary injunction in favour of the plaintiffs) was of the view that posting the DeCSS program on a website infringed the DMCA. DeCSS was considered to have no commercially significant purpose other than to defeat the CSS copy protection system used to protect DVDs from unauthorised access and copying. The defendants were also prohibited from knowingly creating links to websites containing DeCSS.

In the summer of 2001, Russian programmer Dmitry Skylarov was arrested under the DMCA after speaking about software he had written which could crack Adobe's e-book encryption system. In April 2001, it was reported that the Recording Industry Association of America (RIAA) threatened Edward Felten of Princeton University under the DMCA if he made his research on RIAA's digital watermarking technology (part of the SDMI) public.[152]

7.9.3   The UK Position Prior to 31 October 2003

Prior to the 2003 Regulations the CDPA provided protection against those who made or dealt in devices or published information to enable technological measures to be circumvented in certain limited cases. These are set out below. These provisions continue with minor changes for broadcasts (which now include cable programmes). However, section 296 CDPA has been completely rewritten. The changes made to section 296 are discussed below.

(a)   *In the context of broadcasting, cable programmes or transmissions* (Sections 297–299 CDPA). For example, this would include making pirate smart codes used in broadcasting decoders or publishing details on the Internet of how to hack a broadcast conditional access system. The remedies here include both civil rights and criminal offences. In particular, Section 298 CDPA implements the 1998 EU Conditional Access Services Directive (CASD).[153] The CASD is designed to protect 'protected services' ie *paid* online or broadcast services (cable, terrestrial, satellite) protected by a conditional access system. The Directive requires Member States to prohibit persons in their territory from:

   (i)   making, importing, distributing, selling, renting, or possessing for commercial purposes 'illicit devices' ie any equipment or software designed or adapted to give access to a protected service in an intelligible form without the authorisation of the service provider;

---

[151] US District Court Southern District of New York, 82 F. Supp. 2d 211; 2 February 2000.
[152] NewScientist.com: 23 July and 14 August 2001.
[153] Directive 98/84/EC implemented into UK law by the Conditional Access (Unauthorised Decoders) Regulations 2000, SI 2000/1175.

    (ii)   installing, maintaining, or replacing for commercial purposes an 'illicit device';

    (iii) using commercial communications to promote 'illicit devices'.

The UK implementing regulations effectively require the protected service in question to originate within the EU.[154]

(b) *Where copy-protected copies of a copyright work are lawfully issued to the public*, the person issuing the copies has the right to prevent persons from:

    (i)   making, importing, selling etc any device or means specifically designed or adapted to circumvent the form of copy-protection used;

    (ii) publishing any information intended to enable or assist persons to circumvent that form of copy-protection;

    (iii) where such persons know or have reason to believe that it will be used to make infringing copies (Section 296 CDPA; note that from 31 October 2003 a new section 296 applies—see below).[155]

So UK law in this area was aimed at giving broadcasters etc the right to protect access to their services (such as a satellite broadcast) and prohibiting those facilitating the circumvention of copy-protection measures. The law was not specifically directed at protecting content-owners themselves. Furthermore, simply *possessing* (other than for commercial purposes)[156] a circumvention device, or *using* such a device simply to circumvent copy protection or access a restricted service, were not expressly prohibited.

7.9.4 The European Dimension

Until the 2003 Regulations, UK law in this area was more limited than the DMCA. However, following the adoption of the Information Society Directive, the UK was obliged to implement legislation dealing with this whole area. This legislation is also ultimately derived from the WIPO

---

[154] s 298 CDPA.

[155] For a case under the former s 296 CDPA see: *Kabushiki Kaisha Sony Computer Entertainment Inc v Edmonds (t/a Channel Technology)* (23 January 2002, High Court) where the claimants (Sony) successfully obtained summary judgment against the third defendant on the grounds that they were importing into the UK from Russia a computer chip which allowed users to circumvent the copy protection codes applied to computer games used on Sony's Playstation 2 console. This was held to be a clear breach of CDPA, s 296. The copy protection codes used by Sony fell within CDPA, s 296(4) and there was no doubt that the 'messiah' chip in question was specifically designed or adapted to circumvent the copy-protection used by Sony (CDPA, s 296(2)). It did not matter that the messiah chip had other uses than to infringe the claimants' copyright.

[156] s 297A(1)(b); s 298(2)(a)(ii).

Treaties. The 2003 Regulations mean that UK law has moved much more towards the DMCA.

Chapter III of the Information Society Directive deals with the protection of effective technological measures and electronic rights-management information. It is worth setting out how these terms are defined:

(a) *Technological measures* means any technology, device or component that, in the normal course of its operation, is designed to prevent or restrict acts, in respect of works or other subject matter (such as databases), which are not authorised by the right holder of any copyright or database right. Such measures are *effective* where the use of a protected work or other subject matter is controlled by the right holders through the application of an access control or protection process, such as encryption, scrambling or other transformation of the work or other subject matter, or a copy control mechanism, which achieves the protection objective.[157] So these measures include:
  (i)   smart cards (eg for digital television decoders)
  (ii) access control and copy-control software such as CSS and RealNetworks' technology used in its RealMedia products

(b) *Rights management information* means any information provided by right holders which identifies:
  (i)   the work or database
  (ii)   the author or any other right holder
  (iii) information about the terms and conditions of use of the work or database
  (iv)   any numbers or codes representing such information

  So rights management information would include:
  (i)   digital watermarks identifying the copyright owner
  (ii)   on-screen software licences
  (iii) website use terms
  (iv)   classic copyright notices

The Directive requires that Member States provide adequate legal protection against the following:

(c) *Technological measures*
  (i)   circumvention of effective technological measures which the person concerned carries out in the knowledge, or with reasonable grounds to know, that he is pursuing that objective;[158]

---

[157] Art 6(3).
[158] Art 6(1).

    (ii)   the manufacture, import, distribution, sale, rental, advertisement for sale or rental, or possession for *commercial purposes* [emphasis added] of devices, products or components or the provision of services which:

—   are promoted, advertised or marketed for the purpose of circumvention of any effective technological measures;

—   have only a limited commercially significant purpose or use other than to circumvent any effective technological measures; or

—   are primarily designed, produced, adapted or performed for the purpose of enabling or facilitating the circumvention of any effective technological measures.[159]

(d)   *Electronic rights management information (ERMI)*

    (i)   any person knowingly performing without authority any of the following:

—   the removal or alteration of any electronic rights-management information (ERMI), or

—   the distribution, importation for distribution, broadcasting, communication or making available to the public of works or other copyright-protected material or databases *from which electronic rights management information has been removed or altered without authority*.[160]

    (ii)   if the person knows or has reasonable grounds to know that by so doing he is inducing, enabling, facilitating or concealing an infringement of any copyright or related rights or database rights.

Areas of UK debate which overlap with US concerns over the DMCA will include to what extent the Directive permits encryption research aimed at testing the security of access control or copy-protection systems. Recital 48 of the Directive states that the Directive should not hinder research into cryptography. The 2003 Regulations provide that the section 296ZA restrictions on circumventing effective technological measures do not apply 'where a person, for the purposes of research into cryptography, does anything which circumvents effective technological measures unless in so doing, or in issuing information derived from that research, he affects prejudicially the rights of the copyright owner.'[161] This appears to permit commercial research aimed at improving the standard of cryptographic protection (commercial organisations are unlikely to wish to point out defects in any cryptographic protections) but academics who wish to publish critically on this area will not necessarily be protected by this section.

---

[159] Art 6(2).
[160] Art 7(1).
[161] s 296ZA(2).

Also Recital 50 of the Directive would appear to require that the UK ensure when implementing the Directive that the safeguards in Articles 5 and 6 of the Software Directive which allow the decompilation/reverse engineering etc of software in limited circumstances, as discussed in chapter six, are not overridden by the legal protection of software locks/encryption. The 2003 Regulations reflect this by ensuring that software has its own protection regime.

7.9.5   UK Implementation of Effective Technological Measures and ERMI[162]

The implementation of these provisions of the Information Society Directive has required certain changes to the CDPA:

Computer Programs

The circumvention of technical devices applied to computer programs is now dealt with in a stand-alone section 296. Article 1(2) of the Information Society Directive requires that existing Community provisions relating to the legal protection of computer programs are not affected by the Directive. The Software Directive contains specific remedies for circumventing technical devices reflected in section 296.[163]

Section 296 applies where (a) a *technical device*[164] has been applied to a computer program, and (b) a person (A) knowing or having reason to believe it will be used to make infringing copies: (i) manufactures for sale or hire, imports, distributes, sells or lets for hire, offers or exposes for sale or hire, advertises for sale or hire or has in his possession for commercial purposes any means *the sole intended purpose of which*[165] is to facilitate the

---

[162] The first reported case under the 2003 Regulations in this area was *Kabushiki Kaisha Sony Computer Entertainment Inc v Ball* [2004] EWHC 1738 (Ch) where the design manufacture, sale and installation of an electronic chip called 'Messiah 2' which enabled Sony's PS2 games consoles to play foreign and/or unauthorised copies of Sony's computer games was held (on an application for summary judgment) to be an infringement of sections 296, 296ZA, ZD and ZF of the CDPA (in so far as the infringing activities related to the UK).

[163] Directive 91/250/EC: Art 7 (1)(c).

[164] A technical device in relation to a computer program is defined as 'any device intended to prevent or restrict acts that are not authorised by the copyright owner of that computer program and are restricted by copyright' (s 296(6) CDPA) Such a device could be a mechanical or electronic device (eg a 'dongle'—a hardware device which needs to be plugged into a computer port before a program can be run) or (it is submitted) software code itself (eg an encryption algorithm and related software).

[165] This is more narrow than the position for devices and services designed to circumvent technological measures applied to copyright works other than computer programs—see s 296ZD CDPA. See *Kabushiki Kaisha Sony Computer Entertainment Inc v Ball* [2004] EWHC 1738 (Ch) for a discussion of this, where use of the device in question would inevitably facilitate the

unauthorised removal or circumvention of the technical device; or (ii) publishes information intended to enable or assist persons to remove or circumvent the technical device.

A number of persons (not just the person issuing copies to the public) are now given the same rights against A as a copyright owner has in respect of an infringement of copyright:

(a)   a person issuing to the public copies of, or communicating to the public (eg by offering software downloads), the computer program to which the technical device has been applied;

(b)   the copyright owner or his exclusive licensee (if they are not the person specified in (a));

(c)   the owner or exclusive licensee of any intellectual property right in the technical device applied to the computer program.[166]

These rights are concurrent.[167] Delivery up or seizure of certain articles in relation to the means of facilitation of the removal or circumvention of the technical device are also available as remedies.[168] A person bringing an action under section 296 also has the benefit of the presumptions set out in sections 104-106 CDPA.[169]

Circumvention of Technological Measures

Sections 296ZA–296ZF implement the provisions of the Information Society Directive relating to technological measures set out above. These reflect the provisions of the Directive and are not therefore discussed in detail—the reader is referred to 7.9.4 above. As noted above, these provisions do not apply to computer programs, which have their own protection regime.

The effect of the 2003 Regulations is that certain persons are given civil remedies:

(a)   Where technological measures are circumvented the person issuing copies or communicating the work to the public or (if not this person) the copyright owner or their exclusive licensee have the same rights against the person circumventing the measures as a copyright owner has in respect of infringement of copyright (section 296ZA(3)).

---

unauthorised circumvention of a copy protection device resulting in unauthorised copies and therefore clearly fall foul of section 296 (para 33).

[166] s 296(2) CDPA.

[167] s 296(3); see also sections 101(3) and 102(1) to (4) CDPA for the implications of concurrent rights where legal proceedings are brought, eg if one person brings proceedings the other persons entitled to do so must be either joined as a plaintiff or added as a defendant.

[168] s 296(4) and (5) CDPA.

[169] s 296(7); for software which bears a copyright notice a relevant presumption is s 105(3) CDPA: that the named person is the copyright owner unless the contrary is proved.

(b)   Where devices or services designed to circumvent technological measures are supplied by a person then in addition to the persons named
above the owner or exclusive licensee of any intellectual property right
in the effective technological measures also has a right of action (section
296ZD (2)).

It is also a criminal offence to carry out certain acts in relation to the manufacture, import (otherwise than for private or domestic use), or sale, possession, advertising etc (in the course of a business) of any device etc primarily
designed etc for the purposes of enabling or facilitating the circumvention
of effective technological measures. The provision of services in the course
of a business (or if not in the course of a business then to such an extent as
to affect prejudicially the copyright owner) the purpose of which enable or
facilitate the circumvention of effective technological measures is also an
offence.[170] It has been argued that this offence also applies to the protection
of computer programs as well as other copyright works[171] but in the author's
view the definition of 'technological measures' in the 2003 Regulations[172]
(which expressly excludes computer programs from the scope of protection)
means that in practice the offence will be difficult, if not impossible, to apply
where computer programs are protected by technological measures.
   The provisions are drafted so that they also cover the protection of works
to which rights in performances, publication right and database right apply;
they are not just limited to protecting copyright.[173] However, the criminal
offence appears only to apply in relation to copyright works and the protection of copyright.

ERMI

The provisions in the Directive regarding ERMI noted above are implemented by the 2003 Regulations.[174] They also apply to computer programs.
They cover not just ERMI in relation to copyright but also ERMI in respect
of rights in performances, database right and publication right.[175] There are
no specific criminal penalties where a person alters or removes ERMI or
deals in works where the ERMI has been removed or altered. However, the

---

[170]   s 296ZB.
[171]   Cook et al, *The Copyright Directive UK Implementation* (Bristol, Jordans, 2004) 4.28.
[172]   s 296ZF(1) CDPA. Also, according to the Court of Appeal in *R v Higgs* [2008] EWCA
1324, 24 June 2008, a technological measure must not merely discourage or be a general commercial hindrance to copyright infringement, it must be a measure that *physically prevents this*
(para 35).
[173]   See sections 296ZA(6) (circumvention of technological measures) and section 296ZD(8)
(rights and remedies in respect of devices and services designed to circumvent technological
measures).
[174]   s 296ZG CDPA.
[175]   s 296ZG(8).

party issuing copies or communicating the work to the public (or if not the same), the copyright owner or their exclusive licensee have the same rights against such a person as a copyright owner has in respect of infringement of copyright.

7.9.6 Technological Measures and Permitted Acts, Fair Use and Fair Dealing

Technological measures are here to stay. Digital copyright users are increasingly concerned that the trend to copy-protect and control access to copyright works will prevent the fair use or fair dealing of copyright works. In particular, surely private, non-commercial personal use should be permitted?

Both the US and European legislatures have recognised this by building certain safeguards into both the DMCA and Information Society Directive.[176] In particular, in the absence of voluntary measures taken by right-holders, the Directive requires Member States to take appropriate measures to ensure that right-holders make available certain fair use and fair dealing exceptions.[177] The 2003 Regulations make provision for this by allowing the Secretary of State to intervene where a complaint is made that the application of any effective technological measure to a copyright work (other than to a computer program) to which the complainant had lawful access prevents the complainant from carrying out a *permitted act*[178] in relation to the work. Complaints by a representative of members of a class of persons prevented from carrying out a permitted act are also possible.[179] Where the Secretary of State decides to act (there is no obligation on them to do so—they *may* do so) and gives directions to the copyright owner or their exclusive licensee then the complainant (or class of complainants) has the right to enforce the directions on the basis there is a breach of statutory duty.[180]

An outstanding issue is whether such exceptions (or 'permitted acts') can be overridden by contract. For example, online website or software terms and conditions may seek to exclude any fair use or fair dealing rights. The Directive suggests this will be possible.[181] The 2003 Regulations state that the remedy noted above for the Secretary of State to intervene where permitted acts are prevented is *not* available in respect of 'copyright works made available to the public on agreed contractual terms in such a way that members

---

[176] Art 6(4).

[177] Art 6(4).

[178] This is broadly defined—it includes permitted acts in relation to copyright, rights in performances, database right and publication right; the permitted acts are listed in Schedule 5A to the CDPA.

[179] s 296ZE(2).

[180] s 296ZE(6).

[181] Art 6(2), para 4 and Art 9; Recital 53.

of the public may access them from a place and at a time individually chosen by them'.[182] This indicates the importance wherever possible of digital rights owners imposing licence terms on users. In 2011, the Hargreaves Review recommended that legislation be enacted to prevent copyright exceptions being overridden by contract.[183] In the proposed, new exceptions and amendments to existing copyright exceptions noted in section 2.4.1 above which follow on from the Hargreaves Review, there are express provisions that seek to prevent such exceptions being overridden by contract.

7.9.7   The Future of Digital Rights Management (DRM)

The European Commission has been supporting the development of interoperable technical systems to protect copyright such as digital rights management systems (DRMs). According to the Commission, DRMs are technologies that identify and describe digital content protected by intellectual property rights. They can be used to enforce usage rules set by rightholders or prescribed by law for digital content. They can also facilitate legal copying and reuse of content by establishing a secure environment in which right-holders are remunerated for private copying, online content is paid for, and illegal copying is prevented.[184]

The Commission's High Level Group on DRMs presented a Final Report on 8 July 2004 which reflected a consensus on basic principles and recommendations for future actions in three areas:

(a)   DRM and interoperability—open cross-platform DRM systems and standards are imperative and must be fostered;

(b)   migration to legitimate services—the abuse and unauthorised file-sharing of copyrighted content must not be tolerated, and consumers must be encouraged to use legitimate services; and

(c)   private copying levies and DRM—the Commission sees the way forward as a move away from levies on private copying (in some Member States right holders receive compensation for private copying based on levies) to a system based on existing, exclusive copyrights backed by technologies (such as DRM) that ensure a secure environment where such rights can be licensed and enforced.

The Commission's stress on DRMs has been criticised; for example The Foundation for Information Policy Research (FIPR) (www.fipr.org) sees DRMs as displacing the fair use/fair dealing and other protections built into

---

[182]   s 296ZE(9).

[183]   Recommendation 5.

[184]   See European Commission Information Society Factsheet 20 entitled 'Intellectual Property Rights and Digital Rights Management Systems.'

copyright law (a point noted in section 7.9.6 above). The FIPR proposes that the EU must introduce legislation to restrict the 'fruit of the poisoned tree'; that is, that a rights management mechanism, or other technical protection mechanism, which is abused contrary to other settled law, such as competition law or consumer law, should lose its protection under the Information Society Directive.[185] DRM will continue to be controversial to the extent it restricts the fair use/fair dealing of copyright works.

SUMMARY

(a) Digital copyright underpins e-commerce.
(b) Important areas to consider include:
    (i) Do you have the digital rights you need? Are your existing copyright licences sufficient?
    (ii) Are your licence terms and conditions binding? Are copyright notices used? Are they sufficient to protect your IP?
    (iii) Are there commercially attractive ways to copy-protect, manage, and/or track your content, or prevent the use of web crawlers (eg through using meta tags)?
    (iv) Are you proactive in using technology (eg web crawlers) to monitor piracy and is your rights position properly documented so you can take swift action against pirates?

---

[185] See FIPR paper by Ross Anderson entitled 'EU Consultation on Digital Rights Management', 16 September 2004.

8

Digital Copyright, Web 2.0, E-publishing and Apps

Since around 2004 the Internet has been transformed through the growth of Web 2.0, through increased bandwidth and Internet penetration, through the growth of social networking, and the increasing influence of the Internet on everyday life. The previous chapters of this book remain relevant to this new world. This chapter takes the discussion in chapter seven forward by analysing some of the key copyright issues that arise out of Web 2.0 and the continuing development of the Internet since 2004. It looks at:

(a)   Web 2.0 and copyright
(b)   fair dealing and Web 2.0
(c)   liability for hosting and/or distributing user-generated content
(d)   e-publishing
(e)   app development and distribution

8.1   WEB 2.0 AND COPYRIGHT

From a copyright perspective, the key aspects of Web 2.0 are its participatory and 'horizontal nature'. It is horizontal in the sense that content is provided by users themselves, often in a collaborative manner, as opposed to the 'vertical' delivery of content by website providers who distribute either their own or third party content. So for example, blogs and sites such as Wikipedia contain authored text from many users, and sites such as You Tube, Flickr and others contain uploaded text, photos, music, videos and so on. Virtual world content sites such as Second Life enable users to generate their own content in an environment created and therefore 'owned' by the virtual world provider. Web 2.0 is participatory as users are encouraged to create and upload content, often in a collaborative manner (eg Wikipedia).

  In the analysis which follows the assumption is that UK copyright law applies, yet it needs to be borne in mind that there are potentially complex choice of law and jurisdictional issues which are likely to apply in a Web 2.0 environment.

8.1.1   Web 2.0 Legal Issues: Background

Web 2.0 sites raise a number of digital copyright issues including:

(a) copyright ownership and licensing
(b) collaborative and joint authorship
(c) liability for copyright infringement

These issues are considered below. But first, by way of background, some of the complex choice of law and jurisdictional issues which are likely to apply in a Web 2.0 environment are discussed.

Where work is authored online (as opposed to creating the work offline and then uploading it to a website), it will be a common occurrence that the author will reside in one country (let us say for illustration purposes the USA, where they are a US national), yet the work (in computer code on a server) will be located elsewhere (let us say for illustration purposes the UK), and the website is 'published' from the second country (in this case the UK). Given the work is effectively first created and published in the UK, it will automatically benefit from copyright protection in the UK (although its author is a foreign national) and it will also be protected in other countries by virtue of the Berne Convention and Universal Copyright Convention.[1]

At the same time, assuming the author remains the owner of the copyright, for the UK website operator to publish the work lawfully, they must have a licence, either express (eg in writing, for example website terms of use which bind the author) or implied (the author has willingly contributed content which the author expects to see published). What law governs this licence if there is no written licence with an express choice of law clause?

Already potentially complex jurisdictional and choice of law issues arise. Imagine a work with multiple authors in different jurisdictions, or where the website and server are outside the UK; this increases the complexity.

8.1.2   Dealing with the Issues: The Importance of Contractual and/or Licence Terms

One way to reduce the complexity and gain greater legal certainty, both as far as choice of law and jurisdiction is concerned and more generally (as discussed in 8.1.3 below), is for the operator of a Web 2.0 site to require users to agree to clear and binding terms of licensing and use. If properly drafted such terms can:

(a) *Set out the ground rules*
     Such terms can facilitate the creation and exploitation of user-generated content by setting out what the ground rules are for all parties as clearly

---

[1] See Ch IX CDPA and s 175 CDPA.

as possible to avoid future disputes and to give comfort to all parties. For example, it is now common for Web 2.0 sites to require users to grant the site operator (and where appropriate other users) a royalty free non-exclusive licence to use adapt, modify, sublicense, etc any user-generated content in connection with the use and exploitation of the site. In the past some sites have sought to own the copyright in user-generated content but the trend has been for a broad non-exclusive licence to be required by the site operator/provider. This licence will typically be perpetual and irrevocable (so that the user cannot terminate it) and it will be transferable and capable of sublicensing to give the site operator maximum flexibility (so that they can outsource or transfer their operations, for example).

The terms will also clarify what intellectual property rights are retained by the site operator and the scope of any rights granted to the user, which will typically be limited to a nonexclusive revocable (ie it can be taken away at any time) licence to use the site and will contain prohibitions about misusing the site's content (eg through electronically extracting content such as contact details and misusing them). The terms should also deal with moral rights, typically through waivers, as in practice it will be difficult or unreasonable for the operator or indeed other users to comply with these rights, eg where the site operator considers it desirable to remove, adapt or modify user-generated content.

The terms will need to vary in complexity depending on the nature of the site, with virtual worlds which allow users to create complex and potentially valuable content (avatars etc) being at the cutting edge in terms of how these licences are drafted.

(b) *Reduce the risk of liability for the website operator/service provider*
This can be done by including provisions dealing among other things with the following:

   (i)   warranties by the author (backed up by indemnities) about ownership, non-infringement of third party rights, that the work is lawful and not obscene, defamatory, etc;

  (ii)   granting the operator the right to take down and/or edit or modify content preferably for any reason (including by seeking waivers of moral rights where relevant) and (subject to compliance with data privacy laws and other applicable law) to pass on the user's details to rights owners alleging infringement and law enforcement agencies. US website operators typically also set out the notice and takedown procedure under the Digital Millennium Copyright Act (DMCA) as it applies to them.

The importance of clear legal rules (such as a written licence) applying to all Web 2.0 users, participants and providers will be a consistent theme throughout this chapter.

8.1.3   Some Specific Issues

Copyright Ownership and Licensing

As should be clear from the discussion in chapter two, in the UK and, indeed, in general terms throughout the world, copyright arises upon the creation by an author of a work in tangible form (which would include typing text in a blog, for example) and unless the author is employed or otherwise creates the work in circumstances where the author will not be the first owner of copyright or the author agrees in writing to transfer (assign) the copyright to another person, the author retains copyright. This means that in the context of user-generated content the content creator will typically retain ownership. So it is important, as discussed above, for the Web 2.0 site terms of use to address the licensing of this content.

Collaborative and Joint Authorship

As discussed in section 2.5 of chapter two, collaborative working can either lead to a situation where all the authors retain copyright in their sections of a collaborative work where these sections are distinct works (a good example of this is a book which has chapters written by individual authors), or, where the contributions of the authors are not distinct, a work of joint authorship is created. The latter situation would occur in a Web 2.0 context where users are encouraged to submit content to a site which others can edit, revise or correct and so on. The site operator needs to stipulate clear terms explaining how users' rights are to be dealt with otherwise the copyright position will be unclear. The options for the site operator include:

(a)   Users are required to transfer (assign) all copyright and other rights in their content to the site operator in return for a non-exclusive licence back to the user (eg for personal, non-commercial purposes). This means that going forward the site operator can control the use and exploitation of the content. Such a policy is likely to be unpopular unless users are remunerated for their contributions, however.

(b)   Users retain copyright in joint works (or indeed in works for which they are the sole author) but the rights of the users to use, modify and exploit these works together with the scope of the licence granted to the site operator are clarified. An example of this is the approach to copyright of *Wikipedia*. 'Wikis' allow users to create content and the best-known example is *Wikipedia*, the free online encyclopaedia produced collaboratively by its readers.[2] *Wikipedia* takes a similar approach to access to its content as is used in open source software licensing (see section 9.5.4 of chapter nine below). The principle known as 'copyleft' is used—this means

---

[2] http://en.wikipedia.org/wiki/Wikipedia:Introduction (accessed 13 June 2013).

that *Wikipedia* content can be copied, modified and distributed so long as the new version grants the same freedoms to others and acknowledges the authors of the *Wikipedia* article.[3] This principle is given legal force by requiring that all users of *Wikipedia* agree to the Creative Commons CC-BY-SA licence, a 'copyleft' licence similar to the GPL open source software licence and discussed at section 9.5.4 of chapter nine below but which is designed for content generally rather than software.

Liability for Copyright Infringement

The hosting and publishing of user-generated content exposes website operators to potential legal risks—for copyright and other intellectual property right infringement, for defamation and so on. This is because the operator/ service provider is unlikely to have much, if any, control over the content provided by users. This is not a new issue—the Electronic Commerce Directive and the Digital Millennium Copyright Act (DMCA) discussed in chapter two both address this issue. A key aspect of minimising liability, at least in the context of copyright infringement, is to ensure the service provider has put in place a notice and take down policy as discussed in section 2.6 of chapter two and section 7.6 of chapter seven above.

8.2   FAIR DEALING AND WEB 2.0

8.2.1   Google Book Search[4]

Leading search engine Google has a project, the Google Library Project, to scan the text of millions of books and other materials into a searchable database. The materials are in the collections of major research libraries—the Bodleian Library, Oxford, Harvard University Library and so on. Once completed, the project will bring the contents of the world's leading scholarly libraries to a worldwide audience backed up by an impressive search capability.

It is clear from the outset that there are potential copyright issues here. Google was reported as scanning both out of copyright (public domain) materials (where there is clearly no copyright issue) as well as works in copyright (in the US, books first published after 1922). However, for the latter, although Google will copy the entire text into its database, it is understood the search engine used will only extract limited amount of texts ('snippets') as opposed to potentially the entire work for public domain works. These are limited to the sentence that comprises the search term plus the sentences before and after, as well as the book's bibliographic information. Also, copyright owners can seek

---

[3] http://en.wikipedia.org/wiki/Wikipedia:Copyrights (accessed 13 June 2013).
[4] Jordan, 'The Google Book Search Project,' *Michigan Bar Journal* (September 2007). See also the discussion in Netanel, *Copyright's Paradox* (Oxford, Oxford University Press, 2008).

to opt out of the project by notifying Google; in that case Google will either not copy their books or remove any material already copied.

Given that there is potentially copying of copyright works in the project, Google's defence to any allegation of copyright infringement by publishers will be fair use in the USA or fair dealing in the UK (should Google digitise in the UK library books which are in copyright). Google has been subject to several legal actions by authors and publishers in respect of the project in the USA,[5] as well as an action in France and a settled action in Germany.[6] One argument advanced by the claimants in the US action is that Google is deriving commercial benefit from the project, as it will drive viewers to Google's sites and advertisers will want to advertise on Google's site by paying for this. This may militate against Google as regards a finding of fair use. But so far the US cases have not gone to trial. Google will doubtless try to argue that there is fair use and that they should not be found liable for infringement on a number of grounds presumably including that:

(a)   They have sought to limit the amount of copied material presented to the public, their use is highly transformative and of public benefit and in order to provide the service, they have no option but to scan the entire text but they are careful to present only limited search results for those books in copyright, and what they are doing does not compete with publishers and in fact potentially enhances sales of texts in copyright by stimulating interest in them. No doubt Google will also cite the decision in *Perfect 10 v Google* discussed in chapter seven; and

(b)   They have given publishers the option to opt out of the project, although this is controversial and not accepted by many publishers.

As at the date of writing, a US publisher's law suit (by the American Association of Publishers (AAP)) was reported to be settled. However, other suits (in particular by the US Authors Guild) are still ongoing.[7]

8.2.2   Google News[8]

The Google News website uses Google's search engine algorithms to gather news stories from thousands of sources and arrange them in order of importance. Google News displays the headline, less than two sentences of the story, and

---

[5] By the Authors Guild and also a number of publishers in the US District Court for the Southern District of New York.

[6] By French publisher Groupe La Martinière and others, Paris Tribunal de grande instance, 6 June 2006. The German publisher WBG also filed for an injunction in the Regional Court of Hamburg but the petition was dropped in June 2006 as Google promised to withdraw the books from the project; see discussion in European Commission, 'Commission Staff Working Document', Brussels, 30.11.2007, SEC (2007) 1556.

[7] 'Google settles book scanning law suit' BBC News 4, October 2012.

[8] Netanel, *Copyright's Paradox* (Oxford, Oxford University Press 2008) 27–8.

a miniature thumbnail image of a photograph from a press website. The head-line and photo are hyper-linked to the relevant newspaper's or news agency's own website. Again, one of the issues here is that Google's activities potentially drive advertising revenue away from the newspaper sites to Google's sites, as users access the news stories via Google rather than going direct to the newspaper sites, so Google is potentially gaining a commercial advantage from this.

In March 2005, Agence France Presse (AFP) sued Google for copyright infringement on the basis that Google's reproduction and display of the head-lines and story leads as well as the thumbnails constituted wilful infringement of AFP's copyrights. Google has settled this lawsuit but other suits have fol-lowed, including the Belgian case *Copiepresse v Google* where Google lost in the Belgian Court of First Instance on 13 February 2007 and this ruling was upheld on appeal on 5 May 2011.[9]

8.2.3   *Copiepresse v Google*[10]

Copiepresse manages the rights of the Belgian, French and German speak-ing daily press publishers in Belgium. Google made the Google News service available in Belgium in January 2006 under the name 'Google:Actualités'. Copiepresse promptly complained, saying that the service was not a simple search engine but a portal to the written press, with Google reproducing and displaying as it thought fit a significant amount of the text of the articles without prior authorisation. Copiepresse then had a court-appointed expert issue a ruling and by letter requested Google to remove the Belgian news-paper articles complained about, which were present by display in Google News and also stored by Google in its cache memory (created through the use of indexation robots ('Googlebots'), which store a snapshot of web pages on Google's servers, which is then accessible to those using Google's search engine). Google did not respond to this letter and the matter went to trial.

The Court held that the use of a cache and allowing users access to the cache constituted an act of reproduction and communication to the public in breach of copyright and which did not benefit from an exception (eg because it was temporary or transient storage—this was not the case here). The Court also held that the use by the Google News service (which consisted of hyperlinks to the original news articles, together with the reproduction of the title of the article and the first sentence or sentences of it) infringed copyright. This was not because the act of using a hyperlink infringed—the Court noted that it was admitted by both Belgian and international case law and legal doctrine that a hyperlink forwarding to a work protected by copyright does not constitute

---

[9] (La Cour d'appel de Bruxelles) press release of Copiepresse, 5 May 2011.
[10] No 06/10.928/C, The Court of First Instance in Brussels, 13 January 2007 (certified English translation referred to).

a reproduction and that if there was a reproduction, it was made by the Internet user not Google. It was the reproduction and communication to the public on the homepage of Google News of the press article titles and extracts from them that infringed. The court dismissed Google's argument that this text was either not original or too short to merit protection. The court also rejected Google's attempt to benefit from legal exceptions for citation and reporting news under Belgian law. In addition, the court found that Google had infringed the moral rights of the authors of the articles by not naming them as author (right of paternity) and also by modifying their works (right of integrity).

Another interesting aspect of this case is that Google tried to argue that by making the articles available to the public on the Internet, the rights holders had explicitly or implicitly authorised the copying and referencing of their sites. In particular, the publishers could have used meta tags and robot.txt files to prevent Googlebots automatically copying and indexing their sites. This was rejected by the Court—copyright is not a right to oppose copying, but a right to authorise copying prior to copying taking place.

In December 2012, Google announced they were partnering with Belgian news publishers to bring an end to all litigation between them.[11]

8.2.4   The UK Position

The UK has a narrower approach to fair use than the US courts, so as far as the Google Library project is concerned, it is difficult to see how Google's activities as a commercial organisation would benefit from the fair dealing exception for private study or research, nor do its activities appear to easily fall within other UK exceptions.

As far as Google News is concerned, caching of articles is likely to be problematic as well, but it can be debated whether reproducing the titles and a limited amount of text is copyright infringement on the basis either that there is a lack of substantial copying or what is copied is not protected by copyright as it is too short in length (see the discussion in section 7.2.2 of chapter seven above, although recent cases weaken any argument that the text is not protected by copyright[12]). As far as the linking in Google News is concerned, this is still an open area in the UK (see section 7.2.2 of chapter seven). Google would also want to try to rely on the fair dealing defence for reporting current events, discussed in section 2.4.1 of chapter two. The other area that one would want to consider in UK law is the extent of any express or implied licence from the newspaper sites and whether the website terms of use prohibited trawling, scraping or other unauthorised data extraction.

---

[11] Google Europe Blog, 12 December 2012.
[12] See in particular *Newspaper Licensing Agency Ltd v Meltwater Holding BV* [2011] EWCA Civ 890 which applied the CJEU case C-5/08 *Infopaq*.

If so, this would strengthen the content owners' position not least as such restrictions might help negate any fair dealing argument Google might raise.

8.3   LIABILITY FOR HOSTING AND/OR DISTRIBUTING INFRINGING CONTENT

Sections 7.5 and 7.6 of chapter seven have discussed this issue with a focus on file sharing and the supply of technologies that can facilitate copyright infringement. Going forward it is likely that there will continue to be important cases in this area, especially in the USA where at the time of writing, *Viacom v Google* continues towards trial. This section looks at this area, including powers available against ISPs and users to prevent infringement by blocking access to infringing content.

8.3.1   *Viacom v Google*

On 13 March 2007, Viacom and several other plaintiffs launched a copyright action against Web 2.0 site YouTube and its parent Google because of the high level of infringing media content available on YouTube (eg TV programmes and motion pictures).[13] YouTube is a website that is a forum for users to share their own user-generated content. The plaintiffs see it less as a forum for 'user-generated' content and more as an attempt by its owners (Google) 'to wilfully infringe copyrights on a huge scale' and it 'appropriates the value of creative content on a massive scale for YouTube's benefit without payment or licence'. The plaintiffs claim that the defendants are infringing copyright by:

(a)   direct copyright infringement through publicly performing and authorising others to perform the plaintiffs' copyright works;
(b)   direct copyright infringement through publicly displaying and purporting to authorise the public display of the plaintiffs' works;
(c)   direct copyright infringement through reproducing the plaintiffs' works;
(d)   inducing the infringing acts of YouTube users by promoting the use of YouTube to infringe the plaintiffs' copyrights and YouTube are aware of the infringing acts of its users;
(d)   contributory copyright infringement—defendants have actual and constructive knowledge that YouTube users are using the website to infringe the plaintiffs' rights and acting with this knowledge the defendants enable, facilitate and materially contribute to YouTube users' infringements; and

[13] *Viacom International and Others v YouTube Inc, YouTube LLC and Google, Inc.* (US District Court, Southern District of New York, 13 March 2007—complaint for declaratory relief and injunctive relief and damages).

(e)   vicarious copyright infringement as the defendants have both the right and ability to supervise YouTube users' infringing conduct and prevent this but fail to do this for the plaintiffs' works and YouTube significantly and directly benefits from this infringement.

The legal action followed on from the submission by Viacom to YouTube of 100,000 notice and take down requests under the DMCA, asking for the removal of content held on YouTube which Viacom said was infringing its rights.[14] The outcome will be a landmark decision as far as the development of the Internet is concerned, for Google's technology is capable of being used for infringing and non-infringing purposes and Google puts the responsibility for complying with copyright on its users, although Google could use filtering technology to try to screen out infringing content, and indeed has now started to implement such a system which requires copyright owners to supply copies of their content to Google for identification purposes.[15] The current status is that in 2010, the judge held that YouTube was protected by the safe harbour provisions of the DMCA (section 512). Viacom appealed but lost (on the basis the appeals court largely affirmed the earlier decision).[16] However, the case is reported as continuing.[17]

8.3.2   Co-regulation: A Future Approach to Illicit P2P Copying of Material?

The Viacom action against YouTube and Google and the *Napster* and *Grokster* cases discussed in chapter seven highlighted some of the recent issues for rights holders who have found their content available for distribution on P2P networks or via social networking and other user-generated content sites. Later cases continue this trend as infringers move to new platforms, services or industries.

One approach rights holders can take is that of Viacom in vigorously pursuing those involved in the distribution chain, including Google. Needless to say, those on the receiving end of such actions, including Google, will say they are merely intermediaries and providing a useful service for public benefit, and that they should not be found liable for the infringing activities of their users. Ultimately the winners and losers of such an approach will be determined by the courts applying some of the principles discussed in this book. Another approach is for rights holders to work with service providers such as Google and also ISPs to develop voluntary, technological measures (such as

---

[14]   www.eff.org/deeplinks/2007/02/unfairly-caught-viacoms-dragnet-let-us-know.

[15]   'No more copyrighted clips on Google', theage.com.au, 16 October 2007.

[16]   See comments on the case at www.eff.org/cases/viacom-v-youtube (accessed 15 June 2013).

[17]   www.eff.org/deeplinks/2013/04/victory-youtube-viacom-v-youtube-case-anyone-think (accessed 15 June 2013).

filtering) to assist in stemming the tide of copyright infringement. The latter approach is something the UK government has been keen to help facilitate, with a preferred regulatory solution that will ensure an appropriate balance is struck between the interests of rights holders, ISPs and consumers, and that embodies both high level regulation and self-regulation ('co-regulation').[18] However, there are limits to the effectiveness of voluntary measures and so the Digital Economy Act 2010 was controversially passed.

8.3.3   Online Infringement and the Digital Economy Act

As noted in chapter one, there have been moves in a number of countries to give content owners stronger legal powers to prevent online copyright infringement. One approach discussed below is to make use of Article 8(3) of the Information Society Directive whereby content owners can obtain injunctions against ISPs to block access to infringing content. Another approach that has found favour in a number of countries is a so-called 'three strikes and you are out' law, where content owners can send notices to users hosting infringing content and in a graduated approach if content is not taken down, then ultimately the user can have their access to the Internet denied. This is clearly controversial as it limits freedom of expression, is a broad brush approach and can seem Draconian. Nevertheless, it has the potential to be effective against 'repeat offenders'. It is also clear that ISPs have a key role here. They know the identity of alleged infringers so are best placed to issue warning emails etc; it is much more efficient for them to do so and it also protects the user's privacy (at least initially). In the UK the Digital Economy Act 2010 (DEA) addressed this area. Its background was:

> The provisions in the DEA impose new responsibilities on Ofcom to implement and administer measures aimed at significantly reducing online copyright infringement. These measures form part of a multi-pronged approach by Government aimed at reducing online copyright infringement through a complementary mix of enforcement, consumer education and encouragement to industry to develop and promote online services offering lawful access to copyright works.[19]

Key to the Act is a code (Code). The DEA provisions insert amendments to the Communications Act 2003 (CA03) to create two new obligations for Internet service providers. These are referred to as the 'initial obligations'. They are to:

— notify their subscribers if the internet protocol (IP) addresses associated with them are reported by copyright owners as being used to infringe copyright; and

---

[18] Department for Business Enterprise and Regulatory Reform, Consultation on Legislative Options to Address Illicit Peer-to-Peer (P2P) File-Sharing, July 2008.

[19] Para 1.2, Proposed Ofcom DEA Code (http://stakeholders.ofcom.org.uk/consultations/infringement-notice/summary (accessed 11 May 2013)).

— keep track of the number of reports about each subscriber, and compile, on an anonymous basis, a list of those subscribers who are reported on above a threshold to be set in the Initial Obligations Code. This list is referred to as a 'Copyright Infringement List' (CIL). After obtaining a court order to obtain personal details, copyright owners will be able to take action against those included in the list.

The DEA provides that the implementation and regulation of the initial obligations must be set out in a Code. In the absence of an approved code drawn up and agreed by industry, it falls to Ofcom to make a Code in accordance with the requirements of the DEA. The current proposed Code was announced in June 2012.[20] The Code will initially only apply to providers of fixed Internet access supplying services over more than 400,000 broadband-enabled lines and includes a 'three strikes' approach.

It should be noted that in addition to the initial obligations outlined above, the DEA also provides for the imposition of further 'technical obligations' designed to reduce levels of online copyright infringement. These would oblige ISPs to take technical measures (eg bandwidth throttling, limiting or blocking access or temporary account suspension) against relevant subscribers in certain circumstances. However, the Secretary of State cannot impose these technical obligations on ISPs until the Code has been in force for a minimum of 12 months and he/she has obtained an assessment by Ofcom of whether one or more technical measures should be imposed. The introduction of a technical measures framework by the Secretary of State, including a right of appeal to the First Tier Tribunal (a judicial body), will require additional secondary legislation. So, while the imposition of technical measures to cut off Internet access, for example, could ultimately form part of the framework under the DEA, they do not form part of the draft Code. In any event, existing powers noted in 8.3.4 below give content owners the ability to obtain injunctions against ISPs to order them to block existing content so query how necessary such powers under the DEA are.

8.3.4 Injunctions Against Service Providers

The Information Society Directive requires Member States to provide appropriate sanctions and remedies in respect of activities which infringe the rights granted by the Directive, including the ability for rights holders to obtain injunctions against intermediaries whose services are used by a third party to infringe copyright.[21] In the UK Article 8 was implemented in part by s 97A

---

[20] Online Infringement of Copyright and the Digital Economy Act 2010, Notice of Ofcom's proposal to make by order a code for regulating the initial obligations, Ofcom, 26 June 2012.
[21] Article 8.

CDPA which gives the courts the power to grant injunctions against service providers where that service provider has actual knowledge of another person using their service to infringe copyright. This has opened the door for rights holders to obtain 'blocking' injunctions against service providers to prevent access to third party infringing content and services through their services. So for example, in *Twentieth Century Fox Film Corp v British Telecommunications plc*,[22] the court made a blocking order against BT with respect to a website called Newzbin2. Other similar orders were made against Sky and TalkTalk.[23]

8.4   E-PUBLISHING

8.4.1   Introduction

The UK publishing industry is being transformed through the take-up by readers of e-books. At the start of 2013, it was reported that e-book sales at the top UK trade publishers doubled in 2012, meaning that the UK e-book market grew to £250m.[24] In addition academic publishers have had to come to terms with new licensing models for journals with so-called 'open access' publishing on the rise. Publishers have also found themselves needing to deal with online copyright infringement just as the music and film industries have had to. This section looks at some current issues.

8.4.2   E-books

A number of e-book formats are well established with specific reading devices and smartphone and tablet reading apps available to allow ease of purchase and access—for example, Amazon's Kindle device and app, the devices and app provided by Kobo, and Barnes and Noble's Nook device and app. E-books raise a number of legal issues.

What is an E-book?: Licensing and Acquiring Rights
There are a variety of e-book types, the classic format being a digital version of the printed text and illustrations (if any) with very limited interactivity (limited to a table of contents, search facility and ability to add notes). Other e-books ('enhanced e-books') contain much more content and are more akin to multimedia works. The definition is important, as in a typical author—publisher contract, the author will grant exclusive rights to the publisher to

---

[22] [2011] EWHC 1981 (Ch).
[23] See the discussion by Arnold J in *Dramatico Entertainment Ltd and Others v British Sky Broadcasting and Others* [2012] EWHC 268 (Ch), paras 1–5.
[24] *The Bookseller*, 18 January 2013.

exploit his or her work together, typically, with the right for the publisher to also sublicense others to do so (through so-called subsidiary rights). These rights need to be defined as the royalty payable to the author will typically vary. The publisher also needs certainty that it has acquired the rights it needs to create an e-book and then sell it through an online platform.

Licensing/Distribution Models

Having acquired the rights and created the e-book, the publisher then needs to 'sell' the book. As discussed in chapter five, the publishing industry has been finding its way as to how best to sell e-books. For example, are they sold to a distributor like Amazon and then resold (with Amazon being free to set prices) or does the distributor act as an agent rather than a reseller, allowing the publisher to set the end-user price? In academic publishing it is also important to understand the role of content aggregators and online libraries.

In fact, e-books are not strictly speaking sold (they cannot be sold as they are not a piece of tangible property although the expression is still used)—they are licensed (in the US 'rented'). The purchaser acquires a limited non-exclusive licence to read the e-book much as in the same way that software is licensed with resale or transfer of the licence to another person typically being prohibited (unless the publisher or platform provider permits this).

There is an ongoing debate about whether 'used' e-books can be 'resold' (just as used/second-hand books and records/CDs can be lawfully resold through the application of the first sale/exhaustion of rights doctrine). Certainly it is common for such resale/transfer to be prohibited in the user licence terms. For example, the Amazon Kindle terms state: 'Unless specifically indicated otherwise, you may not sell, rent, lease, distribute, broadcast, sublicense, or otherwise assign any rights to the Kindle Content or any portion of it to any third party'.[25] A recent US case (dealing with digital music rather than e-books) has considered this area and found that copying a music file in order to resell it infringed copyright (in the case a copy of the music file was made through transferring it from the seller's computer/device to ReDigi's servers) and this was not protected by the US first sale doctrine/defence under section 109(a) Copyright Act.[26] The judge did however say that the first sale defence would apply to digital copies where the physical device storing the copy (eg iPod) was resold as here no copy was made. It was for the

---

[25] Amazon Kindle Store Terms of Use (Last updated: 24 October 2012): www.amazon.co.uk (accessed 7 April 2013).

[26] 17 USC § 109 see *Capitol Records LLC v ReDigi Inc*, US District Court, Southern District of New York, No. 12-00095 (30 March 2013). Section 109(a) says: 'Notwithstanding the provisions of section 106(3), the owner of a particular copy or phonorecord lawfully made under this title, or any person authorized by such owner, is entitled, without the authority of the copyright owner, to sell or otherwise dispose of the possession of that copy or phonorecord.'

legislature not the courts to extend the first sale doctrine beyond what section 109(a) currently provided. The judge commented:

> Put another way, the first sale defense is limited to material items, like records, that the copyright owner put into the stream of commerce. Here, ReDigi is not distributing such material items; rather, it is distributing *reproductions* of the copyrighted code embedded in new material objects, namely, the ReDigi server in Arizona and its users' hard drives. The first sale defense does not cover this any more than it covered the sale of cassette recordings of vinyl records in a bygone era.[27]

In the UK one would expect the courts to take a similar view subject to the caveat that the recent CJEU decision in *UsedSoft GmbH v Oracle International Corp*[28] (see chapter five) has potentially opened the door for the exhaustion of rights doctrine to be revisited in the context of the resale of digital products. However, given the limited, non-perpetual and revocable nature of many e-book end-user licences and also, that as discussed in chapter 5, the *UsedSoft* case is arguably specific to software, it can be queried how applicable this case is. Certainly one would expect e-book platforms to seek to ensure to the extent possible that their licence terms and business models are constructed to try to avoid any potential application of *UsedSoft v Oracle*.

Copyright Infringement

The growth in unlawfully copied digital books online has encouraged the UK publishing industry to develop automated tools to assist publishers in sending notifications of copyright and take down notices to those hosting and/or providing infringing content. For example, the Publishers Association's (PA) Copyright Infringement Portal is a web-based tool for serving take down notices to ISPs and Webmasters hosting content that infringes copyright.[29]

8.4.3   Open Access[30]

Background

The practice of providing no-cost online access ('open access') to scholarly (typically peer reviewed) journals (as well as papers and other works) has grown rapidly in recent years. The two largest players are BioMedCentral in the UK (part of the commercial publisher Springer Science+Business Media)[31] and the Public Library of Science (PLoS) (a nonprofit publisher

---

[27] Page 12.
[28] Case C-128/11, 3 July 2012.
[29] www.copyrightinfringementportal.com/ (accessed 6 April 2013).
[30] For a recent review of this area see the Finch Report ('Report of the Working Group on Expanding Access to Published Research Findings', June 2012) (Finch Report).
[31] www.biomedcentral.com/ (accessed 8 April 2013).

and advocacy organisation)[32] in the USA. But many publishers now provide open access journals alongside more traditional subscription-based publishing (where the subscriber funds publication). Creative Commons licences are typically used to clarify the usage rights users have. In open access publishing often the author, their institution or their research funding body will pay to have the article published through open access rather than on subscription, as clearly the publication of the article has to be funded in some manner.

The Finch Report[33] has characterised open access in terms of a number of potentially interlocking strands:

— free access (ie access without payment) to a version of a publication via a repository (for example at an academic institution eg the UCL Discovery repository (institutional repository) or a discipline or subject based repository eg The Social Science Research Network (SSRN)[34]), often after an embargo period (often called *green* open access);
— free access to the version of record of a publication via the publisher's own platform (often called *gold* open access);
— the removal of any payment barrier, so that users have a right to read some version of an article (often called *gratis* open access); and
— the removal of most if not all of the restrictions on the use and reuse of articles (often called *libre* open access).

It is important to understand what versions of articles are involved in open access. These can range from the author's original article as submitted to peer review through to the 'version of record' (ie as actually published in the journal) or variants of these.

UK Experience

On 16th July 2012 Research Councils UK (RCUK) launched its new Open Access policy. This was informed by the Finch Report—the policy harmonised and made significant changes to existing Research Councils' Open Access policies.[35] The new policy applies to all qualifying publications being submitted for publication from 1 April 2013, and states that peer reviewed research papers which result from research that is wholly or partially funded by the Research Councils:

— must be published in journals which are compliant with the RCUK policy on Open Access,[36] and;

[32] www.plos.org/ (accessed 8 April 2013).
[33] Finch Report, 120.
[34] www.ssrn.com (accessed 8 April 2013).
[35] www.rcuk.ac.uk/media/news/2012;/Pages/120716.aspx (accessed 9 April 2013).
[36] www.rcuk.ac.uk/documents/documents/RCUKOpenAccessPolicy.pdf (policy dated 8 April 2013) (accessed 9 April 2013).

— must include details of the funding that supported the research, and a statement on how the underlying research materials such as data, samples or models can be accessed

Criteria which journals must fulfil to be compliant with the RCUK Open Access policy are detailed within the policy, but include offering either a 'pay to publish' option or allowing deposit in a subject or institutional repository after a mandated maximum embargo period (which, depending on the subject area, can be up to 6 or 12 months) where no payment is required to publish. In addition, the policy mandates use of the Creative Commons 'Attribution' license (CC-BY) when a payment—an Article Processing Charge (APC)—is levied. The CC-BY licence allows others to modify, build upon and/or distribute the licensed work (including for commercial purposes) as long as the original author is credited (for more information on this licence see section 9.5.5 below).

The Research Councils are to provide block grants to eligible UK Higher Education Institutions, approved independent research organisations and Research Council Institutes to support payment of the APCs associated with 'pay-to-publish'. In parallel, eligible organisations will be expected to set up and manage their own publication funds. The Research Councils will work with eligible organisations to discuss the detail of the new approach to funding APCs and to ensure that appropriate and auditable mechanisms are put in place to manage the funds.

Copyright and Licensing Issues

Open access turns the traditional publishing model on its head. In the traditional model the author licences the publisher content in return for a royalty, the publisher publishes and charges for access to the content through an up front fee or through subscription charges. The publisher funds the publication by in effect charging readers or their institutions/libraries. In fact, in academic publishing, especially for journals, the author does not expect a royalty/fee—being published in a peer-reviewed journal is reward in itself. In open access the author (more typically their institution/research funder) can in effect be asked to pay to be published where they want the article to be available free in its final 'version of record' form, through 'Gold' open access. Given the recent shift in Research Councils UK policy, academic institutions, learned societies (who are often heavily involved with a number of leading journals which they own) and UK publishers are finding their way here. Certainly the RCUK Open Access Policy will need to be carefully reviewed, as will the licensing models of publishers to ensure they are compliant with this policy to the extent relevant. In particular where Gold open access is used (where an APC may be charged) then the journal article must be made available online through a Creative Commons Attribution (CC BY) licence. Where 'Green' open access is opted for, then the journal must consent to deposit of the final 'Accepted Manuscript'[37] in any repository, without restriction on non-commercial reuse and within a defined period: no APC will be payable to the publisher in that case. It should also be noted that in the context of green open access the RCUK policy states:

> Where Open Access is achieved through deposit of the final Accepted Manuscript in a repository (the 'Green' route) in order to maximise the opportunities for access to and reuse of repository content, the Research Councils would like research papers to be made available using the most liberal and enabling licences, ideally CC BY. However, the RCUK policy requires only that the manuscript is made available without restriction on non-commercial reuse. The policy does not specify a particular licence, and the requirement can be met by use of the Creative Commons Attribution-non-commercial licence (CC BY NC). Publisher-specific licences are acceptable providing they support the aims of the policy, and allow reuse including non-commercial text and data mining.[38]

Finally, it should be noted that RCUK recognises that copyright in the manuscript itself normally remains with the author, as reflected in the historical right and tradition of authors to publish online manuscript versions of their papers even before submission, and this will continue and is unaffected by the RCUK Open Access Policy.[39]

8.5 APP DEVELOPMENT AND LICENSING

8.5.1 Introduction

The growth in the use of smartphones and tablets has led to the rapid development and availability of apps. In this book 'app' is used to refer to application programmes available for use on Apple's smartphones and tablets via the App Store, through the Android Play Store for use on Android devices and those available via other platforms (eg the Kindle Fire tablet). The legal issues in developing, distributing and licensing apps are similar to those for software except that there are additional issues relating to privacy law and the collection of user data which are outside the scope of this book. Setting privacy law to one side, apps are just software although they may also contain or create content (music, graphics, animation, text etc) or may operate to link to online content in order to display it. So the discussion elsewhere in this book about the need to clear the rights to use content and about issues relating to linking is also relevant.

---

[37] The Accepted Manuscript is the version of a journal article submitted by an author that has been accepted for publication in a journal, and that has been through a peer review process.
[38] RCUK Open Access Policy, 8.
[39] RCUK Open Access Policy, 2.

8.5.2   App Development and Licensing

An app developer will need to make use of a software development kit (SDK) provided and licensed by the relevant platform and in addition for iOS apps (for Apple devices) Xcode, Apple's integrated development environment (IDE). In the past there has been controversy about the terms of Apple's SDK licence and restrictions imposed on developers.[40] Certainly it is important to review carefully the SDK licence terms and the relevant distribution terms noted below to ensure that the app development complies with these terms. For example, there is likely to be a conflict between the use of software in the app developed under open source terms (see chapter nine) and any SDK licence or distribution terms which restrict or prevent modifications to the app.

Once developed, the app will need to be tested and then accepted for distribution by the relevant platform. The platform will have its own distribution terms. In addition the developer can usually specify their own end-user licence agreement (EULA) terms provided they do not conflict with the distribution terms of the platform. It is quite common for developers to use their own EULAs, especially for content-rich apps where rights owners may require specific protections or where the developer wants to impose restrictions that go beyond any 'default' licence terms specified by the platform.

The platform will typically take a percentage of the developer's revenue from online licence 'sales' of the app.

SUMMARY

(a)   Digital copyright underpins Web 2.0 and user-generated content;

(b)   Online terms dealing with the ownership and licensing of user-generated content, as well as the right to edit and/or remove content where necessary is essential to manage risk in hosting user-generated content;

(c)   Further cases are likely which will clarify liability for hosting infringing user-generated content and the scope of any monitoring obligations.

(d)   Legislation has been enacted in a number of countries allowing strong sanctions to be obtained against online infringers including the possibility of the denial of Internet access.

(e)   E-books and open access are transforming the publishing industry.

---

[40]   See eff (USA) (www.eff.org, 9 March, 2010 (accessed 12/11/13)).

9

Protecting and Managing Your Digital Copyright Assets

This final chapter looks at the practical legal issues for organisations creating, exploiting or licensing digital copyrights. The first part looks at the issues for specific industries and also looks at the important role of collecting societies. The second part contains precedent checklists and precedents dealing with some of the more common licensing situations. In this chapter 'digital copyright assets' are taken to include all digital copyright, database and related rights, whether the person concerned owns them or uses them under licence.

9.1   GENERAL

All industries will make use of digital copyright in some shape or form, whether it is computer software or online information. As in the case of any other asset, care needs to be taken to ensure the organisation concerned has the right to use and exploit the asset to the extent required for its operations. It also needs to be protected against unauthorised use.

Some organisations will deal with digital copyright like any other intellectual property (IP) asset. Their existing corporate IP policies will deal with it. But organisations that are heavy users of digital content, or are significant creators of digital copyright works, or both, need to consider developing specific policies.

The following issues are of general application:

9.1.1   Acquiring Rights: Ownership of Digital Copyright

Where the organisation wants to own all rights to digital works/content the following must be borne in mind:

(a)   **The work is created by an employee in the course of their employment:** the employee will have no moral rights and the copyright will automatically vest in their employer. Nevertheless it is advisable for standard form employment contracts to expressly deal with these issues as well, not least to deal with any international IP issues and to protect the company's confidential information.

(b) **The work is commissioned:** it is imperative a written assignment of copyright and waiver of moral rights are obtained from the creator backed up by warranties and appropriate indemnities where possible. Failure to do this potentially leaves an uncertain ownership/licensing situation.

(c) **The maker of a database is located outside the EEA:** as discussed in chapter three, section 3.3, database right is only available within the EEA and the maker of the database must also have a connection with the EEA (eg through residence or nationality). US and other non-European businesses must give careful thought to protecting their databases in the EEA before making them available in Europe, especially via the Internet. If database right protection is not readily available then contract law (ie binding use terms) and technical protection measures must be actively investigated.

9.1.2   Acquiring Rights: Licensing Digital Copyrights

Those acquiring rights by way of a licence need to consider:

(a) Are all rights included and properly described?

(b) Have all rights been properly cleared?

(c) Are the existing rights licensed sufficient for the digital use and exploitation of the work in question? Old licences will need to be carefully reviewed.

(d) Have the implications of using software/content subject to any open source/copyleft licences been thought through?

(e) What 'quality' warranties should be sought from the licensor (eg accuracy of data, performance of software)?

9.1.3   Protecting and Exploiting Digital Copyrights

Digital copyright must be protected:

(a) Has documentation been kept evidencing such matters as:

    (i) date of creation, name of creator (including their status (employee/contractor) and terms of engagement), details of work created and (where possible) originality (ie independent creation) of the work in question?

    (ii) investment put into creating any databases?

(b)   When the rights are used or exploited are copyright and database rights notices used?

(c)   Any supply/licensing (whether in/out) should be on binding license terms; this includes carefully reviewing any website terms and conditions and the terms that should apply to any UGC. Are the terms sufficient for your use (eg purpose, quality issues) (if a user/licensee)? Are they sufficiently protective, if a licensor? Are they binding?

(d)   Have technical steps to include rights management information or copy protection measures and/or the use of 'no archive' meta tags etc been considered?

(e)   Are the employment or consultancy contracts in standard use sufficient both to deal with ownership/moral rights waivers and to protect against the misuse of confidential information such as source code after termination of the relationship?

Further issues of particular relevance to specific industries are now considered in detail.

9.2   ISSUES FOR SPECIFIC INDUSTRIES

9.2.1   General Industrial

These industries are likely to have or require at least the following digital copyright assets:

(a)   software, both 'off the shelf' and possibly bespoke
(b)   corporate websites
(c)   e-business website(s), possibly
(d)   databases:
  (i)   technical information—know-how, design drawings, test results, etc
  (ii)   customer and supplier details
  (iii) financial information and employee data

Additional issues which may arise include:

(a)   need for coordination between those procuring software and Internet content, and those eg, in marketing and sales wanting to use this for websites: eg content obtained for trade catalogues/printed materials may require further copyright licenses for electronic use;

(b)   care to be taken to ensure technical databases and customer lists are only accessed on a 'need to know' basis under strict confidentiality terms;

(c)   if technical data is to be made available to customers in electronic form, eg as part of an after sales service or to facilitate the sales process, steps

must be taken to properly protect and license the company's copyright
and database rights;

(d)   ensuring software and content licences anticipate wherever possible any
future outsourcing or corporate reorganisation.

9.2.2   Financial and Professional Services

These industries are likely to have or require at least the following digital
copyright assets:

(a)   software: 'off the shelf' and for financial institutions, probably a significant amount of bespoke software
(b)   corporate websites
(c)   e-business website(s), possibly
(d)   databases:
      (i)   know-how—precedents, internal manuals/data, source code etc
      (ii)   customer and supplier details
      (iii)   financial information and employee data
(e)   financial information—typically supplied real-time using data feeds,
including RSS feeds

Additional issues which may arise include:

(a)   need for co-ordination between those procuring software and Internet
content, and those eg in marketing and sales wanting to use this for websites: eg content obtained for catalogues/printed materials may require
further copyright licenses for electronic use;
(b)   security as well as content protection issues if material is made available
in electronic form eg for electronic banking purposes;
(c)   ensuring software and content licences anticipate wherever possible any
future outsourcing or corporate reorganisation;
(d)   ensuring any data acquisition/data feed licences are sufficient for the number of likely users and their contemplated use. Particular care is required
if the data is to be resold (even in altered form or aggregated/transformed)
or used other than for the user's internal business purposes. The risks in
using RSS feeds as data sources for further distribution and/or resale need
to be considered as this may breach the terms of use of the feed provider.

9.2.3   Telecommunications and ISPs

These industries are likely to have or require at least the following digital
copyright assets:

(a)   software, both 'off the shelf' and very probably bespoke
(b)   corporate websites

(c) e-business website(s), possibly
(d) databases:
    (i) technical information—know-how, source code, etc
    (ii) customer and supplier details
    (iii) financial information and employee data
(e) third party content to be transmitted/hosted/cached etc

Additional issues which may arise include:

(a) need for co-ordination between those procuring software and Internet content, and those eg, in marketing and sales wanting to use this for websites: eg content obtained for trade catalogues/printed materials may require further copyright licenses for electronic use;
(b) care to be taken to ensure technical databases and customer lists are only accessed on a 'need to know' basis under strict confidentiality terms;
(c) if technical data is to be made available to customers in electronic form, eg as part of an after sales service or to facilitate the sales process, steps must be taken to properly protect and license the company's copyright and database rights;
(d) ensuring software licences anticipate wherever possible any future out-sourcing or corporate reorganisation;
(e) ensuring the business benefits from any 'safe harbours' or exclusions/limitations from liability in respect of illegal or unlawful content it may happen to transmit, store, host, etc. Where the US is relevant this means complying with the notice and take down regime under the Digital Millennium Copyright Act 1998 and considering similar voluntary and possibly statutory measures in Europe in light of the Electronic Commerce Directive.

9.2.4 Software and Computer Games

These industries are likely to have or require at least the following digital copyright assets:

(a) software, both 'off the shelf' and bespoke
(b) corporate websites
(c) e-business website(s), possibly—including software downloads via the web
(d) databases:
    (i) technical information—know-how, source code, etc
    (ii) customer and supplier details
    (iii) financial information and employee data
(e) content (music, video, etc) used in conjunction with, or comprised within, the game software (possibly in database format)

Additional issues which may arise include:

(a)   need for co-ordination between those procuring software and Internet content, and those eg, in marketing and sales wanting to use this for websites: eg content obtained for trade catalogues/printed materials may require further copyright licenses for electronic use;

(b)   care to be taken to ensure technical databases and customer lists are only accessed on a 'need to know' basis under strict confidentiality terms;

(c)   if technical data/software/code is to be made available to customers in electronic form, eg as part of an after sales service or to facilitate the sales process, steps must be taken to properly protect and license the company's copyright and database rights;

(d)   ensuring any internal software and content licences anticipate wherever possible any future outsourcing or corporate reorganisation;

(e)   establishing careful rights acquisition, UGC and management policies and online terms EULAs and if necessary assigning dedicated personnel to this area. Moral rights must also be dealt with;

(f)   use of technical measures to prevent digital piracy eg, redundant code included in source materials, copy protection technologies, digital watermarking use of meta tags to prevent caching/archiving, etc.

9.2.5   Publishing and Information Providers

These industries are likely to have or require at least the following digital copyright assets:

(a)   software, both 'off the shelf' and possibly bespoke

(b)   corporate websites

(c)   e-business website(s), possibly—including software /content downloads via the web eg, for e-books

(d)   databases:
   (i)   content (in addition this may also be in non-database format)
   (ii)   technical information—know-how, source code, etc
   (iii) customer and supplier details
   (iv)   financial information and employee data

Additional issues which may arise include:

(a)   need for co-ordination between those procuring software and Internet content, and those eg, in marketing and sales wanting to use this for websites: eg content obtained for trade catalogues/printed materials may require further copyright licenses for electronic use;

(b)   ensuring any internal software and content licences anticipate wherever possible any future outsourcing or corporate reorganisation;

(c) establishing careful rights acquisition, UGC and management policies and online terms EULAs and if necessary dedicated personnel to this area. Moral rights must also be considered and dealt with. Open access may be relevant;

(d) use of technical measures to prevent digital piracy eg, copy protection technologies, digital watermarking, use of meta tags to prevent caching/archiving

9.2.6 Broadcasting, Entertainment and Music

These industries are likely to have or require at least the following digital copyright assets:

(a) software, both 'off the shelf' and possibly bespoke

(b) corporate websites

(c) e-business website(s), possibly—including software/content downloads via the web (eg MP3 files) and content streaming (eg video on demand), online broadcasting, m-commerce, user-generated content

(d) databases:
  (i)   technical information—know how, source code, etc
  (ii)   customer and supplier details
  (iii) financial information and employee data
  (iv)   content (probably in non-database form too)

(e) digital broadcast transmissions/services

Additional issues which may arise include:

(a) need for co-ordination between those procuring software and Internet content, and those eg, in marketing and sales wanting to use this for websites: eg content obtained for trade catalogues/printed materials may require further copyright licenses for electronic use;

(b) care to be taken to ensure technical databases and customer lists are only accessed on a 'need to know' basis under strict confidentiality terms;

(c) ensuring any internal software and content licences anticipate wherever possible any future outsourcing or corporate reorganisation;

(d) establishing careful rights acquisition and management policies and online terms to deal with digital content distribution and reuse and UGC and if necessary, assigning dedicated personnel to this area;

(e) use of technical measures to prevent digital piracy eg, copy protection technologies, use of conditional access systems, use of meta tags to prevent caching/archiving, etc.

9.2.7   Gaming and Betting

These industries are likely to have or require at least the following digital copyright assets:

(a)   software, both 'off the shelf' and probably bespoke
(b)   corporate websites
(c)   e-business website(s)—for online gaming
(d)   databases:
    (i)   technical information—know-how, source code, etc
    (ii)   customer and supplier details
    (iii)   financial information and employee data
(e)   content (music, video, etc) used in conjunction with the gaming site and data feeds (eg racing data)

Additional issues which may arise include:

(a)   need for co-ordination between those procuring software and Internet content, and those eg, in marketing and sales wanting to use this for websites: eg content obtained for trade catalogues/printed materials may require further copyright licenses for electronic use;
(b)   ensuring any internal software and content licences anticipate wherever possible any future outsourcing or corporate reorganisation;
(c)   establishing careful rights acquisition and management policies especially for content and data (eg racing data) and if necessary assigning dedicated personnel to this area if there is a heavy content element;
(d)   use of technical measures to prevent digital piracy eg, copy protection technologies employed if there is a heavy content element, use of meta tags to prevent caching/archiving, etc.

9.2.8   Auction Houses and Collectibles Sites

These industries are likely to have or require at least the following digital copyright assets:

(a)   software, both 'off the shelf' and bespoke
(b)   corporate websites
(c)   e-business website(s)—eg online databases of auction information, digital photographs of items sold
(d)   databases:
    (i)   technical information—know-how, source code, etc
    (ii)   customer and supplier details
    (iii)   financial information and employee data
    (iv)   content (typically digital images generally supplied by users) and current and historic sales and price information

Additional issues which may arise include:

(a)   need for co-ordination between those procuring software and Internet content, and those eg, in marketing and sales wanting to use this for websites: eg content obtained for trade catalogues/printed materials may require further copyright licenses for electronic use;

(b)   care to be taken to ensure technical databases and customer lists are only accessed on a 'need to know' basis under strict confidentiality terms;

(c)   ensuring any internal software and content licences anticipate wherever possible any future outsourcing or corporate reorganisation;

(d)   establishing careful rights acquisition and management policies to deal with digital reuse of data and materials (including images): any use of images beyond that required to advertise the sale of an artistic work will probably need to be licensed.[1] User terms and conditions will need to expressly deal with any content supplied by users and appropriate warranties and indemnities sought including moral rights as well as copyright;

(e)   use of technical measures to prevent digital piracy eg, redundant code included in any source materials, 'seed entries' in any auction or other data, possibly using copy protection technologies and watermarking images; also only using low resolution images and use of meta tags to prevent caching/archiving, etc.

9.2.9   Museums, Galleries, and Picture Libraries

These cultural industries are likely to have or require at least the following digital copyright assets:

(a)   software, both 'off the shelf' and possibly bespoke
(b)   corporate websites
(c)   e-business website(s)—eg online galleries
(d)   databases:
    (i)   technical information—know-how, source code, etc (of more relevance to picture libraries) customer and supplier details
    (ii)   financial information and employee data
    (iii)   content (often supplied in-house eg by in-house photographer)
    (iv)   consideration of moral rights position where images are being used

Additional issues which may arise include:

(a)   need for co-ordination between those procuring software and Internet content, and those eg, in marketing and sales wanting to use this for

---

[1] s 63, CDPA. Query however if s 63 applies to online images.

websites: eg content obtained for trade catalogues/printed materials may require further copyright licenses for electronic use;

(b)   ensuring any internal software and content licences anticipate wherever possible any future outsourcing or corporate reorganisation;

(c)   establishing careful rights acquisition and management policies to deal with digital reuse of existing materials (including images). The collecting society DACS (see section 8.3 below) may also need to be consulted regarding digital rights to their artists;

(d)   use of technical measures to prevent digital piracy eg, the use of copy protection technologies and watermarking images; also only using low resolution images where possible on any 'public' websites; consider only allowing subscribers access to better quality images possibly in encrypted form and consider where appropriate the use of meta tags to prevent caching/archiving.

9.2.10   Pharmaceutical, Biotechnology and Bio-information/ Bio-informatics Industries

These industries will make use of significant databases of chemical, genetic and clinical information and data. They are likely to have or require at least the following digital copyright assets:

(a)   software: 'off the shelf' and probably a significant amount of bespoke software for data collection, analysis, cataloguing and storage

(b)   corporate websites

(c)   e-business website(s), possibly

(d)   databases:
    (i)   know-how—research results, genetic information
    (ii)   clinical data—some of this information may be 'bought-in' or co-developed

Additional issues which may arise include:

(a)   need for co-ordination between those procuring software and Internet content, and those eg, in marketing and sales wanting to use this for websites: eg content obtained for catalogues/printed materials may require further copyright licenses for electronic use;

(b)   security as well as content protection issues if material is made available in electronic form;

(c)   ensuring software and content licences anticipate wherever possible any future outsourcing or corporate reorganisation;

(d)   ensuring any data acquisition licences are sufficient for the number of likely users and their contemplated use. Particular care is required if the data is to be resold (even in altered form or aggregated/transformed) or used other than for the user's internal business purposes;

(e) copyright and database right ownership issues as well as patent and confidentiality issues must be carefully addressed when setting up research programmes especially with third parties.

9.2.11 Universities/Higher Education Sector

These organisations are likely to have or require at least the following digital copyright assets:

(a) software, both 'off the shelf' and possibly bespoke (eg accounting systems)
(b) websites
(c) e-business website(s), possibly—including software/content downloads via the web eg for distance/e-learning
(d) databases:
    (i) content (in addition this may also be in non-database format); it may also include works (including original manuscripts) held by the institution's libraries
    (ii) technical and research information—know-how, source code, research results, etc
    (iii) student data
    (iv) financial information and employee data

Additional issues which may arise include:

(a) need for co-ordination between those procuring software and content, and those eg, wanting to use this for websites: eg content obtained for printed materials may require further copyright licenses for electronic use;
(b) ensuring any internal software and content licences anticipate wherever possible any future outsourcing or academic reorganisation;
(c) establishing careful rights acquisition, UGC and management policies and if necessary, dedicated personnel to this area. This will include dealing with the ownership of copyright in books, journal articles etc produced by staff and students. Moral rights must also be considered and dealt with;
(d) use of technical measures to prevent digital piracy where content is exploited for profit/fund-raising purposes eg copy protection technologies, digital watermarking use of meta tags to prevent caching/archiving, etc.

(e)   joint/co-authorship issues are likely to be involved where e-learning materials are produced.[2]

9.3   THE ROLE OF COLLECTING SOCIETIES IN THE DIGITAL ENVIRONMENT

It will be apparent from the discussion so far that clearing digital rights for copyright purposes is potentially an enormous task. Consider a digital radio station. Does the copyright and performer's right position for each piece of music broadcast need to be cleared for each piece of music played? Surely not—securing individual rights for each three-minute track would be a bureaucratic nightmare for user and owner alike.

In fact, since 1851, when SACEM in France was founded, 'collecting societies' have been established around the world to act as clearing houses for a range of copyright and related rights. Members of these societies (who own the rights to be licensed) typically either transfer the rights to be licensed to the society or empower the society to act as their agent in granting licences of their works. The society remits royalties (typically on agreed scales) to members and administers licences of members' rights.

The various collecting societies that operate in the UK have grown out of the analogue world. Nevertheless, they are becoming increasingly important in helping to manage the copyright licensing of works in the digital environment.

There are many collecting societies operating in the UK. The functions of some of the more important ones are set out below. Collecting societies are particularly important to the music industry.

Of course, collecting societies are generally voluntary in nature so not all authors or publishers may choose to use them either in whole or in part. Also, the societies may not have devised comprehensive licensing models for digital works or if they have, these may still be limited in scope. So collecting societies are not a panacea for either authors or users. Nevertheless, they should always be considered in developing any strategy to protect, use or exploit digital works, as should recent initiatives in the areas of orphan works and extended collective licensing noted in 9.4 below. In addition, a number now operate internationally by working with foreign equivalent organisations on a reciprocal basis. For example, the International Federation of the Phonographic Industry (IFPI) has developed a reciprocal agreement to allow webcasting across national borders. There are also moves for collecting

---

[2] See section 2.5, ch 2.

societies to co-operate to provide a 'one-stop shop' for clearing multimedia rights (see 9.3.1 below). Digital technology itself may assist collecting societies in these activities.

It should also be noted that the activities of collecting societies are potentially regulated by:

(a) **Competition law:** inevitably collecting societies involve co-ordinated behaviour and contracting between undertakings and may also have a dominant position as far as licensing rights is concerned;[3]

(b) **CDPA:** the Copyright Tribunal currently has power over collecting societies and can, for example, intervene when issues relating to certain licensing schemes and royalties become contentious. For example, the PRS and MCPS Joint Online Licence was the subject of a reference to the Tribunal by the British Phonographic Industry Ltd (BPI) and others including iTunes, MusicNet, Sony, and a number of mobile phone network operators. One of the key points at issue was how the definition of gross revenue in the licence should be defined, and the Tribunal held that even where the music had been fully paid for, it was appropriate for some advertising revenue thereby generated to be included in the definition of gross revenue;[4]

(c) **Codes of practice/regulation:** at the time of writing the UK government has recently enacted legislation to allow for the regulation of collecting societies (termed 'licensing bodies') through the adoption by the body of a code of practice (see Part 1 of Schedule 22 of the Enterprise and Regulatory Reform Act 2013). In addition, as noted below, there is also a recent EU proposal for a Directive that among other things will also address the operation of collecting societies.

9.3.1   The Future of Collecting Societies in the Digital Environment

Digitisation makes it much easier to exploit rights across borders. It is therefore increasingly important to ensure that collecting societies can readily adapt to new developments, such as the increasing demand for community-wide copyright and related rights licences (but at the same time avoiding monopolistic situations). In April 2004, the European Commission published a Communication[5] that was to provide a broad basis for the reform

---

[3] See for example: *SACEM* [1989] ECR 2565 (ECJ).

[4] *BPI Ltd v MCPS Ltd* [2008] EMLR 5.

[5] Communication from the Commission to the Council, the European Parliament and the European Economic and Social Committee on the Management of Copyright and Related Rights in the Internal Market, COM (2004) 261 final, Brussels 16 April 2004.

of collecting societies. The Commission, which considered that a common, EU-wide approach was required, has now proposed legislation dealing with the collective management and good governance of collecting societies. A Recommendation was made (in 2005—see below) together with a proposed Directive, noted below. Issues considered by the Commission prior to the proposed Directive included the need for adequate external control mechanisms for collecting societies; requirements as to the publication of tariffs and the grant of licences; and the application of principles of good governance, non-discrimination, transparency and accountability of each society in relations with its members.

In particular, the Commission considered the important role played by EU competition law in regulating the behaviour of collecting societies in order to achieve a 'level playing field' for the collective management of copyright and related rights in the internal market. Until now the Commission had tolerated monopolies, or quasi-monopolies, by collecting societies, as long as the assumption could be made that such structures would be the only means of effective protection of the rights of individual owners. However, the Commission—whilst recognising that intellectual property rights provide incentives to innovate and create—was concerned that anti-competitive practices could impede the development of new technologies, as the Commission believes is currently the case in some new media sectors. In contrast, some of the major UK collecting societies have cautioned that competition between societies might devalue creators' rights.

The Commission had in the past also permitted the territorial protection of licensing rights, provided it did not lead to market partitioning within the EU. However, as new possibilities have opened up, territorial restrictions in the administration of rights can no longer in the Commission's view be considered indispensable for the effective management of rights. The exploitation of rights can be restricted to national territories. The administration of these rights, however, cannot, except where it can be proven that, as the only means of effective protection, such a restriction is indispensable.

In future (subject to the provisions of the proposed Directive noted below) the Commission is likely to look favourably at one-stop shopping arrangements and any related reciprocal agreements between collective rights management systems, so long as they do not perpetuate the monopoly structures of the past (except where they are indispensable). In particular, according to the Commission in the Communication (and as reflected in the proposed Directive), owners of intellectual property rights must have a choice in selecting the collecting society that will license their rights. Users must have the choice of a one-stop shop platform when acquiring licences for cross-border operation. Territorial restrictions must not be used to prevent the creation of new global and regional one-stop shop arrangements.

At around the time of the Communication being issued, the Commission objected to 16 national royalty collection organisations in relation to agreements for the collective licensing of music copyrights for online use (collectively known as the Santiago Agreement).[6] The Commission stated it will continue to scrutinise such operations under competition law to ensure that arrangements are not entered into with the main objective of extending dominant positions in traditional media markets into new markets.

Also, the use of new technologies, such as digital rights management systems, for the management of individual rights must be kept open, and the Commission stated it would be particularly vigilant as regards bundling arrangements that prevent users from combining the offerings of collective rights management with individual administration of rights.

The Commission expressed the intention to build on the following set of principles:

(a) the principle of competition between one-stop shop arrangements built on reciprocal rights agreements;
(b) the prohibition on territorial customer allocation, where no longer justified;
(c) transparency requirements, for example, in relation to accounting and separation of administrative from royalty fees.

The Commission's Communication also discusses digital rights management (DRM) systems and individual (ie non-collective) rights management, but it did not envisage any need for new legislation in these areas.[7]

The Communication was followed up in 2005 by a specific recommendation on the management of online rights in musical works[8] which largely follows the approach of the Commission's previous Communication. In its Recommendation, the Commission recommended that right-holders and commercial users of copyright-protected material should be given a choice as to their preferred model of licensing. Different online services might require different forms of EU-wide licensing policies. The Recommendation therefore proposed the elimination of territorial restrictions and customer allocation provisions in existing licensing contracts while leaving right-holders who do not wish to make use of those contracts the possibility to tender their repertoire for EU-wide direct licensing. The Recommendation also included provisions on governance, transparency, dispute settlement and

---

[6] Commission press release IP/04/586 (3 May 2004).

[7] A separate but related initiative of the European Commission is to facilitate the use of DRM: a High-Level Group on DRMs was established in March 2004 as part of the Europe 2005 Action Plan (see ch 7 section 7.9.7).

[8] Commission Recommendation of 18 May 2005 on collective cross-border management of copyright and related rights for legitimate online music services (2005/737/EC).

accountability of collective rights managers, which was intended to introduce a culture of transparency and good governance enabling all relevant stake-holders to make an informed decision as to the licensing model best suited to their needs.[9]

The principles outlined above were also applied by the Commission in 2008 when action was taken against a group of EEA collecting societies involved in music licensing—this is discussed in section 5.5.12 of chapter five.

In a further significant development to follow up the Recommendation, in July 2012 the Commission proposed a Directive 'on collective management of copyright and related rights and multi-territorial licensing of rights in musical works for online uses in the internal market.'[10] The objectives of the Directive are:

— To promote greater transparency and improved governance of collecting societies through strengthened reporting obligations and right-holders' control over their activities, so as to create incentives for more innovative and better quality services.
— And, building upon this—and more specifically—to encourage and facil-itate multi-territorial and multi-repertoire licensing of authors' rights in musical works for online uses in the EU/EEA.[11]

In giving background to the proposal and seeking to address questions, the Commission helpfully sets out the complex position as regards digital music licensing in the EU which the Directive is seeking to help address:

> Today, if an online music provider like iTunes wants to provide a music track for download, it needs to obtain a licence to do so from three separate entities: the track's author (the composer and lyricist), the record producer, and the performer. Collecting societies manage one of these: the author's rights. (The record producer and the performer's licences are usually both managed by the record producer.) It is the functioning of the licence of authors' rights for online use which is set to be improved by the Directive proposed today.[12]

9.3.2   The Major Collecting Societies in the UK

This section briefly considers collecting societies of broad relevance in the UK; the websites referred to were accessed on 8 June 2013.

---

[9] Commission press release, IP/05/1261, Brussels (12 October 2005).
[10] Brussels, 11.7.2012, COM(2012) 372 final.
[11] Commission press release, IP/12/772, Brussels, 11 July 2012.
[12] Question 14, Proposed Directive on collective management of copyright and related rights and multi-territorial licensing—frequently asked questions, Brussels, 11 July 2012.

The Copyright Licensing Agency Limited (CLA) (http://cla.co.uk)

The CLA was formed in 1983 and deals with licensing content for reproduction by reprographic means which includes photocopying, digitally reproducing and scanning. Its owners are the Authors' Licensing and Collecting Society (ALCS) and the Publishers Licensing Society Limited, which represent authors and publishers, respectively. The content is from books, journals and magazines and includes electronic and digital publications as well. Through an agency agreement with DACS (see below) it also licenses the copying of artistic works. A CLA licence (for business, the public sector or education) enables organisations to gain a blanket ('collective') clearance for the materials licensed by the CLA for the specified uses set out in the licence.

The Newspaper Licensing Agency Limited (NLA) (www.nla.co.uk)

The NLA was formed in 1996 by UK national newspapers in order to license the copying of newspaper articles. These licenses extend to paper and digital copying

Design and Artists Copyright Society Limited (DACS) (www.dacs.org.uk)

This society was founded in 1983 and deals with works of visual art including photographs on behalf of DACS' members. DACS's licences cover a wide range of uses (including online/in digital format including apps) from merchandise or an advert, to a book, film or website.

PRS for Music (Formerly the Performing Right Society (PRS) founded in 1914); The Mechanical-Copyright Protection Society (MCPS) (www.prsformusic.com)

The PRS has historically owned and controlled the 'performing right' in musical works. This includes the right to:

(a) perform the work in public (in general in any public place or outside the home)
(b) communicate the work to the public (including by way of broadcast)
(c) authorise others to do these activities

The MCPS has historically dealt with the 'mechanical rights' in musical works (ie the right to reproduce the musical work either as a physical product (which right the MCPS continues to licence eg, for CDs, computer games, DVDs, novelty toys etc) or when music is reproduced for broadcast or online use (the latter now being dealt with through PRS for Music—see below).

More recently the PRS has cooperated with the MCPS and from 2009 rebranded itself as 'PRS for Music'. PRS for Music represents PRS and MCPS members' performing rights and the mechanical rights when a piece of music is reproduced for broadcast or online use.

PRS for Music offers a wide range of licences including for online music (download or streaming), podcasts, ringtones and so on.

PPL and VPL (www.ppluk.com)

As noted in chapter two, under the CDPA there is a separate copyright for sound recordings as opposed to musical works. PPL deals with the public performance right (section 19 CDPA—see chapter two). In practice this is the playing of music outside of a domestic setting and the broadcasting rights for sound recordings. These sound recordings can be in any format (CD, audio files, etc). PPL manages these sound recording rights on a collective basis on behalf of its members—thousands of record companies and performers. PPL also deals with the payment of 'equitable remuneration' to performers where recordings of their performances are played in public or broadcast (see section 2.2.8 above). It has two classes of member—recording rights-holder members (typically record companies) and performer members.

It should be noted that because PPL and PRS for Music are two separate independent companies, in most instances a licence is required from both organisations in order for recorded music to be lawfully played in public, as PPL and PRS represent different rights-holders. PPL collects royalties on behalf of performers and record companies (or any other relevant right-holders in respect of public performances of recorded music) and PRS for Music collects on behalf of songwriters, publishers and composers.

PPL also has a 'sister' company, VPL, which carries out a very similar collective licensing function on behalf of record companies in respect of music videos when they are played in public or broadcast on TV.

9.4   ORPHAN WORKS, EXTENDED COLLECTIVE LICENSING AND DIGITAL COPYRIGHT EXCHANGES/COPYRIGHT HUBS

The huge increase in the exploitation of copyright works online and in digital formats has posed challenges as to how rights for such uses are cleared, as noted elsewhere in this work. In recent years, attention has focused both on ways to enable the efficient identification (through databases—being able to efficiently identify works together with related rights management information is crucial) and clearance of rights (for example, through digital copyright exchanges or copyright hubs) and the related questions of how copyright owners can be traced to give permission and if they cannot be traced (for example, in the case of so-called 'orphan works' where the copyright owner cannot readily be located), whether UK copyright law should offer protections to copyright users who need to exploit such works. For example, by providing under statute for a blanket licence or exception to copyright to permit the use of orphan works. Such users are often cultural institutions such as museums and libraries with valuable archives and collections they wish to make available online.

Orphan works have already received attention at EU level: on 25 October 2012 a Directive on certain permitted uses of orphan works was adopted.[13]

This Directive provides an exception to the right of reproduction (but only for the purposes of digitisation, making available, indexing, cataloguing, preservation or restoration) and communication to the public for the use of orphan works—copyright works or phonograms being considered to be orphan works where none of the right-holders can be identified (or if identified, located) despite a diligent search being carried out in accordance with the Directive (Article 3) which includes a search of relevant sources listed in the Annex to the Directive. These works and phonograms must be protected by copyright or related rights and be first published in a Member State or, in the absence of publication, first broadcast in a Member State. So a work first published in the USA but now in an EU collection would not benefit from the Directive.

Uses of orphan works permitted by the Directive are limited to certain uses made of orphan works by 'publicly accessible libraries, educational establishments and museums, as well as by archives, film or audio heritage institutions and public-service broadcasting organisations, established in the Member States, in order to achieve aims related to their public-interest missions'.[14] The permitted uses are 'to achieve aims related to their public-interest missions, in particular the preservation of, the restoration of, and the provision of cultural and educational access to, works and phonograms contained in their collection. The organisations may generate revenues in the course of such uses, for the exclusive purpose of covering their costs of digitising orphan works and making them available to the public.'[15]

Right-holders are able at any time to put at an end orphan work status and where this is done they are to be entitled to fair compensation for the use that has been made of their works. The Directive must be transposed into national law by 29 October 2014.

It is fair to say the Directive is deliberately of narrow scope. It focuses on non-commercial, public interest uses of orphan works by a limited set of organisations and right-holders remain able to opt out. In parallel with the adoption of the Directive, the UK had already started exploring ways of addressing the orphan works issue. In May 2011, the Hargreaves Review had recommended:

> The Government should legislate to enable licensing of orphan works. This should establish extended collective licensing for mass licensing of orphan works, and a clearance procedure for use of individual works. In both cases, a work should only

---

[13] Directive 2012/28/EU (OJ L 299, 27 October 2012) 5.
[14] Article 1(1).
[15] Article 6(2).

be treated as an orphan if it cannot be found by search of the databases involved in the proposed Digital Copyright Exchange.[16]

At the time of writing (March 2013) the proposed Digital Copyright Exchange has been the subject of further study and industry consultation and the current proposal is for a voluntary industry-led 'Copyright Hub' to be established:

> The main recommendation of our report is the creation of a not-for-profit, industry-led Copyright Hub based in the UK that links interoperably and scalably to the growing national and international network of private and public sector digital copyright exchanges, rights registries and other copyright-related databases, using agreed cross-sectoral and cross-border data building blocks and standards, based on voluntary, opt-in, non-exclusive and pro-competitive principles. The Copyright Hub will serve in the UK and beyond a wide range of copyright licensors (rights holders, creators and rights owners in both commercial and cultural worlds) on the supply side and a wide range of copyright licensees/users on the demand side ... The Copyright Hub's particular focus will not be on the low volume of customised, high monetary value licensing transactions at the top of the market (for example Universal Music Group's licensing of Spotify) but on the very high volume of automatable, low monetary value transactions coming mostly from the long tail of smaller users—the small digital start-up company wanting to use music and images and text creatively for its customers, the teacher in the classroom, a user posting a video on YouTube. Larger companies have told us that they also have requirements for access to easy to use high volume, low monetary value, low transaction cost copyright licensing systems, for example a broadcaster wanting a particular film clip or a publisher wanting a specific diagram or image.[17]

Also the UK government has put forward legislation for orphan works licensing and extended collective licensing in the Enterprise and Regulatory Reform Act 2013—the Act permits the Secretary of State to make regulations to license the use of orphan works much broader than the Directive provides for (covering commercial as well as non-commercial use potentially) and most controversially, the Act enables the Secretary of State to make regulations for licensing bodies such as collecting societies to offer extended collective licensing (ie they are authorised to grant copyright licences in respect of works not owned by or licensed to the licensing body). Extended collective licensing certainly will have a role in addressing the orphan works issue but there are concerns by some right-holders that the Act allows the Secretary of State to extend extended collective licensing beyond orphan works. It can also be questioned why the UK government thinks it necessary to go further than the Orphan Works Directive in this regard.[18]

---

[16] Recommendation 4.

[17] 'Copyright Works: Streamlining Copyright Licensing for the Digital Age'—an independent report by Richard Hooper CBE and Dr Ros Lynch, IPO, July 2012.

[18] For criticisms of the Bill see eg: http://artists-bill-of-rights.org/news/campaign-news/breaking!-uk-content-creators'-call-to-action/ (accessed 5 April 2013).

9.5   PRECEDENT CHECKLISTS AND PRECEDENTS[19]

9.5.1   Checklist—Acquiring Software (Digital Copyright User Focus)

Define What You Are Acquiring

(a)   Clearly define the software, including technical and user documentation that will set out the functionality of the software. This is to ensure that you are acquiring software that will actually do what it is you need it to do.

(b)   Are there provisions setting out acceptance testing procedures and criteria? Do you have a period of time in which you can reject the software (without incurring a fee) if it does not perform in accordance with the criteria?

Delivery

(a)   Is the vendor installing the software for you? What are the timeframes for installation and what happens if the vendor delays?

Intellectual Property: Own or Take a Licence?

(a)   Are you acquiring the intellectual property rights in the software (this is often the case if the software is being developed specifically for you) or are you only licensing the software (much more common)? It is imperative that if you want ownership of the intellectual property rights in the software, that the vendor/developer assigns those rights to you in writing signed by the vendor/developer. In this instance, you will also need to ensure that the vendor/developer has the legal right to assign the intellectual property rights to you—the vendor/developer should provide at least a warranty to this effect.

Taking a Licence

(a)   What are the terms of the licence? Do you require a perpetual licence or only require the software for a limited term? Most software licenses will continue until the agreement terminates.

(b)   Is the definition of who is authorised to use the software acceptable? For example, does it include employees, contractors and authorised agents? Will it allow outsourcing, for example?

(c)   What are the limitations on your use of the software? Are there limitations on the number of users of the software, or is the licence limited

---

[19] There are a number of copyright and e-commerce precedent books, for example, Bond, *Software Contracts* (London, Tottel, 2007). Stokes, *Art and Copyright* (Oxford, Hart Publishing, 2nd edn, 2012) contains a sample copyright assignment and a short form licence. This book contains similar but less extensive precedents.

to use of the software at a particular location (ie unlimited users, but limited to a nominated workstation)?

(d)   If a 'site' licence, is the definition of 'site' clearly expressed? For example, the definition may include on-site facilities and off-site locations. Is the site definition acceptable?

(e)   Are there restrictions on the rights of users—for example, restrictions that disallow the copying or downloading of the software without the express written permission of the vendor or transfer to another computer or back up copies? Or are there limitations on the user's rights to enhance or reformat the software? Are these restrictions acceptable?

Payment

(a)   How is payment of the licence fees structured? Is it a one-off licence fee (for perpetual use until the agreement is terminated) or an annual licence fee? Is payment of the licence fee after successful completion of acceptance testing?

Other Services/Software

(a)   Depending on the software, you may want to include maintenance and support services and upgrades and new releases.

(b)   If the software is high value or business critical, you should certainly consider source code escrow (the source code is lodged with an escrow agent such as the National Computing Centre and will be released on certain defined events eg, the vendor becomes insolvent or fails to maintain the software).

Warranties

(a)   Ensure that there are at the very least some standard warranties included in the contract, including a warranty that the software will operate in accordance with user manuals and other technical specifications. Also seek a warranty and indemnity from the licensor that your use of the software will not infringe the intellectual property rights of a third person.

Limitations of Liability/Exclusions

(a)   The vendor will generally try to limit their liability heavily should things go wrong. You need to consider what loss or damage you might suffer should the software be defective. You then need to try to negotiate some sensible provisions ensuring reasonable compensation in such an eventuality.

Governing Law/Jurisdiction/Dispute Resolution

(a)   What is the governing law of the contract? Depending on the bargaining position of the parties, it is preferable that the governing law is the country in which you reside.

(b) Is it clear which courts are empowered to determine any disputes?

(c) Do you require alternative dispute resolution provisions? For example, arbitration or mediation. This may be useful in avoiding disputes going to court.

9.5.2 Checklist: Acquiring Internet Content (Digital Copyright User Focus)

Intended Use: Do I Need a Licence?

(a) The use of most content obtained from the Internet will be subject to copyright protection.

(b) What is your intended use? Is it permitted by any relevant copyright/use licences or by any exceptions to copyright (eg fair use/fair dealing)?

(c) Do you need a licence at all?

Intellectual Property: Own or Take a Licence?

(a) You need to determine whether you want a licence to use the content or to own all the intellectual property rights in the content. If the content is for Internet use, often you may only require a licence. However, you should consider this issue if you wish to have unlimited rights to the content. If so, you will need a written assignment from the copyright owner of all intellectual property rights in the content.

(b) From whom are you acquiring the content? For example, if employees or sub-contractors are creating the content, you should ensure that it is clearly spelt out what rights you have to the content (either as owner or licensee (whether exclusive or non-exclusive)) and that the vendor can grant what he purports to supply.

(c) Consider whether moral rights are relevant. If necessary or if the position is unclear, obtain a waiver of moral rights.

Taking a Licence

(a) What are the terms of the licence? Are you limited to how you can use the content? For example, you may be restricted in reformatting, editing or revising the content. The contract should expressly set out what rights you have.

(b) What other obligations are there? For example, the copyright owner may require that an acknowledgement appear with the content that it is the author of the content.

Payment

(a) Are the payment terms (if any) clear?

Warranties

(a) Ensure that there are standard warranties included in the contract, including a warranty and indemnity from the licensor that your use and/or republication of the content will not infringe the rights of any third person. Also include a warranty that the licensor is authorised to licence the content to you (either as copyright owner himself or under a sub-licence).

(b) What comfort are you given about the quality and (if relevant) availability of the content/data?

Governing Law/Jurisdiction/Dispute Resolution

(a) What is the governing law of the contract? Depending on the bargaining position of the parties, it is preferable that the governing law is the country in which you reside.

(b) Is it clear which courts are empowered to determine any disputes?

(c) Do you require alternative dispute resolution provisions? For example, arbitration or mediation. This may be useful in avoiding disputes going to court.

9.5.3 Checklist: Digital Copyright Distribution and Licensing (Digital Copyright Licensor Focus)

Sections 9.5.1 and 9.5.2 above look at acquiring software and Internet content from a user/licensee perspective.

On the basis you have acquired the necessary rights (either you own them or have a licence with a right to sub-license others), what must you bear in mind when you are acting as a *licensor*? For example, you are a supplier and you want to license others to use the content or software.

To some extent the issues here are variants of what has already been discussed in the context of a user/licensee acquiring rights to use software or content. From a licensor's perspective, all licences will address at least the following:

Ensure the Licence is Binding

What licensing model discussed in section 7.2.1 of chapter seven (written, shrink wrap, click wrap, bare licence) meets your business requirements?

Define What You are Licensing

You can only license what you are entitled to and should only license what you want to—an obvious point but one that is often forgotten about.

Delivery/Acceptance

Do you need to specify how/when delivery will take place eg, Internet download. This will typically be linked to acceptance in the case of off the shelf/

non-bespoke software. Otherwise acceptance will be dealt with separately for bespoke software.

Licence Scope
(a) A licensor will generally be as restrictive as possible in order to:
>   (i)   protect their IP from misuse, reverse engineering etc (to the extent permitted by the Software Directive);
>   (ii) extract additional payment from the licensee eg, if new/additional users are required, the scope of use changes, the user wishes to dispose of or outsource that part of its business.

   Particular care must be taken in defining what electronic/digital rights are granted—do you want to give the licensee rights in respect of now unknown technologies or do you want to limit the rights granted to existing exploitation methods? If so, avoid overly broad grants and be as specific as possible.

      Whilst care must be taken to comply with competition law, who will own the IP in any works derived from the licensed content?
(b) A reservation of rights clause is quite typical ie the licensor (and/or its suppliers) retain ownership of everything licensed and no rights are granted except those expressly granted by the licence.
(c) A clause is also often added to ensure that any use outside the scope of the licence is a clear breach of contract to enable termination of the licence and a contractual damages claim in addition to any copyright/ IP infringement claim.
(d) If the licensee is allowed to copy or redistribute the content, ensure they include your copyright and other proprietary rights notices on any copies or relevant sites.

Responsibilities of the User/Licensee
In addition to any restrictions within the licence, are there any other obligations or responsibilities you need to put on the licensee eg, they must procure the appropriate hardware, software and Internet connection at their expense and liability in order to make use of the content licensed.

Payment
(a) How is payment of the licence fees structured? Is it a one-off licence fee (for perpetual use until the agreement is terminated) or an annual licence fee? Or will there be a royalty basis? Can you increase the fees in subsequent years if relevant?
(b) Payment terms will be specified and VAT/tax aspects dealt with (eg withholding taxes if there is a foreign element).

Other Services/Software

Do you wish to offer any additional products or services and if so how will they be charged for and/or licensed?

Technical Measures/Audit/Inspection/Record Keeping

(a)   You should expressly reserve the right to employ technical measures including by remote access/control to protect and/or disable your content. This is to help you to comply with the Computer Misuse Act 1990.

(b)   Consider audit rights to check any misuse and where appropriate to check royalty payments.

(c)   Consider obliging the licensee to keep full records of all copies and licensing of the content. This is essential if you are being paid on a royalty basis.

Warranties

What comfort do you wish to offer users as to:

(a)   quality of material supplied (including performance if it is software)

(b)   non-infringement of third party IP and that the material is not obscene, defamatory, unlawful, illegal, etc

(c)   that your IP is valid

(d)   that all moral rights have been waived

Limitations of Liability/Exclusions

Licensors should always seek to exclude or limit their liability. Loss of profit, revenue and goodwill is typically excluded, as are indirect and consequential damages. A monetary cap on liability is often set at the value of the licence fees. Terms which may be implied by law (eg as to quality/fitness for purpose) are also typically excluded in favour of the express terms of the contract. In any event, regard must be had to general English contract law principles regarding the lawfulness of excluding/limiting liability in light of the Unfair Contract Terms Act 1977 (which potentially applies to both business and consumer contracts) and other relevant consumer protection legislation.

Termination

(a)   Is it clear how the agreement can be terminated? At the very least, an un-remedied breach by the licensee of the agreement or their insolvency ought to allow the licensor to terminate.

(b)   Clarify what happens on termination eg, what clauses survive, what accrued rights continue, the content/material to be erased from the user's systems, etc.

Boilerplate Clauses

(a)   Ensure you are not liable for force majeure ie an event outside your reasonable control prevents you from performing the contract.

(b)   Make clear how the licence terms can be waived or varied.

(c)   Include a provision ('severance clause') which seeks to remove any unlawful provisions from the agreement. This is particularly important if there is bona fide uncertainty about the competition law aspects of the agreement.

(d)   Restrict the licensee from assigning or sub-licensing the agreement without your consent. Consider also whether it might be in your interest to be able to terminate the agreement if the licensee is taken over ('change in control') and in particular if they are acquired by a competitor.

(e)   Give your affiliates, associated companies and suppliers the benefit of the exclusions/limitations of liability in the licence by making use of the Contracts (Rights of Third Parties Act) 1999 and prevent anyone else apart from you and the licensee, as appropriate, benefiting from the contract.

(f)   How will the parties communicate eg to serve notice of termination?

(g)   If you are supplying confidential information (eg source code) ensure the licensee is bound by obligations of confidence.

(h)   Include an entire agreement clause to seek to exclude any prior terms or representations made by the licensor concerning the licence and to ensure no other documents or discussions set out the agreement of the parties. Liability for fraud should not, however, be excluded.

Governing Law/Jurisdiction/Dispute Resolution

(a)   What is the governing law of the contract? Depending on the bargaining position of the parties, it is preferable that it is the governing law in the country in which you (licensor) reside.

(b)   Is it clear which courts are empowered to determine any disputes? Licensor will prefer its courts but with the right to sue in licensee's jurisdiction eg for non-payment or misuse of IP.

(c)   Do you require alternative dispute resolution provisions? For example, arbitration or mediation. This can be useful in avoiding disputes going to court and arbitration may be useful in an international agreement.

9.5.4   Open Source Licences: Checklist of Licensing options

There are numerous open source or free software licences. They vary considerably in their approach, in particular whether developments can be kept 'private' or whether all derived software must be made freely available going forward. There is also some uncertainty about whether such licences are contracts or simply licences.[20] Some of the more common licences are briefly reviewed below.

Open source Licensing Checklist

Before either acquiring 'free' or open source software[21] or making your software available to others 'open source', it is imperative that careful thought is given to the following and as to whether the use and/or licensing of open source model fits in with your business model:

(a)   If the software is being acquired for further development and redistribution, or simply redistribution with other products, do the terms of the open source licence that run with the software:

   (i)   Require that any customer software bundled with or distributed with the open source software be made 'open' as well?

   (ii)   Require that any derived works or improvements to the open source software the customer creates also be made 'open'?

   (iii)   Clearly set out what use and redistribution rights you have?

   (iv)   Give any comfort on intellectual property ownership and non-infringement? This is unlikely so you will need to take a view about the risks of using the software, although attempts have been made in the GPLv3 (discussed below) to try to address software patents which may apply to the software. In particular, it is becoming more common for software to benefit from patent protection and the existence of possible blocking patents should not be ruled out. Unlike typical commercial software, where the user will generally get some comfort in this regard, open source software typically comes 'as is', although again the GPLv3 does attempt to deal with software patents by ensuring that users of the GPLv3 in relation to software protected by their patents license these patents under the GPLv3 so the patents are not asserted in the future but licensed upfront.

   (v)   Impose onerous restrictions in terms of requiring you to bind your licensees to the open source terms? Can you comply with the mechanics of informing users of the terms of any open source software licences? This may be tricky if what you are supplying consists of a mix of open and proprietary software.

   (vi)   Restrict the commercial terms (pricing etc) upon which you can distribute the software?

---

[20] See the discussion by Andres Guadamuz in 'Free and Open-Source Software' in Edwards and Waelde (eds), *Law and the Internet'* (Oxford, Hart Publishing, 3rd edn, 2009) ch 11.
   [21] See Glossary for the distinction between free and open source software, although in this section they are used interchangeably.

(vii)   Deal with any DRM restrictions that may apply? This is a feature of the GPLv3 which seeks to prevent DRM being used to prevent users of GPLv3 licensed software from modifying it.

Some Open Source Licences

The list below indicates some examples of open source licences, of which the GPL is the most heavily promoted and now comes in two versions, v2 and v3. v3 is an updated version of v2 and among other things attempts to deal with the growing issue of software patents potentially blocking the use of open source software and it also has provisions dealing with DRM. However, v2 remains very popular. If choosing an open source licence, it is important to find an up-to-date licence that will be widely accepted, recommended and/or understood and GPLv3 is being promoted on this basis.

(a)   **GPL** (The GNU General Public Licence[22])—Software under this licence cannot generally be mixed with proprietary software, and modifications may not be made private, or withheld, or obfuscated. It is very widely used. It is 'copyleft.'[23]

(b)   **LGPL** (The GNU Lesser General Public Licence (formerly the GNU Library General Public Licence[24]))—This allows certain software libraries to be mixed with non-free/proprietary software. However, as with the GPL, there is no right to make modifications private. It is also copyleft.

(c)   **BSD** (Berkeley System Distribution), **MIT** (also referred to as **Expat**), **X** and **Apache** Licences—These licences allow open source software to be mixed with proprietary software and allow modifications to be made private. They are not copyleft licences.

(d)   **NPL** (Netscape Public Licence)/**MPL** (Mozilla Public Licence)—In 1998 Netscape dedicated its Navigator browser software to the public by giving it over to a company called Mozilla. The MPL has become quite common as a model for distributing and using open source software.

(e)   **Affero GPL**—This is designed for use where software is used on servers. The licence seeks to ensure the redistribution of code in such circumstances. It does not, however, address the issue of software as a service (SaaS)/cloud computing which open source advocates view as problematic.[25]

---

[22] See: www.gnu.org—these comments relate to GPLv2.
[23] See Glossary for a definition.
[24] See: www.gnu.org.
[25] www.guardian.co.uk/technology/2008/sep/29/cloud.computing.richard.stallman (accessed 15 June 2013).

9.5.5   Creative Commons

The organisation Creative Commons is promoting the use of various 'Creative Commons' licences that apply some of the principles of open source software licensing to non-software content: text, images, videos, etc, in order to allow users to retain certain rights but also create a space, a 'creative commons', for others to make use of their work. According to its creators, 'Creative Commons defines the spectrum of possibilities between full copyright—*all rights reserved*—and the public domain—*no rights reserved*. Our licenses help you keep your copyright while inviting certain uses of your work—a "some rights reserved" copyright.'[26] There are now Creative Commons licences governed by the law of England and Wales.[27] Anyone thinking of using a Creative Commons licence (or indeed an open source licence for that matter) needs to review it carefully to make sure it is appropriate.

The Finch Report has helpfully summarised Creative Commons (CC) licences as being built around four sets of conditions which authors and other creators can choose to apply (in combination if they wish), based on standardised sets of CC licences:

— *Attribution (BY)*, which allows users to copy, distribute, display and perform the work and make derivative works based on it only if they give the authors credit (ie 'attribution') in the form they prescribe .

— *Non-commercial (NC)*, which allows users to copy, distribute, display, and perform the work and make derivative works based on it only for non-commercial purposes.

— *No Derivative Works (ND)*, which allows users to copy, distribute, display and perform only verbatim copies of the work, and not any derivative works based on it. (In other words the work cannot be modified, altered or reused or any other derivative works created or 'derived' from it.).

— *Share-alike (SA)*, which allows users to distribute derivative works only under a licence identical to the licence that governs the original work.

As noted above, the conditions may be combined in a number of ways, reflecting the conditions the authors/creators wish to impose. The CC-BY licence imposes the fewest conditions, although there is also a CC Zero ('CC0') 'licence'(in fact called a 'tool' by CC) under which creators waive all copyrights and related interests that they may have over a work, in effect

---

[26] http://creativecommons.org/about/.
[27] http://creativecommons.org/international/uk/.

dedicating it to the public domain. Creative Commons (CC) has six standard licences in total in addition to 'CC0' described by CC as follows:[28]

— **Attribution 'CC BY':** This licence lets others distribute, remix, tweak, and build upon your work, even commercially, as long as they credit you for the original creation. This is the most accommodating of licenses offered. Recommended for maximum dissemination and use of licensed materials.

— **Attribution-NoDerivs 'CC BY-ND':** This licence allows for redistribution, commercial and non-commercial, as long as it is passed along unchanged and in whole, with credit to you.

— **Attribution-NonCommercial-ShareAlike 'CC BY-NC-SA':** This licence lets others remix, tweak, and build upon your work non-commercially, as long as they credit you and license their new creations under the identical terms.

— **Attribution-ShareAlike 'CC BY-SA':** This licence lets others remix, tweak, and build upon your work even for commercial purposes, as long as they credit you and license their new creations under the identical terms. This licence is often compared to 'copyleft' free and open source software licences. All new works based on yours will carry the same licence, so any derivatives will also allow commercial use. This is the licence used by *Wikipedia*, and is recommended for materials that would benefit from incorporating content from *Wikipedia* and similarly licenced projects.

— **Attribution-NonCommercial 'CC BY-NC':** This licence lets others remix, tweak, and build upon your work non-commercially, and although their new works must also acknowledge you and be non-commercial, they do not have to license their derivative works on the same terms.

— **Attribution-NonCommercial-NoDerivs 'CC BY-NC-ND':** This licence is the most restrictive of our six main licences, only allowing others to download your works and share them with others as long as they credit you, but they cannot change them in any way or use them commercially.

9.5.6 Cloud Computing/Software as a Service (SaaS)

In recent years, many software applications are now provided as a service rather than licensed to the user; in other words, the user does not have a copy of the program to run under its own control on its own machine. Instead, the user

---

[28] See: http://creativecommons.org/licenses/ (accessed 9 April 2013). The text describing the six licences set out below is taken from the CC website noted earlier and is accordingly licensed from CC under a Creative Commons Attribution 3.0 Licence—see http://creativecommons.org/terms (accessed 9 April 2013).

subscribes with a service provider to receive services using the software over the cloud/the Internet. Here the program is under the control of the service provider and resides on their machine. So the primary responsibility for obtaining rights to use the software under licence rests with the service provider. The service provider needs to ensure its licence is broad enough to allow it to provide the relevant services to its users. The user meanwhile (if he/she does not have access to the software in order to copy and run it) has a services agreement rather than a software licence. However, the situation will be different if the service provider is simply hosting the software on behalf of the user with the user having the right to access it and run it remotely. Here both the service provider and the user will need to be licensed if the software is proprietary.

9.5.7   Linking Agreement[29]

HYPERLINK POLICY

*[*Insert Company name]* does not necessarily endorse websites that link to any of *[*insert Company name]* websites. *[*Insert Company name]* will not be held liable for the content of any site from which its sites are hyperlinked.

In order to establish a hyperlink from a *[*insert Company name]* website you must at least fulfill the following criteria:[30]

[(a)   Your site must be reviewed and/or updated with current and accurate information on an 'as needed' and regular basis.

(b)   Your site must be available 24 hours a day, seven days a week, and be hosted on a server with adequate capacity to meet visitor demands reasonably (eg download times of home page must be consistent with competitive sites).

(c)   Your site must not include offensive, obscene and/or libellous material or any other material that may lead to civil or criminal liability and must not be directly linked to any other sites that may include offensive, obscene and/or libellous material or any other material that may lead to civil or criminal liability.

(d)   You must commit to hyperlink back to the related *[*insert Company name]* website from your site within 10 business days.

(e)   Your website must not be a personal homepage. Links from *[*insert Company name]* websites will not link directly to any personal web pages.]

---

[29] Note: care must be taken to ensure these terms are binding. See section 7.2.1 of ch 7.
[30] Customise as appropriate—additional or fewer criteria may be required as appropriate.

Terms and Conditions of Hyperlink[31]

IMPORTANT NOTICE

In order to establish a hyperlink to the home page of *[*insert Company name]* website you must first apply for and be granted permission from *[*insert Company name]* which permission may be granted in *[*insert Company name's]* absolute discretion and you must also accept and acknowledge the following terms and conditions. By selecting 'I ACCEPT' below, you hereby accept and agree to, and represent that you have the authority to enter into, this Agreement.[32]

TRADEMARKS

You acknowledge and agree that:

(a) *[*insert Company name]* trade marks, trading, business and brand names, including, but not limited to *[insert details about relevant trade marks]* (collectively, the 'Marks'), *[*Insert Company name]* website and its contents are and shall remain the sole property of *[*insert Company name]*.

(b) Nothing in this Agreement shall give you any right of ownership in the Marks or *[*insert Company name]* website.

(c) You shall not take any action that would impair the value or goodwill associated with the Marks or *[*insert Company name]* image or reputation and you shall not use the Marks in any way that might be misleading.

LICENCE TO USE TRADEMARKS

Subject to the terms and conditions of this Agreement, *[*insert Company name]* gives you a non-exclusive, limited license to use the Marks on your website solely for the purpose of providing a hyperlink to *[*insert Company name]* website [or their inclusion in meta tags].[33] You may only use the text and images provided by *[*insert Company name]* in the manner and locations specified by *[*insert Company name]*.

You may not use the Marks for any other purpose whatsoever including the promotion, advertising or publicity of your website. You shall not state or imply in any way that *[*insert Company name]* has endorsed you or your products, service or website.

NO DEEP LINKING

Any link you establish must transfer the user directly to the home page of *[*insert Company name]* website to enable viewing of the site as posted by *[*insert Company name]* without the imposition of any of your content or frames, browser windows or third party content.

---

[31] Ensure these terms are binding—see section 7.2.

[32] This assumes the linking Agreement is in electronic form.

[33] Consider whether this is appropriate.

DISCLAIMER
You expressly agree that the use of *[*insert Company name]* materials, Marks and website is at your sole risk. *[*Insert Company name]* does not warrant that its service will be uninterrupted or error free, *[*insert Company name]* provides this access 'as is' without warranty of any kind. *[*insert Company name]* disclaims all warranties, expressed or implied, including, but not limited, to the implied warranties of satisfactory quality and fitness for a particular purpose to the fullest extent permitted by law.

LIMITATION OF LIABILITY
Except to the extent it is unlawful to exclude or limit such liability, in no event will *[*insert Company name]* be liable for any direct, indirect, incidental, special or consequential damages including, but not limited to, loss of profit, loss of data, loss of business or any other loss arising out of or resulting from this Agreement or the use of any of the materials or Marks under this Agreement or access to any of the services described in this Agreement even if *[*insert Company name]* has been advised of the possibility of such damages. The foregoing shall apply regardless of the negligence of *[*insert Company name]* and regardless of whether such liability is found in contract, negligence, tort or any theory of liability except for fraud.

INDEMNITY
You agree to defend, indemnify and hold harmless *[*insert Company name]*, its trustees, officers, employees and agents from and against any claims, demands, damages, causes of action, loss or judgments arising from your breach of this Agreement or your hyperlink to *[*insert Company name]* website.

TERMINATION
[*insert Company name] reserves the right to terminate this Agreement in its sole discretion with or without cause at any time. If *[*insert Company name]* terminates this Agreement, you shall remove any and all links to the *[*insert Company name]* website within twenty-four hours of receipt of notice from *[*insert Company name]*.

GOVERNING LAW AND JURISDICTION
This Agreement is governed by and shall be construed in accordance with the laws of England. You hereby submit to the [exclusive][34] jurisdiction of the English courts.

---

[34] Non-exclusive jurisdiction may be appropriate depending on where the parties reside.

APPLICATION FOR HYPERLINK

In order to establish a hyperlink, in addition to accepting the terms and conditions, you must submit an application form (written or via email) to the Manager *[insert title, for eg Information Systems Department]* at the following address *[insert relevant addresses including email]*:

(a)   The name of your website(s) (including URL) and date of commencement

(b)   The name and address of the producer and registered administrative contact of your website

(c)   Profile of the Company Name/Organisation including contact persons, address and email

['I ACCEPT' AND 'I DO NOT ACCEPT' BUTTONS]

9.5.8   Website Terms

IMPORTANT NOTICE

[Please read the following terms of use carefully as your access to and use of this website and various web pages ('the Website') will be deemed as acceptance by you of the terms of use *[alternatively, place an 'I agree' and 'I do not agree' box here and require the user to click on the 'yes' box as indicating acceptance of the terms before allowing the user to proceed]]*.[35]

DATA PROTECTION AND PRIVACY

See the Data Protection statement at *[insert link or insert material here]* for information relating to the collection and use of your information.][36]

ACCOUNT, PASSWORD AND SECURITY [OPTIONAL]

If a particular website or web page requires you to open an account, you must complete the registration process by providing current, complete and accurate information as prompted by the applicable registration form. You will then choose a password and a user name. You are entirely responsible for maintaining the confidentiality of your password and account. Furthermore, you are entirely responsible for any and all activities that occur under your account. *[*Insert Company name]* is not liable for any loss that you may incur as a result of someone else using your password or account.

---

[35] Note: care must be taken to ensure that terms are binding—see section 7.2.1 of ch 7.

[36] Data protection is outside the scope of this book but will need to be dealt with either here or separately.

COPYRIGHT, DATABASE RIGHTS AND TRADEMARKS

The information, graphics, artwork, text, audio, video, animation, images, trademarks, names, software, other content and logos ('Content') contained in the Website are protected by copyright, database right and/or trademark laws. They are also proprietary to *[*insert Company name]* or its licensors and may be protected by rights in confidence. For database right purposes *[*insert Company name]* is the maker of the Website. This Website is Copyright © *[*insert Company name][date]*.

PERMITTED USE[37]

Access to and use of the Website is permitted only by individuals for personal and/or educational use and non-commercial purposes. You may access and download the Content and store a copy on a temporary basis for the sole purpose of viewing such Content without alteration or addition. You may print Content (other than third party copyright material) in whole or in part provided that such reproduction is to be used for personal and/or educational but not commercial purposes only.

NON-PERMITTED USE

Other than as expressly permitted by these terms of use, you may not modify, copy, distribute, communicate to the public, extract, reutilise, download, reproduce, display, republish, post, licence, transmit, manipulate, add to, delete from, adapt or otherwise use any Content in whole or in part, without *[*insert Company name]* prior written permission. In addition, users shall not be entitled to reproduce Content (or any part thereof) without any identification mark or other mark of origin relating thereto and also a copyright notice identifying *[*insert Company name or proprietor][and a database right notice identifying [*insert Company name as the maker of the database]]*.

No Content, or any part thereof, may be permanently copied or reproduced in any form or reproduced on any other system, device or website, or stored in or transmitted to or from any other electronic or digital form in whole or in part.

NO UNLAWFUL USE

As a condition of your use of this Website, you must not use the Website for any purpose that is unlawful or prohibited by these terms. You must not use the Website in any manner that could damage, disable, overburden or impair any site or service (or the network connected to the Website). You must not attempt to gain any unauthorised access to the Website or other accounts,

---

[37] Consider if this is sufficient.

computer systems, devices or networks connected to the Website through hacking, password mining or any other means.

PERMISSION REQUIRED TO LINK

Our prior written permission is required in order for any links to be made to the Website. Please e-mail *[insert details]* for any requests.[38] *[*Insert Company name]* reserves the right to require the removal of any link established by a third party between the Website and any third party website.

LINKS TO THIRD PARTY SITES

The Website may contain links to third party websites ('Linked Sites'). *[*Insert Company name]* does not sponsor, endorse or otherwise approve of any information or statements appearing in the Linked Sites (nor in sites referred to in or linked to the Linked Sites). *[*Insert Company name]* is not responsible for webcasting or any other form of transmission received from any Linked Site nor is *[*insert Company name]* responsible if the Linked Site is not working properly. It is your responsibility to enter into and comply with any software or other licences required to access and use any Linked Sites and any material they contain or link to.

DISCLAIMER

The Content included on the Website has been compiled by *[*insert Company name]* from a variety of sources. *[*Insert Company name]* reserves the right to change the terms and conditions of use of this Website without notice and at any time. The Website is provided for information purposes only and the Website and its content are made available 'as is' and 'as available'.

*[*Insert Company name]* excludes to the fullest extent permitted by law all warranties and conditions in relation to the Website and Content whether express or implied, including but not limited to the implied warranties of satisfactory quality and fitness for a particular purpose.

*[*Insert Company name]* makes no representations and does not warrant:

(a)   that the information selected for the Website is comprehensive, complete, verified, organised or accurate;

(b)   that it is licensed by the copyright or database right owner of any third party Content to include or reproduce such Content in the Website;

(c)   that the Website or its Content will be uninterrupted or error-free; and that the server from which the Website is available is free of viruses or bugs.

---

[38] Alternatively use Linking Agreement precedent or similar.

You specifically agree that *[*Insert Company name]* shall not be responsible for unauthorised access to or alteration of your transmissions or data, any material or data sent or received or not sent or received, or any transactions entered into through the Website. You specifically agree that *[*Insert Company name]* is not responsible or liable for any threatening, defamatory, obscene, offensive, unlawful or illegal content or conduct of any other party or any infringement of another's rights, including intellectual property rights.

LIMITATION OF LIABILITY

Except to the extent it is unlawful to exclude or limit such liability, in no event will *[*insert Company name]* be liable for any direct, indirect, incidental, special or consequential damages including, but not limited to, loss of profit, loss of data, loss of business or any other loss arising out of or resulting from access to the Content or the Website or breach of this agreement even if *[*insert Company name]* has been advised of the possibility of such damages. The foregoing shall apply regardless of the negligence of *[*insert Company name]* and regardless of whether such liability is found in contract, negligence, tort or any theory of liability except for fraud.

INDEMNITY

You agree to defend, indemnify and hold harmless *[*insert Company name]*, its trustees, officers, employees and agents from and against any claims, demands, damages, causes of action, loss or judgments arising from your breach of these terms of use.

TERMINATION AND ACCESS RESTRICTION

[*Insert company name] reserves the right, in its sole discretion, to terminate your access to the Website and the related services or any portion thereof with or without cause at any time.

GOVERNING LAW AND JURISDICTION

This agreement is governed by and shall be construed in accordance with the laws of England. You hereby submit to the non-exclusive jurisdiction of the English Courts.[39]

Further Information

[Company address, Phone, Fax, Email]

---

[39] See earlier comments about choice of jurisdiction/dispute resolution.

9.5.9   Sample Assignment of Copyright, Moral Rights Waiver/ Assertion and Licence

This section includes some short form clauses that may be useful in the context of assigning or licensing copyright or database right. However it comes with the caveat that legal (and potentially tax) advice should be taken as to whether the clauses are fit for their intended purpose and in any event they need to be included in the context of a legally binding agreement.[40] In particular no warranties or indemnities or further assurance provisions are included.

Assignment of Copyright (and Database Right)

[In consideration of the payment of £ [x] to Party A by Party B] Party A hereby assigns to Party B all Party A's entire right title and interest in the [[worldwide] copyright [and database right] [(including in relation to any future copyright and database right by way of a present assignment of future copyright and other applicable rights)][41] in [*define the work*] for the full period of such rights, together with any and all renewals, revivals, reversions and extensions of such rights [throughout the world] now or in the future [and also including the right to sue for past infringements of these rights].[42]

Waiver of Moral Rights

[In consideration of the payment of £ [x] to Party A by Party B] Party A irrevocably and unconditionally waives to the fullest extent permitted by law and in favour of Party B, its successors, assigns and licensees any moral rights to which Party A may be entitled under any laws now existing or in future enacted in any part of the world (including without limitation rights pursuant to the Copyright, Designs and Patents Act 1988 Sections 77, 80, 84 and 85).

Assertion of Moral Rights

Party A's moral right to be identified as the author or director of the [*define the work*] under section 77 Copyright, Designs and Patents Act 1988 is asserted.

---

[40] See Stokes, *Art and Copyright* for a more detailed presentation of these clauses in sample agreements.

[41] Define nature of rights assigned. Under UK law future copyright (ie copyright in work to be created) can be assigned prior to the creation of the work.

[42] If Party B is to acquire the right to sue for past infringements this language needs to be included.

Licence

[Subject to the payment of £[*x*] and Party B's compliance with the terms of this licence,] Party B is hereby granted the [exclusive/non-exclusive] right by Party A [under the applicable copyright [and database right] controlled by Party A][43] to [use][44] the [*define material licensed*] ('Licensed Material) for [*give purpose of use*] in the following territory [worldwide)] for the following period [*give duration of licence*]. Party B agrees not to use the Licensed Material other than as expressly permitted by this licence. Party A shall retain ownership of all rights in the Licensed Material and all rights not expressly granted by this licence are reserved to Party A.

SUMMARY

(a)   All industries will have digital copyright assets they need to properly acquire, protect and manage.

(b)   Contract as well as technical measures such as encryption and the use of meta-tags to prevent the use of web crawlers (where it is desirable to do this) will remain an important way in which to protect and manage content.

(c)   A number of organisations are making use of open source software and/or Creative Commons licences but they should only be used as long as the user is comfortable that the rights granted to others are appropriate and all such licences should be carefully reviewed before use.

(d)   The checklists in this chapter are designed to help all organisations and digital copyright users deal with the challenges of digital copyright.

---

[43] Define nature of rights licensed.

[44] Use denotes broad rights depending on the purpose and context. Consider limiting this to more specific rights eg, 'to reproduce', 'to communicate to the public' etc if these can be readily defined and it is clear what these rights should be.

INDEX

Introductory Note

References such as '178–9' indicate (not necessarily continuous) discussion of a topic across a range of pages. Wherever possible in the case of topics with many references, these have either been divided into sub-topics or only the most significant discussions of the topic are listed. Because the entire volume is about 'digital copyright', the use of this term (and certain others occurring throughout the work) as an entry point has been minimized. Information will be found under the corresponding detailed topics.